Praise for th

"These are fa ... on
and beautiful ... ne
Strode, *Daily Sun*

"Dit is gebruikersvriendelik, nuttig en omvattend en het 'n groot opvoedkundige waarde"—***Die Beeld***

"Handy travel companions ... these guides may be small but they're literally jam-packed with information ... making these guides holiday must-haves for an informed and more enjoyable trip"
—***Longevity* magazine**

"These handy books are accessible to everyone from the lay person to geologists and scientists, answering all your questions regarding these sites"—***Saturday Dispatch***

"... compact pocket guides packed with info, maps and colourful pictures"—***50/50***

"They are a celebration of various aspects of South African culture, including our historical inheritance and the land on which we live"—**Diane de Beer, *Pretoria News***

"There's this marvellous new collection of pocket guides by Southbound, each highlighting a specific World Heritage Site in South Africa ... Easy to use and fun to read, the pocket guides are a must for anyone remotely interested in our country's heritage"
—***Independent on Saturday***

"These books reveal fascinating parts of our country that many of us aren't properly aware of. They'd make excellent gifts, singly or collectively, and are great primers for planning a holiday"
—**Bruce Dennill, *The Citizen***

"All [eight] of South Africa's World Heritage Sites are covered, each in a manageable pocket guide which provides a remarkable amount of information for the edification of the serious ecotourist ... comprehensive contents ... an extensive amount of information ..."
—**Carol Knoll, *Environmental Management***

"... intensely practical ... fantastic series to buy ..."
—**Jenny Crwys-Williams, *Talk Radio 702***

"... these are among the best we have—opinionated and full of personality"—
Patricia McCracken, *Farmers Weekly*

Southbound Travel Guides

South Africa

2010 Travel Guru

compiled by Kerrin Cocks

With special thanks to Alicia, Aulette, Ntombi and Chris

Published in 2010 by 30° South Publishers (Pty) Ltd.
3 Ajax Place, 120 Caroline Street, Brixton, 2092
Johannesburg, South Africa
www.30degreessouth.co.za
info@30degreessouth.co.za

Copyright © Kerrin Kay Cocks, 2010

Design and origination by 30° South Publishers (Pty) Ltd.

Printed and bound by Pinetown Printers, Durban

ISBN 978-0-958489-11-9

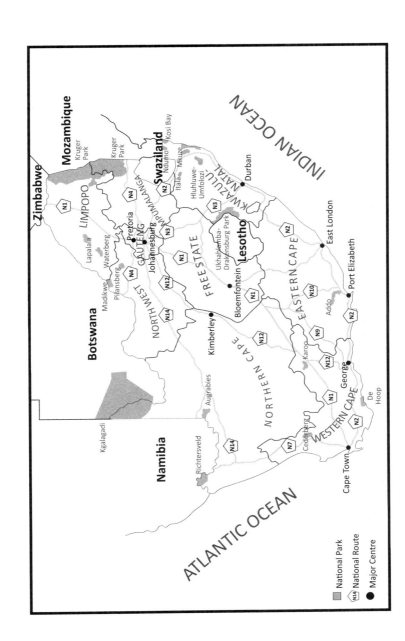

CONTENTS

INTRODUCTION

If this book were comprehensive it would run to volumes; each province is worthy of a book on its own, but then it would not be handy or user-friendly. Just a comprehensive list of the restaurants of Gauteng or the B&Bs of the Western Cape would run to volumes. So we know what the book isn't and what not to expect.

What you can expect is a very detailed directory of listings of places to stay, places to go, things to do and how to get there. If your stay in South Africa is brief but you have time between meetings and want to maximize that time by seeing some of the sites, this book is what you need. You'll find some restaurants listed in and around the suburb you're staying in, museums, galleries and an alternative place to put your feet up should you not, for some reason, find your accommodation to your liking.

For each province a top ten has been selected; these are the top ten places I recommend you visit should you find yourself in that province. They are diverse and range from natural beauty to man-made 'beauty', museums and other places of specific interest. It may come as a suprise to some to find that Gauteng has a top ten to rival most. So don't touch down at OR Tambo International and then get on the fastest flight out of Jo'burg to Cape Town.

A 30-minute drive out of any of South Africa's major centres is guaranteed to take you to any number of places of interest. If you are spending some time in South Africa then this book is a must as it not only offers a quick guide to the must-sees but also provides a deeper insight into the coutry's less-known, but no-less-interesting places.

It is an ideal companion to the more wordy travel guides to South Africa and, because we are hosting the 2010 World Cup, it's a must for all foreign tourists. This guide tells you where the stadiums are, what's been done to jack them up for their big moment in FIFA history and various other trival facts. Plus, when there's no game to watch you can decide over your morning coffee what, besides a field, a relatively small round ball, 22 men with varying hairstyles and ref, can be done and seen in this beautiful country.

The notes section at the back is for those who never have someting to write on when making calls from the car about reservations or tarriffs.

F A C T B O X

Official name: Republic of South Africa (RSA)
Head of State: President Jacob Zuma
Government: Multi-party democracy
GDP: US$467.8 billion
Inflation: 12.3%
Currency: South African rand
Exchange rate: R7.50 = US$1.00
Population: 48,782,756
Area: 1,219,912 sq km
Dialling code: +27
Regional codes:
  Johannesburg 011
  Pretoria 012
  Durban 031
  Cape Town 021
  Port Elizabeth 044
  East London 043
  Bloemfontein 051
Time: GMT +2
Electricity: 15A
Flag: Adopted on Freedom Day, 27 April 1994 and flown for the
  first time when Nelson Mandela was inaugurated as president on
  10 May 1994.
National animal: Springbok (*Antidorcas marsupialis*)
National bird: Secretary bird (*Anthropoides paradisia*)
National fish: Galjoen (*Coracinus capensis*)
National flower: Giant or King protea (*Protea cynaroides*)
National tree: Real yellowwood (*Podocarpus latifolius*)
Languages: South Africa has 11 official launguages:
  English
  Afrikaans
  IsiNdebele
  IsiXhosa
  IsiZulu
  SiPedi

Sesotho
Setswana
SiSwati
Tshivenda
Xitsonga

National anthem:

Nkosi sikelel' iAfrika
Maluphakanyisw' uphondo lwayo
Yizwa imithandazo yethu
Nkosi sikelela, thina lusapho lwayo
Morena boloka setjhaba sa heso
O fedise dintwa la matshwenyeho
O se boloke, O se boloke setjhaba sa heso
Setjhaba sa South Afrika - South Afrika
Uit die blou van onse hemel
Uit die diepte van ons see
Oor ons ewige gebergtes
Waar die kranse antwoord gee
Sounds the call to come together
And united we shall stand
Let us live and strive for freedom
In South Africa our land

Public holidays:
New Year's Day (1 January)
Human Rights Day (21 March)
Freedom Day (27 April)
Workers' Day (1 May)
Youth Day (16 June)
National Women's Day (9 August)
Heritage Day (24 September)
Day of Reconciliation (16 December)
Christmas Day (25 December)
Day of Goodwill (26 December)

TRAVEL AND TRANSPORT

Domestic Travel:

Airports

www.airports.co.za

Bloemfontein Airport—051-407 2240
Cape Town International Airport—021-934 2240
Durban International Airport—031-451 6666
East London Airport—043-706 0306
George Airport—044-876 9310
Kimberley Airport—053-830 7100
Lanseria Airport (Johannesburg)—011-951 2000
OR Tambo International Airport (Johannesburg)—011-921 6911
Port Elizabeth Airport—041-507 7204
Upington Airport—054-332 2161

Domestic Airlines

1time
www.1time.co.za
0861-345 345

British Airways
www.britishairways.com
011-441 8600

Comair
www.comair.co.za
011-921 0111

Kulula
www.kulula.com
0861-585 852

Mango
www.flymango.com
0861-162 646

South African Express Airways (SAX)
www.flysax.com
011-978 5577

SAX flies to:

- Bloemfontein
- Cape Town
- Durban
- East London
- George
- Hoedspruit
- Kimberley
- Mafikeng
- Mala Mala
- Manzini
- Margate
- Maseru
- Mtata
- Nelspruit
- Phalaborwa
- Pietermaritzburg
- Polokwane
- Port Elizabeth
- Richards Bay
- Upington

South African Airways
www.flysaa.com
011-978 1000

Shuttles

Airport Shuttle—transfers to and from the airports in Gauteng, Western Cape, Limpopo and the North West. This includes transfers to Sun City and regional tours.
www.airportshuttle.co.za
0861-748 8853

EZ Shuttle—services Gauteng, the Western Cape and KwaZulu-Natal (KZN) as well as arranging day tours and coach hire.
www.ezshuttle.co.za
0861-397 488

Magic Bus—scheduled transfers from Johannesburg, Cape Town and Durban airports.
www.magicbus.co.za
011-548 0822

Way 2 Go Transfers—24 hour door-to-door shuttle service to and from Cape Town International Airport and the entire Cape peninsula.
www.way2gotransfers.co.za
021-638 0300

Cape Town Airport Shuttles—drop off and collect from all areas of the Western Cape to Cape Town International Airport.
www.capetownshuttleservice.co.za
021-559 5467

Airport Shuttle Service—covers the Johannesburg and Pretoria areas as well as transfers to and from the Kruger National Park and Sun City.
www.airportshuttle.co.za
0861-748 8853

@Shuttles—airport shuttle, transfers to and from events and chauffeur services. Operational in Gauteng and surrounds.
www.shuttles.co.za
0861-111 610

A2B Transfers—operate in Johannesburg, Pretoria, Mpumalanga, KZN and the Western Cape. Transfers and shuttle services to and from airports, resorts, cities, events, etc.
www.a2btransfers.com
012-345 5906

Buzz Around—door-to-door transfers, airport shuttle service, short and long tours and group transfers for events, parties and corporate functions.
www.buzzaround.co.za
083-651 6700

Guinea-Fowl Shuttle Service—door-to-door shuttle service to OR Tambo International and Lanseria aiports, as well as to Sun City, game reserves, guesthouses and lodges.
www.guineafowlshuttle.co.za
072-970 4618

Silverstone Shuttle Service—to and from locations within Gauteng as well as to Bloemfontein, Kruger National Park, Pretoria, Hartbeespoort Dam, Sun City, Clarens, Nelspruit, Vereeniging, Sasolburg and Parys.
www.s-s-s.co.za
011-781 6817

African Shuttle—shuttle service in and around Gauteng.
www.africanshuttle.co.za
082-805 7919

Johannesburg & Pretoria/Tshwane Chauffeur Drive/Shuttle Services—shuttle service in and around Gauteng.
www.jpshuttle.co.za
011-888 6509

Car Rentals

Avis
www.avis.co.za
0861-021 111 / 0861-600 414 / 011-923 3402

Budget
www.budget.co.za
0861-016 622 / 011-398 0123

Europcar
www.europcar.co.za
0861-131 1000 / 011-574 1000

Hertz
www.hertz.co.za
0861-600 136 / 011-935 4800

First
www.firstcarrental.co.za
0861-011 323 / 011-230 9999

Tempest
www.tempestcarhire.co.za
0861-836 7378 / 011-532 3900

Buses

Greyhound—inter-city buses to all major South African cities as well as
to Gaborone, Bulawayo, Harare and Maputo.
www.greyhound.co.za
083-915 9000

Luxliner Intercity Passenger Coaches—Johannesburg's East Rand to
Durban as well as from Witbank and Middleburg to Durban and from
Pretoria to Margate.
www.intercity.co.za
011-914 4321

InterCape—inter-city buses to all major South African destinations as
well as through Namibia to Windhoek and Walvis Bay, north to Etosha,
through the Caprivi into Zimbabwe.
www.intercape.co.za
021-380 4400

Taxis (meter)

Current meter-reading fares are charged as follows: an initial fare of
R2.00, then R5.50 per kilometre and 10 cents per 20-second period of
engine idling time. There is no charge for the distance travelled by the
taxi to the client, so the fares mentioned must cover that distance as
well. Some taxi companies also offer special rates of up to 50% discount
for disabled passengers and pensioners.

Cape Town
Shuttle Excellence CC—021-462 0272
Cab X Press—021-448 1616
Grab a Cab—021-556 6344
Citi Hopper—021-934 4440

Durban
Rasools Taxi Services—031-401 6450
Eagle Taxis—031-337 8333
Mjrc Cabs—031-561 4590
UCabs—031-561 1846

Johannesburg
AAA Diamond Taxis—076-328 0405
A Class Cabs—0800-204 693
Corporate Cabs—011-771 2200
Lehobye & Sons Cab—011-443 6536
Moonlight Cabs—011-462 9668
NTTS Transport Services—071-146 8925
PWV Taxis—011-683 7111
Rose Radio Taxis—011-403 9625
SA Cab—0861-172 222

Safe Cab—0861-665 566
Village Cab—011-887 2207
Village Vision Cab—011-887 3612

Pretoria
Rixi Taxis—012-362 6262
Jakaranda Cab and Tours—082-515 2656

Nelspruit
City Bug—013-753 3392

Taxis (public)

Public mini-bus taxis dominate 90% of the taxi market in South Africa. Until 1977 a law restricted taxis in South Africa to sedan meter taxis, but now these popular mini-buses account for 65% of South African public transport. Although many South Africans travel by taxi every day, for those who do not make frequent use of their services, hailing a taxi can be somewhat daunting. There are hundreds of taxi ranks all over the cities; larger ones in the city centres and smaller ones in the suburbs. Ask a local to direct you to the nearest taxi rank.

There are variations between catching a taxi in different South African cities. Generally taxi drivers in Cape Town will shout out their destinations to you as you walk down the street, but in Jo'burg an intricate sign 'language' exists, made up of more than a dozen hand signals, all referring to different destinations.

However, regardless of what city you are in, a raised index finger will generally get you to the CBD. If you're using mini-bus taxis you're either travelling on a shoestring budget or want to get to know the people of South Africa. Either way, you can't go wrong by asking a local what hand sign will get you to your destination.

Fares are vastly cheaper than meter taxis. Travelling from Roodepoort on the West Rand of Jo'burg into the CBD will cost you a mere R6.50.

Visas and Documents

Visas

South African visa fees are set at US$47 or €43. You should obtain your visa before leaving for South Africa as visas are not issued at South African border posts and you will not be allowed on board an aircraft without one. It is suggested that you apply four weeks before your departure.

Nationals of the following countries are **exempt** from obtaining a visa if visiting South Africa for **90 days or less**:

African Union laissez-passer

Andorra	Iceland
Argentina	Israel
Australia	Italy
Austria	Jamaica
Belgium	Japan
Botswana	Liechtenstein
Brazil	Luxemburg
Canada	Malta
Chile	Monaco
Czech Republic	Netherlands
Denmark	New Zealand
Ecuador	Norway
Finland	Paraguay
France	Portugal
Germany	San Marino
Greece	Singapore
St Vincent & the Grenadines	Spain
Sweden	Switzerland

United Kingdom of Great Britain and Northern Ireland, British Islands Bailiwick of Guernsey and Jersey, Isle of Man and Virgin Islands, Republic of Ireland, and British Overseas Territories.*

Uruguay
Venezuela
United States of America

*The following British Dependent Territories **do** require a visa:
Anguilla, Bermuda, British Antarctic Territory, British Indian Ocean Territory, Cayman Islands, Falkland Islands, Gibraltar, Montserrat, Pitcairn, Henderson, St Helena, Ducie and Oeno Islands, the Sovereign Base Area of Akrotiri and Dhekelia and the Turks and Caicos Island.

Nationals of the following countries are exempt for obtaining a visa if visiting South Africa for **30 days or less**:

Antigua and Barbuda
Barbados
Belize
Benin
Bolivia
Cape Verde
Costa Rica
Cyprus
Gabon
Guyana
Hong Kong (only with regard to holders of Hong Kong British National Overseas passports and Hong Kong Special Administrative Region passports)
Hungary
Jordan
Lesotho
Macau (only with regard to holders of Macau Special Administrative Region passports (MSAR)
Malaysia
Malawi
Maldives
Mauritius
Mozambique
Namibia
Peru
Poland
Seychelles
Slovak Republic
South Korea

Swaziland
Thailand
Turkey
Zambia
Zimbabwe (only in respect of government officials, including police on
   cross-border investigations)

Other Documents

If you plan to hire a car in South Africa make sure you have a valid
international driver's licence. If you plan to travel with your own car
in South Africa you will have to obtain a carnet de passage. If you're a
student, it is always a good idea to carry your hostel and student card
with you as you may qualify for discounts at certain places. In terms of
vaccinations, only a yellow fever vaccination certificate is needed when
entering South Africa from an infected country.

Taxes and Refunds

South Africa has 14% Value Added Tax, but foreign visitors are able
to claim a portion of this back when leaving the country, provided the
goods purchased are also leaving the country. So although receipts kept
from your meal at the Cape Town Fish Market won't be considered,
any items in your suitcase with their corresponding receipts (over
a total value of US$42) will be inspected by a customs official and
the VAT component refunded to you, once you have passed through
immigration.

Borders and Neighbouring States

South Africa is bordered by Mozambique, Zimbabwe, Botswana,
Swaziland and Namibia, with Lesotho falling within South Africa's
borders. When travelling by road one can enter or exit South Africa
through different border posts:

Eastern Cape
Qacha's Nek (between RSA and Lesotho)

Free State
Caledonspoort (between RSA and Lesotho)
Ficksburg Bridge (between RSA and Lesotho)
Maseru Bridge (between RSA and Lesotho)
Van Rooyens Gate (between RSA and Lesotho)

Limpopo
Beitbridge (between RSA and Zimbabwe)

Mpumalanga
Golela (between RSA and Swaziland)
Jeppes Reef (between RSA and Swaziland)
Lebombo (between RSA and Mozambique)
Mahamba (between RSA and Swaziland)
Nerston (between RSA and Swaziland)
Oshoek (between RSA and Swaziland)

North West
Grobler's Bridge (between RSA and Botswana)
Kopfontein (between RSA and Botswana)
Ramatlamba (between RSA and Botswana)

Northern Cape
Nakop (between RSA and Namibia)
Vioolsdrif (between RSA and Namibia)

Embassies

Albania
Shop G57, Fourways Mall, Fourways, Johannesburg 2191
011-465 3871
nrose@tiscali.co.za

Algeria
950 Arcadia Street, Hatfield, Pretoria 0083
012-342 5074 / 5

Angola
1030 Schoeman Street, Hatfield, Pretoria 0083
012-342 0049

Argentine Republic
200 Standard Plaza, 440 Hilda Street, Hatfield, Pretoria 0083
012-430 3524 / 7

Australia
292 Orient Street, cnr Schoeman Street, Arcadia, Pretoria 0083
012-423 6000

Austria
1109 Duncan Street, Brooklyn, Pretoria 0181
012-452 9155
pretoria-ob@bmeia.gv.at

Bangladesh
410 Farenden Street, Sunnyside, Pretoria 0002
012-343 2105-7
bangladeshpta@iburst.co.za

Belarus
327 Hill Street, Arcadia, Pretoria 0002
012-430 7664 / 7707 / 9

Belgium
625 Leyds Street, Muckleneuk, Pretoria 0002
012-440 3201 / 2
cosbeljb@isdailcom

Benin
900 Park Street, cnr Orient Street, Arcadia, Pretoria 0083
012-342 6978
embbenin@yebo.co.za

Bolivia
No. 2 Meadowbrook Close, French Lane, Morningside, Johannesburg 2196
011-883 3416
seabeco@tiscali.co.za

Bosnia & Herzegovina
25 Stella Street, Brooklyn, Pretoria 0181
012-346 5547
bih@mweb.co.za

Botswana
24 Amos Street, Colbyn, Pretoria 0083
012-430 9640

Brazil
1st Floor, Woodpecker Place, Hillcrest Office Park, 177 Dyer Road, Pretoria 0083
012-366 5200
pretoria@brazilianembassy.org.za

Bulgaria
1071 Church Street, Hatfield, Pretoria 0083
012-342 3720 / 1
embulgsa@iafrica.com

Burkina Faso
849 Government Avenue, Arcadia, Pretoria 0083
012-342 2246 / 2243

Burundi
20 Glyn Street, Colbyn, Pretoria 0083
012-342 4881 / 4883

Cameroon
800 Duncan Street, Brooklyn, Pretoria 0075
012-362 4731
hicocam@cameroon.co.za

Canada
1103 Arcadia Street, Corner Hilda Street, Hatfield, Pretoria 0083
012-422 3000

Central African Republic
20 Monument Road, Kempton Park, Johannesburg 1619
011-970 1355
erikson@lia.co.za

Chile
1st Floor, Block B, Brooklyn Gardens, 235 Veale Street, Niuew Muckleneuk, Pretoria 0002
012-460 8090
consulate@chile.org.za

China (People's Republic of)
965 Church Street, Arcadia, Pretoria 0083
012-431 6500

Colombia
3rd Floor, Park Corner Building, 1105 Park Street, Hatfield, Pretoria 0083
012-342 0211 / 4
emcolsf@mweb.co.za

Comoros
817 Thomas Street, cnr Church and Eastwood Streets, Arcadia, Pretoria 0083
012-343 9483

Congo
960 Arcadia Street, Arcadia, Pretoria 0083
012-342 5508

Congo (Democratic Republic of)
791 Schoeman Street, Arcadia, Pretoria 0083
012-344 6475/6

Costa Rica
14 Taiton Road, Forest Town, Johannesburg 2193
011-486 4716
bish@mega.co.za

Côte d'Ivoire
795 Government Avenue, Arcadia, Pretoria 0083
012-342 6913 / 14

Croatia
1160 Church Street, Colbyn, Pretoria 0083
012-342 1206 / 1598

Cuba
45 Mackenzie Street, Brooklyn, Pretoria 0181
012-346 2215
pretoria@embassy.mzv.cz

Cyprus
cnr Hill & Church Street, Arcadia, Pretoria 0083
012-342 5258
cyprusjb@mweb.co.za

Czech Republic
936 Pretorius Street, Arcadia, Pretoria 0083
012-431 2380

Denmark
Block B2, Iparioli Office Park, 1166 Park Street, Hatfield, Pretoria 0083
012-430 9340
pryamb@um.dk

Djibouti
138 West Street, Sandton, Johannesburg 2196
011-719 9111

Dominican Republic
270 Delphinus Street, Waterkloof Ridge, Pretoria 0181
012-346 3937
embajadadominicana@telkomsa.net

Ecuador
Suite 3, Selatipark, 36 Selati Street, Alphen Park, Pretoria 0081
012-346 1162

Egypt
270 Bourke Street, Muckleneuk, Pretoria 0002
012-343 1590 / 1
egyptemb@global.co.za

Equatorial Guinea
48 Florence Street, Colbyn, Pretoria 0083
012-342 9945 / 6470 / 7087 / 5076

Eritrea
1281 Cobham Road, Queenswood, Pretoria 0186
012-333 1302

Estonia
16 Hofmeyer Street, Welgemoed, Bellville, Cape Town 7530
021-913 3850
jrknipe@iafrica.com

Ethiopia
47 Charles Street, Bailey's Muckleneuk, Brooklyn, Pretoria 0181
012-346 3542

European Union
2 Green Park Estates, 27 George Storrar Drive, Groenkloof, Pretoria 0181
janine.pretorius@ec.europa.eu

Finland
628 Leyds Street, Muckleneuk, Pretoria 0002
012-343 0275
sanomat.pre@formin.fi

France
250 Melk Street, Cnr Middle Street, New Muckleneuk, Pretoria 0181
012-425 1600
france@ambafrance-rsa.org

Gabon
921 Schoeman Street, Arcadia, Pretoria 0083
012-342 4376 / 7

The Gambia
Block A, Lower Ground, Grayston Ridge, 144 Katherine Street, Sandown, Johannesburg 2146
011-430 7640

Georgia
7th Floor, Southern Life Centre, Cape Town 8001
021-421 6355

Germany
180 Blackwood Street, Arcadia, Pretoria 0083
012-427 8900
GermanEmbassyPretoria@gonet.co.za

Ghana
1038 Arcadia Street, Hatfield, Pretoria 0083
012-342 5847-9

Greece
1003 Church Street, Arcadia, Pretoria 0083
012-430 7351 / 2 / 3
embgrsaf@global.co.za

Grenada
3rd Floor, Digital House, Park Lane, Sandton, Johannesburg 2196
083-461 6559

Guatemala
16th Floor, 2 Long Street, Cape Town 8001
021-418 2020

Guinea
336 Orient Street, Arcadia, Pretoria 0083
Tel: 012-342 7348 / 4906
embaguinea@l.africa.com

Guinea-Bissau
1st Floor, Lakeside 2, Bruma Lake, Ernest Oppenheimer Drive, Bruma,
    Johannesburg 2198
011-622 3688

Guyana
The Decision Centre, Hurlingham Manor, Sandton, Johannesburg 2199
011-789 9760
raebenz@compuserve.com

Haiti
808 George Street, Arcadia, Pretoria 0007
012-430 7560

Holy See (The Vatican)
800 Pretorius Street, Arcadia, Pretoria 0083
012-344 3815 / 6

Hungary
959 Arcadia Street, Hatfield, Pretoria 0083
012-430 3020 / 30
mission.prt@kum.hu

Iceland
Building A2, iParioli Office Park, 1166 Park Street, Hatfield, Pretoria 0083
012-342 5885

India
852 Schoeman Street, Arcadia, Pretoria 0083
012-342 5392
hcipta@iafrica.com

Indonesia
949 Schoeman Street, Arcadia, Pretoria 0083
012-342 3350
indonemb@intekom.co.za

Iran
1002 Schoeman Street, Hatfield, Pretoria 0083
012-342 5880 / 1
office@iranembassy.org.za

Iraq
803 Duncan Street, Brooklyn, Pretoria 0181
012-362 2049
abrtmb@iraqmofamail.net

Ireland
1st Floor, Southern Life Plaza, 1059 Schoeman Street, cnr Festival Street,
  Arcadia, Pretoria 0083
012-342 5062

Israel
428 King's Highway, cnr Elizabeth Grove Street, Lynwood, Pretoria 0081
012-470 3500 / 348 6389 / 0470
cao-sec@pretoria.mfa.gov.il

Italy
796 George Avenue, Arcadia, Pretoria 0083
012-423 0000
ambital@iafrica.com

Jamaica
1119 Burnett Street, Hatfield, Pretoria 0083
012-362 6667 / 366 8500
jhcpretoria@telkomsa.net

Japan
259 Baines Street, cnr Frans Oerder Street, Groenkloof, Pretoria 0181
012-452 1500
enquiries@embjapan.org.za

Jordan
252 Olivier Street, Brooklyn, Pretoria 0181
012-346 8615 / 2
embjordpta@telkomsa.net

Kenya
302 Brooks Street, Menlo Park, Pretoria 0081
012-362 2249 / 50 / 51

Korea (Democratic Peoples' Republic of)
958 Waterpoort Street, Faerie Glen, Pretoria 0081
012-991 8661
dprkembassy@lantic.net

Korea (Republic of)
GreenPark Estates, Building 3, 27 George Storrar Drive, Groenkloof, Pretoria 0081
012-460 2508
korrsa@smartnet.co.za

Kuwait
890 Arcadia Street, Arcadia, Pretoria 0083
012-342 0877
safarku@global.co.za

Latvia
The Reserve, 54 Melville Road, Illovo, Johannesburg 2196
011-750 1600
consul@neishlos.com

Lebanon
788 Government Street, Arcadia, Pretoria 0083
012-430 2130
embassyoflebanon@telkomsa.net

Lesotho
391 Anderson Street, Menlo Park, Pretoria 0081
012-460 7648

Liberia
Suite 9, Section 7, Schoeman Street Forum, 1157 Schoeman Street, Hatfield, Pretoria 0083
012-342 2734 / 35
libempta@pta.lia.net

Libya
900 Church Street, cnr Balmoral Street, Arcadia, Pretoria 0083
012-342 3902
libyasa@telkomsa.net

Lithuania
1st Floor, Killarney Mall, Riviera Road, Killarney, Johannesburg 2193
011-486 3660
heidi@garbjoffe.co.za

Luxembourg
1st Floor, Fulnam House, Hampton Park, 20 Georgian Crescent, Bryanston Ext 5,
Johannesburg 2191
011-463 1744 / 659 0961

Madagascar
90B Tait Street, Colbyn, Pretoria 0083
012-342 0983 / 4 / 5 / 6

Malawi
770 Government Avenue, Arcadia, Pretoria 0083
012-342 0146 / 1759

Malaysia
1007 Schoeman Street, Arcadia, Pretoria 0083
012-342 5990 / 3

Mali
Block B, 876 Pretorius Street, Arcadia, Pretoria 0083
012-342 7464 / 0676

Malta
P O Box 1351, Morningside, Johannesburg 2057
332 Koeberg Road, Milnerton, Cape Town 8744
011-706 3052
maltaconsulate@intekom.co.za

Mauritania
146 Anderson Street, Brooklyn, Pretoria 0181
012-362 3578
rimambapretoria@webmail.co.za

Mauritius
1163 Pretorius Street, Hatfield, Pretoria 0083
012-342 1283 / 4
mhcpta@smartnet.co.za

Mexico
Parkdev Building, Brooklyn Bridge, 570 Fehrsen Street, Brooklyn, Pretoria 0181
012-460 1004
embamexza@mweb.co.za

Monaco
1 Milton's Way, 11 Bell Crescent Close, Westlake Business Park, Westlake, Cape Town 7945
021-702 0991 / 021-702 0992
info@consulate-monaco.co.za

Morocco
799 Schoeman Street, cnr Farenden Street, Arcadia, Pretoria 0083
012-343 0230 / 344 2340
sifmapre@telkomsa.net

Mozambique
529 Edmund Street, Arcadia, Pretoria 0083
012-401 0300

Myanmar
201 Leyds Street, Arcadia, Pretoria 0083
012-341 2557 / 2556
euompta@global.co.za

Namibia
197 Blackwood Street, Arcadia, Pretoria 0083
012-481 9100
secretary@namibia.gov.na

Netherlands
210 Queen Wilhelmina Avenue, Nieuw Muckleneuk, Pretoria 0002
012-425 4500
pre@minbuza.nl

New Zealand
125 Middle Street, Muckleneuk, Pretoria 0181
012-435 9000
enquiries@nzhc.co.za

Nigeria
971 Schoeman Street, Arcadia, Pretoria 0083
Tel: 012-342 0805 / 0663
nhep@iafrica.com

Norway
Iparioli Building A2, 1166 Park Street, Hatfield, Pretoria 0083
012-342 6100
emb.pretoria@mfa.no

Oman
11 Andreson Street, Brooklyn, Pretoria 0181
012-362 8301
emb-oman@telkomsa.net

Pakistan
312 Brooks Street, Menlo Park, Pretoria 0081
Tel: 012-362 4072 / 3 / 3967
pareppretoria@telkomsa.net

Palestine
809 Government Avenue, Arcadia, Pretoria 0083
012-342 6411

Panama
229 Olivier Street, Brooklyn, Pretoria 0181
012-460 6677
panamaembassy@bodamail.co.za

Paraguay
189 Strelitzia Road, Waterkloof Heights, Pretoria 0181
012-347 1047
embapar@iafrica.com

Peru
1st Floor, Block A, Brooklyn Gardens, 235 Veale Street, cnr Middel Street,
   Nieuw Mucleneuk, Pretoria 0181
012-346 8744
embaperu6@telkomsa.net

Philippines
54 Nicholson Street, Muckleneuk, Pretoria 0181
012-346 0451 / 2
pretoriape@mweb.co.za

Poland
14 Amos Street, Colbyn, Pretoria 0083
012-430 2631 / 2
e20@mweb.co.za

Portugal
599 Leyds Street, Muckleneuk, Pretoria 0002
012-341 2340 / 1 / 2
portemb@global.co.za

Qatar
355 Charles Street, Waterkloof, Pretoria 0181
012-452 1700
qatar-emb@lantic.net

Romania
117 Charles Street, Brooklyn, Pretoria 0181
012-460 6940

Russian Federation
316 Brooks Street, Menlo Park, Pretoria 0081
012-362 1337 / 8

Rwanda
983 Schoeman Street, Arcadia, Pretoria 0083
012-342 6536

Saharawi Arab Democratic Republic
801 Merton Avenue, Arcadia, Pretoria 0083
012-342 5532
samoba19@yahoo.com

San Marino
P O Box 2013, Brooklyn Square, Pretoria 0075
012-460 5826
antonlo@telkomsa.net

Saudi Arabia
711 Duncan Street, cnr Duncan Street, Pretoria 0081
012-362 4230 / 4240

Senegal
Charles Manor, 57 Charles Street, Bailey's Muckleneuk, Pretoria 0181
012-460 5263

Serbia
163 Marais Street, Brooklyn, Pretoria 0181
Tel: 012-460 5626 / 6103

Seychelles
Global House. 296 Glenwood Road, Lynnwood Park, Pretoria 0081
012-348 0270
economist.embassy@ymail.com

Singapore
980 Schoeman Street, Arcadia, Pretoria 0083
012-430 6035

Slovak Republic
930 Arcadia Street, Arcadia, Pretoria 0083
012-342 2051 / 2
slovakem@telkomsa.net

Spain
Lord Charles Building, 337 Brooklyn Road, Brooklyn, Pretoria 0181
012-460 0123

Sri Lanka
410 Alexander Street, Brooklyn, Pretoria 0181
012-460 7690 / 7679
slhc@srilanka.co.za

Sudan
1203 Pretorius Street, Hatfield, Pretoria 0083
012-342 4538 / 7903

Suriname
Groenkloof Forum Office Park, 57 George Storrar Drive, Groenkloof, Pretoria 0181
Tel: 012-346 7627 / 45 / 7721
embsur@lantic.net

Swaziland
715 Government Avenue, cnr Blackwood Street, Arcadia, Pretoria 0083
012-344 1910

Sweden
1 Parioli Complex, 1166 Park Street, Hatfield, Pretoria 0083
012-426 6400
ambassaden.pretoria@foreign.ministry.se

Switzerland
225 Veale Street, Parc Nouveau, New Muckleneuk, Pretoria 0181
012-452 0660
vertretung@pre.rep.admin.ch

Syrian Arab Republic
963 Schoeman Street, Arcadia, Pretoria 0083
Tel: 012-342 4701 / 4566

Tanzania
822 George Avenue, Arcadia, Pretoria 0083
012-342 4371 / 93
tanzania@cis.co.za

Thailand
428 Hill Street, cnr Pretorius Street, Hatfield, Pretoria 0028
Tel: 012 342 5470 / 4516 / 4506
info@thaiembassy.co.za

Trinidad & Tobago
258 Lawley Street, Waterkloof, Pretoria 0181
012-460 9688
tthepretoria@telkomsa.net

Tunisia
850 Church Street, Arcadia, Pretoria 0083
012-342 6282 / 83

Turkey
1067 Church Street, Hatfield, Pretoria 0028
012-342 6053-7
pretbe@global.co.za

Uganda
882 Church Street, Arcadia, Pretoria 0083
012-342 6031 / 3

Ukraine
398 Marais Street, Brooklyn, Pretoria 0181
012-460 1946

United Arab Emirates
992 Arcadia Street, Arcadia, Pretoria 0083
012-342 7736
uae@mweb.co.za

UK of Great Britain & Northern Ireland
Greystoke, 255 Hill Street, Arcadia, Pretoria 0083
012-421 7500
media.pretoria@fco.gov.uk

United States of America
877 Pretorius Street, Arcadia, Pretoria 0083
012-431 4000

Uruguay
3rd Floor, Glenrand MIB House, 1119 Burnett Street, 301, Hatfield, Pretoria 0083
012-362 6521 / 22
urusud@pixie.co.za

Vanuatu
Grosvenor Court 1, High Level Road 78, Green Point, Cape Town 8002
021-434 6570
Christian@brendel.co.za

Venezuela
Suite 4, 1st Floor, 474 Hatfield Gables South, Hilda Street, Hatfield, Pretoria 0083
012-362 6593

Vietnam
87 Brook Street, Brooklyn, Pretoria 0181
012-362 8119
vnto@worldonline.co.za

Yemen
329 Main Street, Waterkloof, Pretoria 0181
012-425 0760
info@yemenembassy.org.za

Zambia
Zambia House, 570 Ziervoel Avenue, Arcadia, Pretoria 0083
012-326 1854
zahpta@mweb.co.za

Zimbabwe
Zimbabwe House, 798 Merton Street, Arcadia, Pretoria 0083
012-342 5125

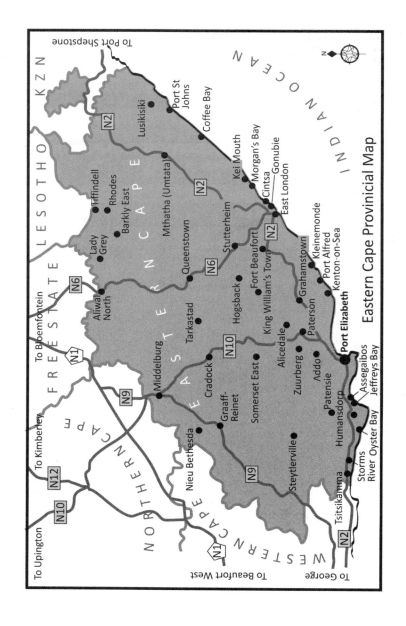

Eastern Cape Provincial Map

Eastern Cape

Tourism Information Offices

East London Tourism Board
Tel: 043-701 9600
URL: www.ectourism.co.za

Eastern Cape Tourism Board
Tel: 047-489 1400
Email: mqingwanac@mbhashemun.gov.za
URL: www.ectourism.co.za

Graaff-Reinet Tourism Bureau
Tel: 049-892 4248
Email: info@graaffreinet.co.za
URL: www.graaffreinet.co.za

Grahamstown Tourism Bureau
Tel: 046-622 3241
Email: info@grahamstown.co.za
URL: www.grahamstown.co.za

Jeffreys Bay Tourism
Tel: 042-293 2923
Email: jbay-tourism@agnet.co.za
URL: www.jeffreysbaytourism.com

Port Elizabeth Tourism Bureau
Tel: 041-585 8884
Email: information@tourismpe.co.za
URL: www.gardenroute.org/pe/index.htm

Wild Coast Tourism Office
Tel: 047-531 5290
URL: www.wildcost.co.za

Top 10

Addo Elephant Park
Tel: 042-233 8600
Email: addoenquiries@sanparks.org
URL: www.addoelephant.com

In 1931, when the original elephant section of the park was proclaimed, only 11 elephants remained. Today, in the beauty of the dense valley bushveld of the Sundays River, 450 elephant find sanctuary in its 164,000 hectares. There are plans to expand Addo into a mega-park and marine reserve. Addo is home to the Cape buffalo, Black rhino and the flightless dung beetle. The park conserves five of South Africa's seven biomes and incorporates the largest coastal dune field in the southern hemisphere and protects the world's largest Cape gannet breeding population on Bird Island. Definitely worth a trip, the bushveld of the Sundays River Valley is beautiful, the park is well managed and has curio and restaurant facilities. You can drive around in your own vehicle or book guided game drives. A range of accommodation is available from hotels to self-catering cottages.

Amakhala Game Reserve
Tel: 046-636 2750
Email: centralres@amakhala.co.za
URL: www.amakhala.co.za

This relatively new addition to South Africa's game parks used to be cultivated farm lands. Since the turn of the century it has been encouraged to reclaim its natural identity. The park aims to re-introduce animals formerly endemic to the area, thereby making a marked contribution to the area's natural heritage. The reserve boasts six independently owned lodges. The lodges are owner-managed by the descendants of the original families who arrived in South Africa, in Algoa Bay, with the British settlers of 1820. The lodges offer various styles of accommodation, which include two gracious colonial homesteads, two classic bush lodges, an historic inn and a settler farmhouse.

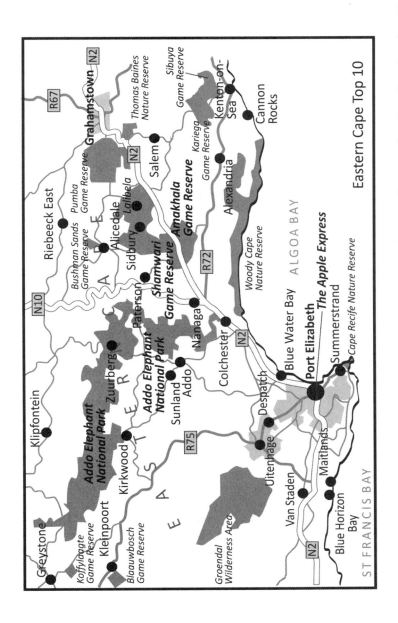

Eastern Cape Top 10

Camdeboo National Park
Tel: 049-892 3453
Email: camdeboo@sanparks.org
URL: www.sanparks.org/parks/camdeboo/

With over 200 national parks, game reserves and wildlife conservancies, South Africa can afford to boast a little, especially in a province as diverse in natural beauty as the Eastern Cape, gripping the semi-arid Karoo in the west and northwest and the lushness of the Zulu kingdom in the northeast. Now, South Africans making the tedious trip from Jo'burg to Cape Town by car may close their eyes and go hell for leather along the N1 through the blazing heat of the Karoo. But stop! Don't see the Karoo as something to get through, see it as a destination. It is breathtakingly beautiful. Camedeboo encircles the town of Graaff-Reinet. The greater portion of the park is situated between 740 and 1480 metres above sea level in the foothills of the Sneeuberg range. The Nqweba Dam lies within the park and covers about 1,000 hectares when full. At some places, dolerites form jointed pillars—the best examples of which are found in the Valley of Desolation where erosion of the softer sedimentary beds has left dolerite pillars which rise to heights of 90 – 120 metres.

Hole in the Wall
Situated in Coffee Bay
URL: www.sa-venues.com/attractionsec/holeinthewall.htm

Literally a hole in a monumental wall of free-standing rock in Coffee Bay, on South Africa's unspoiled, rural stretch of Wild Coast. Hole in the Wall is a pretty much self-contained holiday village, perfect for families with children. There is no shortage of swimming pools, trampolines and beach activities, ideal and safe to let the kids play while the folks chill out on the beach or on the deck overlooking the beach, or at the bar, again with a seaview. This part of the South African coastline, stretching between the Mtamvuna River in the north and the Great Kei River to the south, is characterized by its untamed beauty and yet for the holidaymaker it has all the facilities, activities and accommodation you would find anywhere else; just a little more rustic and a little less gauche, but no less comfortable.

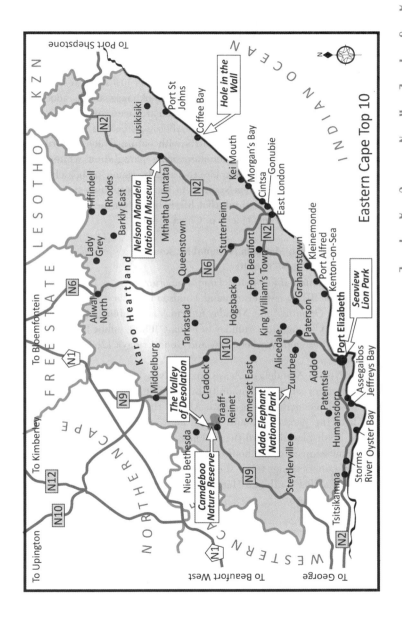

Eastern Cape Top 10

Karoo Heartland
URL: www.karooheartland.co.za

The Karoo Heartland has its southeastern border just northwest of Port Elizabeth, then stretches north through Cookhouse and Cradock. It proceeds north as far as Colesberg and then arcs west and southwest to Murraysburg and then south through Aberdeen, ending its horseshoe journey in Willowmore. History flirts with nature which in turn can only explode in a junction of mountaineering, paragliding, white-water rafting, angling and 4x4ing. Explore this area by canoe, on horseback or on foot. Visit museums, treat yourself to Karoo hospitality and cuisine and don't for one minute think that life is better on the coast. It even has its own annual events calendar. Check it out!

Nelson Mandela National Museum
Tel: 047-532 5110
Email: info@mandelamuseum.org.za
URL: www.nelsonmandelamuseum.org.za
Opening time: Monday to Friday and public holidays 09h00
Closing time: Monday to Friday: 16h00; public holidays
(except Workers' Day and Good Friday): 12h30

Aftern Nelson Mandela's release from prison he received many gifts from the international community in recognition of his life's work for peace and reconciliation in South Africa. He accepted these gifts on behalf of the people of South Africa and expressed a wish that they should be displayed for all the nation to see. Hence the establishment of the museum near his home village of Qunu in the Eastern Cape. The museum occupies three sites: the Bunga Building in Mthatha, the Nelson Mandela Youth and Heritage Centre in Qunu and the Open Air Museum at Mvezo.

Seaview Game and Lion Park
Tel: 041-378 1702
Email: seaview@isat.co.za
URL: www.seaviewgamepark.co.za
Opening Time: Daily: 09h00
Closing Time: Daily: 17h00
Tariffs: Adults: R45; Students and pensioners: R40;
    Children: R20

Established in 1975 the Seaview Game and Lion Park is situated 25 kilometres west of Port Elizabeth in 120 hectares of bush and grassland. Because of the high volume of tourists that South African parks now enjoy, many parks only allow their own game-viewing vehicles to drive in the park itself. The Seaview Game and Lion Park however, still offers its visitors the opportunity to drive themselves around and enjoy some close-up game viewing. There is a restaurant, curio shop and caravan and camping facilities. The park offers the thrilling and unforgettable experience of interacting with the young cubs. A must do!

Shamwari Game Reserve
Tel: 041-407 1000
Email: reservations@mantiscollection.com
URL: www.shamwari.com

Situated along the Bushman's River, between Port Elizabeth and Grahamstown the Shamwari (meaning 'friend' in Shona) Private Game Reserve is about conserving a vanishing way of life and as such has received numerous international awards, including the World's Leading Conservation Company and Game Reserve for many consecutive years. Steeped in settler history, and dating back to the time when a multitude of game roamed wild and free, the 20,000-hectare reserve boasts five eco-systems, thus enabling the support of many forms of plant, animal and bird life.

The Apple Express
Tel: 041-583 4480
Email: bookings@appleexpresstrain.co.za
URL: www.apple-express.co.za

This steam-powered locomotive was started as a tourist train in 1965 and is renowned for its day trips over weekends. The train became renowned in the 1980s with the advent of the Great Train Race, where relays of athletes would complete against the train in a race that took them from Port Elizabeth to Loerie, 70 kilometres away. The Apple Express travels to Assegaaibos and Patensie. The trips are quaint getaways, perfect for the whole family. There are various accommodation options available, from tented camping to graded dinner, bed and breakfast.

Valley of Desolation
Situated near Graaff-Reinet
URL: www.camdeboocottages.co.za/valley.html

Surrounding the town of Graaff-Reinet, the Valley of Desolation is a geological phenomenon. Located within the Camdeboo National Park, it has been declared a National Monument. These sheer, vertical cliffs of dolerite tower a massive 120 metres above the valley floor, the product of volcanic and erosive forces over hundreds of millions of years. Graaff-Reinet is without doubt worth a visit, just for the charmingly restored Karoo-style homes and the historical buildings; and the hamlet of Nieu Bethesda lures even the most cynical tourist.

Activities

Adventure Activities

Areena Riverside
Tel: 043-734 3055
Email: info@areenaresort.co.za
URL: www.areena.co.za

EP Skydivers
Tel: 046-622 3319
Email: joosvos@eastcape.net
URL: www.epskydivers.co.za

Face Adrenalin Bloukrans Bungy
Tel: 042-281 1458
Email: info@faceadrenalin.com
URL: www.faceadrenalin.com

Green Adventures
Tel: 041-581 2727
Email: info@greenadventures.co.za
URL: www.greenadventures.co.za

J-Bay Sandboarding
Tel: 042-296 2974 / 072-294 8207
Email: jaybaysandboarding@hotmail.com
URL: www.jeffreysbaytourism.org

JBay Wind
Tel: 082-507 8887
Email: customworks@intekom.co.za
URL: www.customworks.co.za

Kromme River Expeditions
Tel: 084-506 6396
Email: kipper-skipper@webmail.co.za
URL: www.stfrancistourism.co.za/index.php

Nukakamma PPC Canoe Trail
Tel: 041-468 0238
Email: rwrich@worldonline.co.za
URL: www.trailinfo.co.za/water/
    nukakamma/index.html

SA Adventure Trails
Tel: 033-343 1217
Email: info@wildcoastwalk.co.za
URL: www.wildcoastwalk.co.za

Tiffindell Ski
Tel: 086-178 7909
Email: resort@skisouthafrica.co.za
URL: www.skisouthafrica.co.za

Ulovane Environmental Training
Tel: 083-295 3206
Email: Candice@ulovane.co.za
URL: www.ulovane.co.za

Wild Mountain Adventures
Tel: 045-971 9064
Email: wildmountain@polka.co.za
URL: www.wildmountainadventures.co.za

Outdoor Activities

Beach Horse Rides & Loerie Mountain Trails
Tel: 079-299 8080
Email: info@horsetrails.co.za
URL: www.horsetrails.co.za

Drifters Wild Coast Hiking / Cycling Trail
Tel: 011-888 1160
Email: drifters@drifters.co.za
URL: www.drifters.co.za

Mkulu Kei Horse Trails
Tel: 043-841 1525
Email: Cheryl@mkulukeihorsetrails.co.za
URL: www.mkulukeihorsetrails.co.za

Natural High Outdoor Activities
Tel: 079-636 8949
Email: getit@naturalhigh.co.za
URL: www.naturalhigh.co.za

Strandloper Trails
Tel: 043-841 1046
Email: strandloper@net4u.co.za
URL: www.strandlopertrails.org.za

Wild Coast Horse Trails
Tel: 043-831 1087
Email: julie-ann@sunrayfarm.co.za
URL: www.wildcoasthorsesafari.co.za

Sport

Graaff-Reinet Golf Club
Tel: 049-893 0286
Email: grtgolfclub@wam.co.za
URL: http://golf.ifm2.com/graaffreinet/
contact.html

Grahamstown Golf Club
Tel: 046-622 2106
Email: j.burton@ru.ac.za
URL: www.grahamstown.co.za/golf/

Jeffreys Bay Golf Club
Tel: 042-293 2532
Email: jbaygolf@absamail.co.za
URL: www.g-i.co.za/jeffreysbay

Port Elizabeth Golf Club
Tel: 041-374 3140
Email: admin@pegolf.co.za /
bookings@pegolf.co.za
URL: www.pegolf.co.za

West Bank Golf Course
Tel: 043-731 1523
Email: westbankgolfclub@iafrica.com
URL: www.westbankgc.co.za
Situated in East London

Stadiums

Nelson Mandela Bay Stadium
Tel: 041-508 2010
Email: 2010@wc.mandelametro.gov.za
URL: www.nelsonmandelabay.gov.za

One of five stadiums built from scratch for the 2010 World Cup, this five-tier stadium in Port Elizabeth seats 48,000 fans. The stadium is hailed for its location and view of North End Lake; apparently not many stadiums in the world overlook a lake, although I'm really not sure how this adds value for the teeming hordes of soccer-crazed fans. What it can and should be congratulated for is that it is the first newly-built stadium that was indeed ready to host Confederations Cup games.

Buffalo Park Cricket Ground
Tel: 043-743 7757
URL: www.borderbears.co.za
Situated in East London

St George's Park Cricket Club
Tel: 041–506 6689
Email: shaunayc@cricket.co.za
URL: www.stgeorgespark.nmmu.ac.za
Situated in Port Elizabeth

Culture

Museums

Albany Museum Complex
Tel: 046-622 2312
URL: www.ru.ac.za/static/affiliates/am/?request=affiliates/am/
Situated in Grahamstown

Anderson Museum
Tel: 045-943 1017
URL: www.southafrica.info/travel/cultural/179904.html
Opening Time: Monday to Friday: 09h00
Closing Time: Monday to Friday: 12h00
Situated in Dordrecht

Barkley East Museum
Tel: 045-971 0063
Opening Time: Monday to Friday: 09h00 and again at 15h00
Closing Time: Monday to Friday: 12h00 and again at 17h00

Bathurst Agricultural Museum
Tel: 072-408 4858
Email: hopewell@telkomsa.net
URL: www.bathurst.co.za/Museum.htm
Opening Time: Monday to Saturday: 09h00; Sunday: 15h00
Closing Time: Monday to Friday: 16h00; Sunday: 16h00

Bayworld
Tel: 041-586 1051
Email: svanzyl@icon.co.za
URL: www.bayworld.co.za
Opening Time: Daily: 09h00
Closing Time: Daily: 17h00
Situated in Port Elizabeth

Burgersdorp Cultural Historical Museum
Tel: 051-653 1738
URL: www.southafrica.info.travel/cultural/179904.html
Opening Time: Monday to Friday: 08h00
Closing Time: Monday to Friday: 16h00

Calgary Transport Museum
Tel: 043-730 7244
URL: www.gardenroute.org/eastlondon/index.html#calgary
Opening Time: Daily: 09h00
Closing Time: Daily: 16h00
Situated in East London

C M van Coller Museum
Tel: 045-843 1737
Opening Time: Monday, Tuesday, Thursday, Friday: 10h00; Wednesday: 14h00
Closing Time: Monday, Tuesday, Thursday, Friday: 12h00; Wednesday: 16h00
Situated in Cathcart

East London Museum
Tel: 043-743 0686
Opening Time: Monday to Friday: 09h30; Saturday: 14h30; Sunday: 11h00
Closing Time: Monday to Friday: 17h00; Saturday: 17h00; Sunday: 16h00

F S Malan Museum
Tel: 040-602 2277
URL: www.ufh.ac.za
Opening Time: Monday to Friday: 09h00 and again at 14h00
Closing Time: Monday to Friday: 13h00 and again at 17h00
Situated in Alice

Fort Beaufort Historical Museum
Tel: 046-645 1555
Opening Time: Monday to Saturday: 08h30
Closing Time: Monday to Friday: 17h00; Saturday: 12h45

Gately House
Tel: 043-722 2141
Opening Time: Tuesday to Friday: 10h00; Weekends: 15h00
Closing Time: Tuesday to Friday: 13h00; Weekends: 17h00
Situated in East London

Graaff-Reinet Museum Complex
Tel: 049-892 3801
URL: www.wheretostay.co.za/information/topic/3626

Kerkplein Museum
Tel: 051-633 2441
Email: ectban@intekom.co.za
Opening Time: Monday to Saturday: 09h00
Closing Time: Monday to Saturday: 12h00
Situated in Aliwal North

Ons Erfenis Museum
Tel: 046-684 0290
Opening Time: Monday to Friday: 08h00 and again at 14h00
Closing Time: Monday to Friday: 13h00 and again at 17h00
Situated in Adelaide

Schreiner House
Tel: 048-881 5251
URL: www.places.co.za/html/schreiner.html
Opening Time: Monday to Friday: 09h00 and again at 14h30
Closing Time: Monday to Friday: 12h30 and again at 16h30
Situated in Cradock

The Great Fish River Museum
Tel: 048-881 4509
Opening Time: Tuesday to Friday: 08h00 and again at 14h00; Saturday: 08h00
Closing Time: Tuesday to Friday: 13h00 and again at 16h00; Saturday: 12h00
Situated in Cradock

Theatres

Feather Market Centre
Tel: 041-585 8758
Email: sgibson@mandelametro.gov.za
URL: www.feathermarket.co.za
Situated in Port Elizabeth

Guild Theatre
URL: www.guildtheatre.co.za
Situated in East London

John Rupert Theatre
Tel: 049-891 1042
URL: www.graaffreinettourism.co.za
Situated in Graaff-Reinet

Opera House
URL: www.southafrica.com/eastern-cape
Situated in Port Elizabeth

Potters Place
Tel: 042-293 2500
URL: www.pottersplace.co.za
Situated in Jeffreys Bay

Galleries

De Beers Centenary Art Gallery
Tel: 040-602-2011
Situated in Alice

Epsac Art Gallery
Tel: 041-585 3641
Situated in Port Elizabeth

Ibis Art Centre
Email: IbisArtCentre@SouthAfricanArtists.com
Situated in Nieu Bethesda

King George VI Art Gallery
Tel: 041-586 1030
Situated in Port Elizabeth

Nelson Mandela Metropolitan Art Museum
Tel: 041-506 2000
Email: artmuseum@mandelametro.gov.za
URL: www.artmuseum.co.za
Situated in Port Elizabeth

Owl House
Tel: 049-841 1733
Email: theowlhouse@mweb.co.za
URL: www.owlhouse.co.za
Situated in Nieu Bethesda

Peter's Art Gallery
Tel: 042-293 1671
Email: art@petersgallery.co.za
URL: www.petersgallery.co.za
Situated in Jeffreys Bay

Ron Belling Gallery
Tel: 041-586 3973
Email: ronbelling@mweb.co.za
URL: www.ronbelling.co.za
Situated in Port Elizabeth

The Vincent Art Gallery
Tel: 043-726 4356
Email: vincentart@lantic.net
URL: www.vincentartgallery.co.za
Situated in East London

Walter Battiss Gallery
Tel: 042-243 2079
Email: semuseum@eastcape.net
Situated in Somerset East

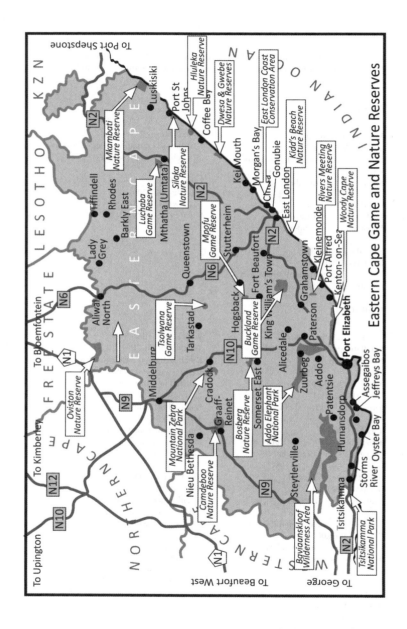

Eastern Cape Game and Nature Reserves

Game and Nature Reserves (including National Parks)

Eastern Cape Parks
Tel: 043-705 4400
Email: reservations@ecparks.co.za
URL: www.ecparks.co.za

Eastern Cape Parks Reserves
Baviaanskloof
Cammando Drift
Dwesa
East London Coast
Fort Fordyce
Great Fish River
Hluleka
Mkhambathi
Mpofu
Oviston
Silaka
Thomas Baines
Tsolwana

South African National Parks
Tel: 012-426 5000
Email: reservations@sanparks.org
URL: www.sanparks.org

SANParks Reserves
Addo Elephant National Park
Camdeboo Nature Reserve
Mountain Zebra National Park

Other Parks

Amakhala Game Reserve
Tel: 046-636 2750
Email: centralres@amakhala.co.za
URL: www.amakhala.co.za

Blaauwbosch Game Reserve
Tel: 041-585 3359
Email: res@blaauwbosch.co.za
URL: www.blaauwbosch.co.za

Bosberg Nature Reserve
Tel: 042-243 0095
Email: bcrm.tourism@lgnet.org.za
URL: www.sa-venues.com/game-reserves/
  ec_bosberg.htm

Bucklands Game Reserve
Tel: 083-775 9655
Email: reservations@bucklandsreserve.co.za
URL: www.bucklandsreserve.co.za

Cape Recife Nature Reserve
Tel: 041-581 7540
Email: info@nmbt.co.za
URL: www.sabirding.co.za/birdspot/
  021013.asp

Dwesa and Cwebe Reserves
Tel: 047-499 0073 / 22 & 047-576 0006 / 7
URL: www.wildcoast.co.za/dwesa

Kariega Game Reserve
Tel: 046-636 7904
Email: reservations@kariega.net
URL: www.kariega.co.za

Kidd's Beach Nature Reserve
URL: www.sa-venues.com/attractionsec/
  kidds-beach.php

Koffylaagte Game Reserve
Tel: 049-836-9188
URL: www.koffylaagtegamelodge.co.za

Kwantu Game Reserve
Tel: 042-203 1400
Email: reservations@kwantu.co.za
URL: www.kwantu.co.za

Luchaba Nature Reserve
URL: www.sa-venues.com/game-reserves/
  ec_luchaba.htm

Pumba Game Reserve
Tel: 046-603 2000
Email: respumba@pehotels.co.za
URL: www.pumbagamereserve.co.za

Shamwari Game Reserve
Tel: 041-407 1000
Email: reservations@mantiscollection.com
URL: www.shamwari.com

Sibuya Game Reserve
Tel: 046-648 1040
Email: reservations@sibuya.co.za
URL: www.sibuya.co.za

Woody Cape Nature Reserve
now part of the Addo Elephant
  National Park
URL: www.sa-venues.com/game-reserves/
  ec_woodycape.htm

Entertainment

Finnezz
cocktail lounge
Tel: 041-586 3233
Situated in Port Elizabeth

Hemimgways Casino
casino
Tel: 043-707 7777
Situated in East London

Imbizo Jazz Café
club / lounge
Tel: 083-493 7002
Situated in East London

Klub Libertas
club
Tel: 049-892 3104
Situated in Aberdeen

Michaela's
cocktail bar
Tel: 043-738 5139
Situated in Cintsa

Numbers Dance Club
club
Tel: 043-748 4425
Situated in East London

Oldest Licensed Pub in South Africa
pub
Tel: 046-625 0673
Situated in Bathurst

Sunshine Bay Beach Club
club
Tel: 042-293 2941
Situated in Jefferys Bay

Tattersalls
club
Tel: 042-293 2232
Situated in Jefferys Bay

The Boardwalk
casino
Tel: 041-507 7777
Situated in Port Elizabeth

Wild Coast Sun
casino
Tel: 039-305 9111
Situated outside Port Edward

Yellow House
cocktail bar
Tel: 083-281 0257
Situated in Grahamstown

Annual Events

Addo Rose & Garden Show
Tel: 042-234 0422
Held in Addo every October

Algoa FM Homemakers Expo
Tel: 041-373 6616
Held in Port Elizabeth every July

Bathurst Agricultural Show
Tel: 046-625 0759
Held in Bathurst every March

Bedford Garden Festival
URL: info@bedford-gardens.co.za
Held in Bedford every October

Billabong Pro Jeffreys Bay (Surfing)
URL: www.billabongpro.com
Held in Jeffreys Bay every July

Biltong Festival
Tel: 042-243 1333
Held in Somerset East every July

Chilli Festival
Tel: 041-484 4540
Held in Port Elizabeth every February

Christian Business Expo
Tel: 011-672 3456
Held in Port Elizabeth every June

East London Bridal Fair
URL: www.sa-venues.com/events/eastern-
  cape-event-description
Held in East London every August

Eastern Cape Fashion Week
Tel: 041-373 9545
Held in Port Elizabeth every September

Fugard Festival
Tel: 049-841 1635
Held in Nieu Bethesda every October

Grahamstown Flower Festival
Tel: 072-244 3863
Held in Grahamstown every November

Grahamstown National Arts Festival
URL: www.nationalartsfestival.co.za
Held in Grahamstown every July

Hogsback Arts Festival
Tel: 045-962 1174
Held in Hogsback every December

Jeffreys Bay Shell Festival
Tel: 082-6333693
Held in Jeffreys Bay every September

Kirkwood Wildlife Festival
Tel: 042-230 0064
Held in Kirkwood every June

Lady Grey Passion Play
Tel: 051-603 0046
Held in Lady Grey every April

Loerie Naartjie Festival
Tel: 042-283 0437
Held in Loerie every September

Nahoon Mile
Tel: 043-735 4181
Held in East London every March

Nelson Mandela Bay Splash Festival
Tel: 041-393 4800
Held in Port Elizabeth every April

New Year's Festival of Lights
Tel: 049-841 1729
Held in Nieu Bethesda every December

Queenstown Annual Easter Family Festival
Tel: 043-743 0799
Held in Queenstown every April

Rhodes Extreme Mountain Bike Race
Tel: 045-971 9144
Held in Rhodes every September

SciFest Africa
URL: www.scifest.org.za
Held in Grahamstown every March

Steytlerville Rainbow Festival
Tel: 049-835 0484
Held in Steytlerville every October

The Collective Graduate Exhibition &
  Fashion Show
Tel: 041-504 3247
Held in Port Elizabeth every October

Uitenhage Street Carnival
Tel: 041-585 0906
Held in Uitenhage every December

Wild Coast Jikileza Country Fair
Tel: 043-734 3123
Held in East London every July

Wild Coast Wet 'n Wild Festival
Tel: 083-653 3111
Held in Cintsa every June

Wine Fair
Tel: 043-726 2320
Held in East London every July

Wordfest
URL: www.wordfest.co.za
Held in Grahamstown every July

Shopping www.mallguide.co.za

Beacon Bay Retail Park
Tel: 043-748 4660
Situated in East London

Binnehof Centre
Tel: 041-363 3621
Situated in Uitenhage

Clearly Park Shopping Centre
Tel: 041-481 5472
Situated in Port Elizabeth

Fountains Mall
Tel: 042-200 2900
Situated in Jeffreys Bay

Hemingways Mall
Tel: 043-721 3181
Situated in East London

Mdantsane City
Tel: 043-762 4110
Situated in East London

Pier 14 Shopping Centre
Tel: 041-484 1228
Situated in Port Elizabeth

Vincent Park Shopping Centre
Tel: 043-727 0990
Situated in East London

Restaurants

Cintsa
Michaela's of Cintsa
Cuisine: Buffet, seafood, international
Tel: 043-738 5139
Address: Steenbras Drive, Chintsa East

Bathurst
Kingston
Cuisine: French, international
Tel: 046-625 0129
Address: Shaw Park Road

East London
Arthurs
Cuisine: Contemporary
Tel: 043-726 7085
Address: 2 Voortrekker Road

Country Bumpkin Restaurant
Cuisine: International
Tel: 043-738 5226
Address: 561 Heron Loop Drive

Grazia Fine Food & Wine
Cuisine: Italian
Tel: 043-722 2009
Address: Upper Esplanade, Beach Front

Le Petit Restaurant
Cuisine: European
Tel: 043-735 3685
Address: 54 Beach Road

Smokey Swallows
Cuisine: Fine Dining
Tel: 043-727 1349
Address: Shop 11, cnr Deverux Avenue
   & Chess Galleria

Zhong Hua
Cuisine: Chinese
Tel: 043-735 3442
Address: 48 Beach Road

Jeffreys Bay
3 Fat Fish
Cuisine: International
Tel: 042-293 4147
Address: 27A Da Gama Road

De Viswijf
Cuisine: Seafood
Tel: 042-293 3921
Address: 55 Diaz Road

Kitchen Windows
Cuisine: International
Tel: 042-293 4230
Address: 23 Diaz Street

Potter's Place
Cuisine: Grill
Tel: 042-293 500
Address: cnr Costerland & St Francis
 Streets

The Mexican
Cuisine: Mexican
Tel: 042-293 2966
Address: 19 Da Gama Street

Port Alfred
Links Coastal Inn Restuarnt
Cuisine: Seafood & grill
Tel: 046-624 2345
Address: 14 Wesley Hill

Port Elizabeth
34° South
Cuisine: Seafood
Tel: 041-583 1085
Address: The Boardwalk, Marine Drive

Barneys Tavern
Cuisine: Grill
Tel: 041-583 4500
Address: Shop 6, The Boardwalk,
 Marine Drive

Blue Orange Garden Café
Cuisine; Bistro
Tel: 041-581 3199
Address: 92 Heugh Road

Blue Waters Café
Cuisine: International
Tel: 041-583 4110
Address: Marine Drive

De Kelder
Cuisine: Grills
Tel: 041-583 2750
Address: cnr 6th Avenue &
 Marine Drive

Elephant Walk
Cuisine: Contemporary
Tel: 041-372 1470
Address: cnr Kragga Kamma & Old
 Seaview Road

El Greco
Cuisine: Greek
Tel: 041-583 2950
Address: Shop 35, The Boardwalk, 2nd Avenue

Farriagers Restaurant & Bar
Cuisine: African
Tel: 041-584 0019
Address: Brooks Hill Drive

Gondwana Café
Cuisine: Fusion
Tel: 041-585 0990
Address: 2 Dolphins Leap, Beach Road

Narai Siam Thai Kitchen
Cuisine: Thai
Tel: 41-363 8126
Address: 20 Worraker Street

Old Austria
Cuisine: Austrian
Tel: 041-373 0299
Address: 24 Westbourne Road

Oystercatcher
Cuisine: Seafood
Tel: 041-582 1867
Address: PE Harbour

Pecorino
Cuisine: Italian
Tel: 041-365 2700
Address: cnr 3rd Avenue & Pickering Street

Royal Delhi Restaurant
Cuisine: Indian
Tel: 041-373 8216
Address: 10 Burgess Street

Thatchwoods
Cuisine: South African
Tel: 041-379 2906
Address: Holmeleigh Farmyard, Kragga
 Kamma Road

The Island Seafood Grill & Bar
Cuisine: Seafood
Tel: 041-583 3789
Address: Marine Drive, Cape Recife

The Verandah Restaurant
Cuisine: Bistro
Tel: 041-583 2161
Address: Marine Drive

Wicker Woods
Cuisine: South African
Tel: 041-374 8170
Address: 99 Cape Road

St Francis Bay
Chokka Block
Cuisine: Seafood & grill
Tel: 042-294 1615
Address: Port St Francis

Tsitsikamma
Fynboshoek Cheese
Cuisine: Bistro
Tel: 042 280 3879
Address: Across from the Tsitsikama Lodge,
   off the N2 (Forest Ferns exit)

Chains and Franchises

Cape Town Fish Market
URL: www.ctfm.co.za

Cappuccino's
URL: www.cappuccinos.co.za

Cattle Baron
URL: www.cattlebaron.co.za

Dros
URL: www.dros.co.za

Dulce Continental Restaurant
URL: www.dulce.co.za

Mugg & Bean
URL: www.themugg.com

Ocean Basket
URL: www.oceanbasket.co.za

Panarotti's
URL: www.panarottis.com

Spur
URL: www.spur.co.za

The Famous Butcher's Grill
URL: www.butchersgrill.com

Wimpy
URL: www.wimpy.co.za

Accommodation

www.eastcape-venues.co.za
www.wheretostay.co.za/ec/
www.accommodation-in-eastern-cape.com
www.stayeastcape.co.za
http://eastern-cape.com
www.south-african-hotels.com/eastern-cape-hotels
www.safarinow.com/destinations/eastern-cape
www.discoverthecape.com/hotels-ec

East London
Hotels

Blue Lagoon Hotel
Tel: 043-748 4821
Email: reservations@bluelagoonhotel.co.za
URL: www.bluelagoonhotel.co.za

Hemingways Hotel
Tel: 043-707 8000
Email: hemingways@southernsun.com
URL: www.southernsun.com

B&Bs, Guest Houses, Self-catering

Benri B&B and Self-Catering
Tel: 043-740 3331
Email: benri@lantic.net
URL: www.benrigonubie.co.za

Bunkers Inn on the Golf Course
Tel: 043-735 4642
Email: bunkersinn@mweb.co.za
URL: www.bunkersinn.co.za

Cozy Nest B&B
Tel: 043-722 8534

Gonubie Manor B&B and Self-Catering
Tel: 043-732 1775

Smart Villa Guest House
Tel: 043-735 3139
Email: info@smartvilla.co.za
URL: www.smartvilla.co.za

Stratfords Guest House
Tel: 043-726 9765
Email: reservations@stratfordsguesthouse.co.za
URL: www.stratfordsguesthouse.co.za

Tidewaters B&B
Tel: 043-740 4505

Wild Rose Villa B&B
Tel: 083-874 0222
Email: info@wildrosevilla.co.za
URL: www.wildrosevilla.co.za

Camping

Areena Riverside Resort
Tel: 043-734 3055
Email: info@areenaresort.com
URL: www.areenaresort.com

Port Elizabeth
Hotels

Humewood Hotel
Tel: 041-585 8961
Email: reservations@humewoodhotel.co.za
URL: www.humewoodhotel.co.za

Kings Tide Boutique Hotel
Tel: 041-583 6023
Email: kingstide@crowncollection.co.za
URL: www.kingstide.co.za

Paxton Hotel
Tel: 041-585 9655
Email: Paxton@iafrica.com
URL: www.paxton.co.za

The Kelway Hotel
Tel: 041-584 0638
Email: reservations@thekelway.co.za
URL: www.thekelway.co.za

Lodges

Kwantu Game Reserve
Tel: 042-203 1400
Email: reservations@kwantu.co.za
URL: www.kwantu.co.za

B&Bs, Guest Houses, Self-catering

Admirals Lodge Guest House
Tel: 041-583 1894
Email: admiralslodge@mweb.co.za
URL: www.admiralslodge.co.za

Anne's Bed & Breakfast
Tel: 041-581 1662

Carslogie House
Tel: 041-583 5251
Email: stay@carslogie.co.za
URL: www.carslogie.co.za

Kaliza's Place
Tel: 041-583 1403
Email: kalizasplace@absamail.co.za
URL: www.kalizasplace.co.za

Keiskama B&B
Tel: 084-585 1888
Email: handicap@webmail.co.za
URL: www.keiskamabnb.co.za

Lemon Tree Lane
Tel: 041-373 4104
Email: info@lemontreelane.co.za
URL: www.lemontreelane.co.za

Manor 38
Tel: 041-583 2328

Other
Hotels

City Lodge Hotels
Tel: 0861-563 467
URL: www.citylodge.co.za
Situated in multiple venues

Drostdy Hotel
Tel: 049-892 2161
URL: www.drostdy.co.za
Situated in Graaff-Reinet

Frontier Country Hotel
Tel: 046-622 7667
Situated in Grahamstown

Garden Court Hotels
Tel: 0861-447 744
URL: www.southernsun.com
Situated in multiple venues

Graham Hotel
Tel: 046-622 2424
Situated in Grahamstown

Hotel Formula 1
Tel: 011-807 0750
URL: www.hotelformula1.co.za
Situated in multiple venues

Ocean View Hotel
Tel: 047-575 2005
Email: oceanview@coffeebay.co.za
URL: www.oceanview.co.za
Situated in Coffee Bay

Premier Hotels
Tel: 0861-115 555
URL: www.premierhotels.co.za
Situated in multiple venues

Protea Hotels
Tel: 0861-119 000
URL: www.proteahotels.com
Situated in multiple venues

Wild Coast Sun Hotel
Tel: 011-780 7800
Email: scvc@za.suninternational.com
URL: www.suninternational.com
Situated on the Wild Coast

Lodges

Hitgeheim Country Lodge
Tel: 042-234 0778
Email: hitgeheim@agnet.co.za
URL: www.hitgeheim-addo.co.za
Situated in Addo

Millard Mountain Lodge
Tel: 045-971 9078
Email: mlodge@eci.co.za
URL: www.millardlodge.co.za
Situated in Barkley East

Misty Mountain Reserve
Tel: 041-373 1599
Email: mistymountainreserve@isat.co.za
URL: www.mistymountainreserve.co.za
Situated in Tsitsikamma

Oceana Wildlife Reserve
Tel: 041-407 1000
Email: reservations@oceanareserve.com
URL: www.oceanareserve.com
Situated in Port Alfred

Olive Park Lodge
Tel: 086-128 3737
Situated in Grahamstown

River Bend Lodge
Tel: 042-233 8000
Email: reservations@riverbendlodge.co.za
URL: www.riverbendlodge.co.za
Situated in Addo Elephant Park

Sederkloof Lodge
Tel: 049-839 1122
Email: thysbaviaans@mweb.co.za
URL: www.sederkloof.co.za
Situated in Baviaanskloof

Shamwari Private Game Reserve
Tel: 041-407 1000
Email: reservations@mantiscollection.com
URL: www.shamwari.com
Situated in Paterson

The Safari Lodge
Tel: 046-636 2750
Situated in Addo

Tsitsikamma On Sea Luxury Lodge
Tel: 042-280 3697
URL: www.tsitsikammaonsea.com
Situated in Tsitsikamma

B&Bs, Guest Houses, Self-catering

18 On Park
Tel: 082-783 1414
Email: jkent@albanynet.co.za
URL: www.18onpark.co.za
Situated in Grahamstown

28 Stones Hill B&B
Tel: 082-784 7685
Situated in Grahamstown

137 High Street
Tel: 046-622 3242
Email: info@137highstreet.co.za
URL: www.137highstreet.co.za
Situated in Grahamstown

Addo Dung Beetle Guest Farm
Tel: 083-399 4129
Situated in Addo

Aquarius B&B
Tel: 042-293 3741
Situated in Jeffreys Bay

Bay Cove Inn
Tel: 042-296 2291
Situated in Jeffreys Bay

Ganora Guest Farm
Tel: 049-841 1302
Email: info@ganora.co.za
URL: www.ganora.co.za
Situated in Graaff-Reinet

Heerenhuys Guest House
Tel: 049-892 6088
Situated in Graaff-Reinet

Marina Martinique B&B
Tel: 042-292 0000
Email: info@mmbnb.co.za
URL: www.mmbnb.co.za
Situated in Jeffreys Bay

Moya Manzi Beach House
Tel: 042-292 0780
Email: info@moyamanzi.com
URL: www.moyamanzi.co.za
Situated in Jeffreys Bay

Oak Lodge Guest House
Tel: 086-128 3737
Situated in Grahamstown

The Cock House
Tel: 046-636 1287
Email: cockhouse@imaginet.co.za
URL: www.cockhouse.co.za
Situated in Grahamstown

Thyme & Again B&B
Tel: 049-892 5413
Situated in Graaff-Reinet

Villa Reinet Guest House
Tel: 049-892 5525
URL: www.villareinet.co.za
Situated in Graaff-Reinet

Windmill Junction
Tel: 049-892 4504
Email: info@windmilljunction.co.za
URL: www.windmilljunction.co.za
Situated in Graaff-Reinet

Camping

Badfontein Guest Farm
Tel: 051-633 2263
Situated in Aliwal North

Green Fountain Farm Resort
Tel: 046-624 2929
Email: info@greenfountain.co.za
URL: www.greenfountain.co.za
Situated in Port Alfred

Morgan Bay Caravan and Camping
Tel: 043-841 1062
Situated on the Wild Coast

Storms River Mouth Rest Camp
Tel: 012-428 9111
URL: www.gardenroute-direct.com/
tsitsikamma/storms-river-mouth-rest-camp
Situated in Tsitsikamma

Tours

African Blue Tours & Travel
tailor-made tours
Tel: 021-438 1900
URL: www.africanbluetours.com

African Ramble
fly-in safaris
Tel: 044-533 9006
URL: www.aframble.co.za

AfriXplorer
tailor-made and scheduled tours
Tel: 012-348 1708
URL: www.afrixplorer.co.za

Bushcat Safaris
tailor-made and scheduled tours
Tel: 083-302 6228
URL: www.bushcatsafaris.com

Calabash Tours
cultural tours
Tel: 041-585 6162
URL: www.calabashtours.co.za

Eastern Cape Tours
tailor-made tours
Tel: 082-824 3124
URL: www.easterncapetours.co.za

Fairfield Group
day tours
Tel: 041-374 0710
 URL: www.fairfieldtours.com

Panorama Tours
tailor-made and scheduled tours
Tel: 021-426 1634
Email: info@panorama.co.za
URL: www.panoramatours.co.za

Springbok Atlas Tours
scheduled tours
Tel: 041-581 2555
URL: www.springbokatlas.co.za

Umzantsi Afrika Tours
tailor-made and scheduled tours
Tel: 041-379 1629
URL: www.umzantsi.co.za

Wimberger SA Tours
tailor-made tours
Tel: 021-913 0801
URL: www.coastingafrica.com

Out to Sea

Bluwater Charters
Tel: 082-822 3202
Email: rfski@operamail.com

Jeffreys Bay Surf School
Tel: 042-293 4214
Email: info@jbaysurfschool.com

Lightleys Holiday Houseboats
Tel: 044-386 0007
Email: info@houseboats.co.za
URL: www.houseboats.co.za

Outdoor Focus
Tel: 046-624 4432
Email: info@outdoorfocus.co.za
URL: www.outdoorfocus.co.za

Raggy Charters
Tel: 041-378 2528
Email: info@raggycharters.co.za
URL: www.raggycharters.co.za

Car Rentals

Avis
Tel: 0861-021 111
URL: www.avis.co.za

Budget
Tel: 0861-016 622
URL: www.budget.co.za

Click Car Hire
Tel: 021-551 9515
URL: www.sa-venues.com/explore/clickcarhire/

Drive South Africa
Tel: 0860-000 060
URL: www.drivesouthafrica.co.za

Europcar
Tel: 0861-131 000
URL: www.europcar.co.za

First
Tel: 0861-011 323
URL: www.firstcarrental.co.za

Hertz
Tel: 0861-600 136
URL: www.hertz.co.za

Tempest Car Hire
Tel: 0861-836 7378
URL: www.tempestcarhire.co.za

Emergency Numbers
Ambulance / Fire
10177

Cell phone Emergency Number
112

National Tourism Information & Safety Line
083-113 2345

Police Emergency number
10111

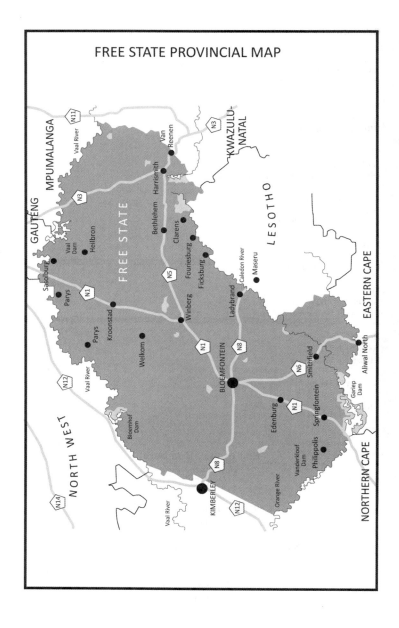

FREE STATE PROVINCIAL MAP

Free State

Tourism Information Offices

Bethlehem Tourism Bureau
Tel: 058-303 5732
Email: info@bethlehem.org.za
URL: www.bethlehem.org.za

Bloemfontein Tourist Offices
Tel: 051-407 3200
Email: info@bloemfonteintourism.co.za
URL: www.bloemfonteintourism.co.za

Free State Tourism Authority
Tel: 051-411 4300
Email: info@freestatetourism.org
URL: www.freestatetourism.org

Harrismith Tourist Information
Tel: 058-662 3525
Email: Victoria@efstatetourism.co.za

Top 10

Basotho Cultural Village
URL: www.drakensberg-tourist-map.com/basutu-cultural-village.html
Opening Time: Daily: 09h00
Closing Time: Weekdays: 16h30; Weekends: 17h00

A traditional South Sotho village, nestled in the sandstone foothills of the Golden Gate National Park, gives visitors a sense of how the South Sotho have lived since the 16th century. Guests must accept a sip of traditional beer from the chief as a sign of hospitality and an invitation to enter his village once they have been on a tour of the outdoor museum. The resident *ngaka* will throw the bones for you, giving you a glimpse into your future. There is traditional fare to be sampled in the village or enjoyed at the restaurant. Concerts are regularly held in the amphitheatre and there is a curio shop in the complex too.

Botanical Gardens
Tel: 051-436 3612
Email: fsnbg@sanbi.org
URL: www.sanbi.org/frames/freestatefram.htm
Opening Time: Daily: 08h00
Closing Time: Daily: 18h00
Tariffs: adults: R12; children and senior citizens: R8;
pre-school children: R5

In 1965 the city of Bloemfontein purchased the farm Winter Valley to cultivate and showcase the province's own floral diversity—a sorely needed attraction for a town whose name literally means 'flower spring'. Militarily, this site saw action in the South African War at the turn of the 20th century; the curator's house was built during the Second World War by Italian prisoners of war. Today, the garden boasts 400 species of plants, a visitor's centre, an educational centre and a restaurant. What's more, it's a paradise for birders and reptile junkies.

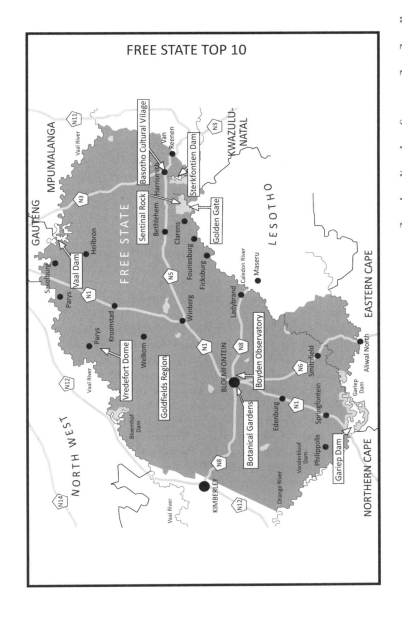

Boyden Observatory
Tel: 051-401 2924
Email: hoffmamj.sci@mail.uovs.ac.za
URL: www.ufs.ac.za/faculties/index.php

The Boyden Observatory is situated 26 kilometres east of Bloemfontein and serves as an astronomical research station and a scientific education centre. In 1879 Uriah A. Boyden bequeathed US$238,000 to Harvard University to be used for astronomical purposes. The observatory was originally established in Lima, Peru, but was moved to South Africa in 1927. It is managed by the University of the Free State and boasts the third-largest optical telescope in South Africa; the largest is in Sutherland.

Golden Gate Highlands National Park
Tel: 058-255 1100
Email: goldengate@sanparks.org
URL: www.detea.fs.gov.za/goldengate.htm

This 11,600ha park can be found in the northeastern Free State in the foothills of the Maluti Mountains, essentially the border, in that region, between South Africa and Lesotho. It derives its name from the brilliant shades of gold cast by the sun on the park's sandstone cliffs, especially against the impressive Brandwag buttress rock formation. Obviously hiking and horse-back riding are the most popular ways to experience the splendour of the park, although you can also view game from the comfort of your own vehicle. Guided tours are offered as well as a variety of hiking options and for the more adventurous visitor there is abseiling and canoeing; although beware of the water temperatures in winter! Of special interest is the Cathedral Cave and the Vulture Restaurant.

Goldfields Region
Tel: 057-352 4222
URL: www.dteea.fs.gov.za

The Goldfields Region of the Free State occupies the northern half of the larger Transgariep Goldfields Region. Gold was first discovered in 1938 and is today rivalled only by those of Gauteng. To the north it includes the town of Welkom and to the south the provincial capital Bloemfontein; south of that, extending as far as the Orange River is the Transgariep region. Welkom, the second-largest city in the Free State, is also situated in the Transgariep Goldfields Region. Welkom was planned by the chairman of Anglo-American and is a garden city with a commercial centre built around a central square. The mines in and around Welkom are very deep and flooding of the shafts is an ever-present threat with large quantities of brackish water being pumped to the surface daily. The water is collected in evaporation pans which have become home to a prolific birdlife including flamingo, the Sacred ibis, Egyptian goose, Muscovy duck, Marsh owl, and seagulls.

Sterkfontein Dam
Tel: 058-622 3520
URL: www.freestatetourism.org/things-to-do/sterkfontein-dam/sterkfontein-dam.html

Part of the Thukela-Vaal Water Project, the Sterkfontein Dam is situated 23 kilometres from the town of Harrismith and is about an hour's drive from either Bloemfontein or Villiers. The dam is situated in a reserve atop the highveld escarpment and hence offers some spectacular views, covering some 18,000ha. Obviously it's perfect for, and utilized for, watersports of all descriptions but since it is located in a reserve it is also home to a host of bird and animal life and offers some great hikes. The Thukela-Vaal Water Project was designed to draw water from the Drakensberg Pumped Storage Scheme to the Vaal catchment area.

Sentinel Rock
URL: www.freestatetourism.org/things-to-do/the-sentinel/
the-sentinel.html

Sentinel Rock rises over Golden Gate National Park in the eastern Free State and is the most northern point of the Drakensberg Mountains. If you want to appreciate the splendour of the rock and the region in which it finds itself you need to put on those hiking boots and do some work. But it's worth every step, no matter how laboured. From the top one has front-row seats to the most spectacular view of the Tugela Falls (the highest in Africa). The trail takes you to above 3,000m on the plateau of the Drakensberg Amphitheatre via two successive sets of chain ladders. For those of you who'd love to see it but can't see yourselves hiking up there, relax; there is an access road through Phuthaditjaba to the parking area that winds up a part of the Drakensberg that forms the border between KwaZulu-Natal and the Free State.

Vaal Dam
Tel: 082-851 1071
Email: adrian@zanet.co.za
URL: www.vaaldam.co.za

The French Riviera of the Free State; a bit of an oxymoron, but you get the picture. It offers everything from nature reserves to holiday resorts, gold estates and the like. The dam has around 800 kilometres of shoreline and covers 300 square kilometres. It is supplied by the Vaal and the Wilge rivers; the latter supplied by the Lesotho Highlands Water Project. In area the Vaal Dam is bigger than Luxembourg; its water is supplied directly to the municipalities of Johannesburg: pure, fresh mountain water, certainly good enough to drink!

Vredefort Dome
Tel: 056-811 2000
Email: support@parysinfo.co.za
URL: www.parys.info

About two billion years ago (that's billion as in 1,000 million) there was a catastrophic event just outside the present-day village of Vredefort. An enormous meteorite measuring between ten and 15 kilometres across smashed into the ground, causing unimaginable destruction and chaos. When the dust had settled, a crater measuring between 200 and 300 kilometres in diameter was left, stretching from Welkom in the southwest to Pretoria in the northeast. At the centre of the crater was a prominent uplift—rather like the splash-back you see when you drop a pebble into a pond. This uplift, originally measuring about 100 kilometres across, is the Vredefort Dome. Today, much of this dome has been eroded away or covered by newer rock layers, but there is a remainder of 'Dome Mountain Land' which can still be seen curling around the present-day town of Parys. The Vredefort Dome is therefore the earliest and largest impact structure found on Earth thus far. Furthermore, it is surmised that the impact effectively buried the gold deposits that were present in the contemporary surface rock and thus protected the Witwatersrand goldfields for future generations. (*David Fleminger, World Heritage Sites of South Africa—The Vredefort Dome, 2006*)

Xhariep Dam
URL: www.countryroads.co.za/content/gariep-dam.html

Topping the charts as South Africa's largest dam, the Xhariep, or Gariep, comes in with a clear win at 360 square kilometres. Situated just northeast of Colesberg the dam forms the southern border between the Free State and the Northern Cape, at the junction of the Western, Northern and Eastern Cape ... or thereabouts. The sheer magnificence of this more than 100-kilometre-long and 24-kilometre-wide dam, is indeed sufficient to testify to the exceptional engineering and success of Africa's largest water-supply scheme. The dam has two main tourist attractions in the Free State, namely the nature reserve and Resort Aventura Midwaters. It is the most central point of the Republic of South Africa and has an airfield with a double tarred runway. International gliding championships are held here annually in December. Overseas gliders agree that Xhariep Dam is the Mecca of gliding where world records are regularly broken.

Activities

Adventure Activities

Ash River Adventures
Tel: 058-256 1358
Email: simon@cranford.co.za

Bloemfontein Skydiving Centre
Tel: 051-451 1143
Email: tandemskydive@gmail.com
URL: www.sa-venues.com

Break Away Trails
Tel: 072-310 1595
Email: info@breakawaytrails.co.za
URL: www.breakawaytrails.co.za

Clarens Adventures
Tel: 058-256 1903
Email: simon@cranford.co.za

Dimalachite White-water Rafting
Tel: 056-818 1860
Email: info@dimalachite.co.za
URL: www.dimalachite.co.za

Goldfields Gliding Club
Email: info@ggc.co.za
URL: www.ggc.co.za

Outrageous Adventures
Tel: 058-256 1792
Email: kallie@outrageousadventures.co.za
URL: www.outrageousadventures.co.za

Whitewater Training
Tel: 056-811 2597
Email: wwt@whitewatertraining.co.za
URL: www.whitewatertraining.co.za

Wild Rides
Tel: 082-491 9788
Email: robsilcock@gmail.com

Outdoor Activities

Hot-Air Ballooning SA
Tel: 083-446 9423
Email: info@hotairballooningsa.co.za
URL: www.hotairballooningsa.co.za

White Mischief
boat trips
Tel: 082-920 5551
Email: gavin1@cherryfestival.co.za

Sport

Bethlehem Golf Course
Tel: 058-303 4656
URL: www.golfoncourse.co.za/index

Bloemfontein Golf Course
Tel: 051-447 0906
Email: golf@bfngc.co.za
URL: www.bfngc.co.za

Harrismith Golf Course
Tel: 058-623 0468
URL: www.golfoncourse.co.za/index

Moolmanshoek Private Game Reserve
horseback rides
Tel: 051-933 2220
Email: info@moolmanshoek.co.za
URL: www.moolmanshoek.co.za
Situated in the eastern Free Sate

Oppenheimer Park Golf Course
Tel: 057-353 2131
Email: opgc@internext.co.za
URL: www.golfwelkom.co.za
Situated in Welkom

Stadiums

Vodacom Park
(Free State Stadium)
Tel: 051-407 1700
URL: www.safarinow.com/destinations/
bloemfontein/places/Free-State-Stadium
Situated in Bloemfontein

Home of the Vodacom Cheetahs, this is the Free State stadium we are glamming up for the 2010 World Cup. By adding a second tier this 38,000-seater will now hold an additional 10,000 fans. The stadium is situated in the same complex as the athletics stadium, the cricket ground and a host of other sporting facilities. Upgrades were complete in time to host South Africa's Confederations Cup match against Spain in 2009.

OUTsurance Oval
Tel: 051-447 5715
Email: Petriw@cricket.co.za
URL: www.fscu.co.za
Situated in Bloemfontein

Culture

Museums

Anglo-Boer War Museum
Tel: 051-447 3447
Email: museum@anglo-boer.co.za
URL: www.anglo-boer.co.za
Opening Time: Monday to Friday: 08h00; Saturday: 10h00; Sunday: 11h00;
    Public Holidays: 09h00
Closing Time: Monday to Friday: 16h30; Weekends and Public Holidays: 17h00
Situated in Bloemfontein

Bethlehem Museum
Tel: 058-303 5076
Opening Time: Monday, Thursday and Saturday: 10h00; Tuesday, Wednesday and Friday:
    10h00 and again at 14h30
Closing Time: Monday and Thursday: 12h30; Tuesday, Wednesday and Friday: 12h30 and
    again at 17h00, Saturday: 12h00

Bram Fischer House
Tel: 051-405 8490
Opening Time: By appointment only
Situated in Bloemfontein

Catharina Brand Heritage Collection
Tel: 051-914 0654
Opening Time: Monday to Friday: 08h00 and again at 18h00; Saturday: 08h00 and again
    at 18h00
Closing Time: Monday to Friday: 17h00 and again at 22h00; Saturday: 14h00 and again at
    22h00
Situated in Ladybrand

First Raadsaal Museum
Tel: 051-447 9609
URL: www.nasmus.co.za/NMSATELL/Satellit.htm#raadsaal
Opening Time: Monday to Friday: 10h00; Weekends and Public Holidays: 14h00
Closing Time: Monday to Friday: 13h00; Weekends and Public Holidays: 17h00
Situated in Bloemfontein

Free State Voortrekker Museum
Tel: 051-881 0130
Opening Time: Monday to Friday: 10h00 and again at 13h00
Closing Time: Monday to Friday: 12h15 and again at 16h00
Situated in Winburg

Freshford House Museum
Tel: 051-447 9609
Email: mimi@nasmus.co.za
URL: www.nasmus.co.za/NMSATELL/Satellit.htm#freshford
Opening Time: Monday to Friday: 10h00; Weekends and Public Holidays: 14h00
Closing Time: Monday to Friday: 13h00; Weekends and Public Holidays: 17h00
Situated in Bloemfontein

National Afrikaans Literary Museum and Research Centre
Tel: 051-405 4034
Email: naln@sac.fs.gov.za
URL: www.fs.gov.za/Departments/SAC/MUSEUM/naln.html
Opening Time: Monday to Friday: 07h30 and again at 13h00; Saturday: 09h00
Closing Time: Monday to Friday: 12h15 and again at 16h00; Saturday: 12h00
Situated in Bloemfontein

National Museum
Tel: 051-447 9609
Email: ornito@nasmus.co.za
URL: www.nasmus.co.za
Opening Time: Monday to Friday: 08h00; Saturday: 10h00; Sunday and Public Holidays: 12h00
Closing Time: Monday to Friday and Saturday: 17h00; Sunday and Public Holidays: 17h30
Tariffs: Adults R5; Children R3
Situated in Bloemfontein

Old Presidency Museum
Tel: 051-448 0949
Opening Time: Tuesday to Friday: 10h00 and again at 13h00; Sunday: 14h00
Closing Time: Tuesday to Friday: 12h00 and again at 16h00; Sunday: 17h00
Situated in Bloemfontein

Oliewenhuis Art Museum
Tel: 051-447 9609
Email: oliewen@nasmus.co.za
URL: www.nasmus.co.za/OLIEWENH/olwh.htm
Opening Time: Monday to Friday: 08h00; Saturday: 10h00; Sunday and Public Holidays: 12h00
Closing Time: Monday to Friday and Saturday: 17h00; Sunday and Public Holidays: 17h30
Tariffs: Free
Situated in Bloemfontein

Riemland Museum
Tel: 058-852 2014
Email: quarta@heilbron.co.za
Opening Time: Tuesday: 08h00; Wednesday: 13h00; Friday: 09h00
Closing Time: Tuesday: 12h00; Wednesday: 16h00; Friday: 12h00
Situated in Heilbron

SA Armour Museum
Tel: 051-402 1777
Email: armourschool@mweb.co.za
URL: www.saarmourmuseum.co.za
Situated in Bloemfontein

The Military Museum
Tel: 051-447 5478
Email: naln@majuba.ofs.gov.za
URL: www.fs.gov.za/Departments/SAC/MUSEUM/military.html
Opening Time: Monday to Friday: 10h00 and again at 13h00; Sunday: 14h00
Closing Time: Monday to Friday: 12h15 and again at 16h00; Sunday: 16h00
Situated in Queens Fort, Bloemfontein

Transgariep Museum
Tel: 015-773 0216
Opening Time: Monday to Friday: 10h00
Closing Time: Monday to Friday: 12h00
Situated in Philippolis

Wagon Museum
Tel: 051-447 9609
URL: www.nasmus.co.za/NMSATELL/Satellit.htm#raadsaal
Opening Time: Monday to Friday: 10h00; Weekends and Public Holidays: 14h00
Closing Time: Monday to Friday: 13h00; Weekends and Public Holidays: 17h00
Situated in Bloemfontein

Welkom Museum
Tel: 057-391 3133
URL: www.fs.gov.za/Departments/SAC/MUSEUM/welkom.html
Opening Time: Monday to Friday: 08h30; Saturday: 09h00
Closing Time: Monday to Friday: 19h00; Saturday: 12h00

Theatres

Performing Arts Centre of The Free State (PACOF)
Tel: 051-447 7772
URL: www.pacofs.co.za
Situated in Bloemfontein

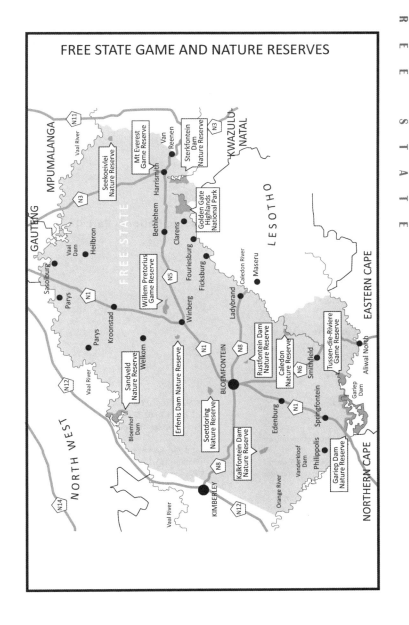

FREE STATE GAME AND NATURE RESERVES

Galleries

Blou Donki Art Gallery
Tel: 058-256 1757
Email: manager@bloudonki.co.za
URL: www.bloudonki.co.za
Situated in Clarens

Gallery 88
Tel: 016-976 2524
Situated in Sasolburg

Johannes Stegman Art Gallery
Tel: 051-401 2706
Situated in Bloemfontein

Game and Nature Reserves (including National Parks)

South African National Parks
Tel: 012-426 5000
Email: reservations@sanparks.org
URL: www.sanparks.org

SANParks Reserves
Golden Gate Highlands National Park

Other Parks

Caledon Nature Reserve
Tel: 051-583 1920
Email: info@routes.co.za
URL: www.tourismmotheo.co.za

Erfenis Dam Nature Reserve
URL: www.sa-venues.com/game-reserves

Gariep Dam Nature Reserve
Tel: 051-713 9300
URL: www.tourismxhariep.co.za

Kalkfontein Dam Nature Reserve
URL: www.sa-venues.com/game-reserves

Mount Everest Game Reserve
Tel: 058-623 0235
URL: www.sa-venues.com/game-reserves

Sandveld Nature Reserve
Tel: 053-433 1702
URL: www.sa-venues.com/game-reserves

Seekoeivlei Nature Reserve
Tel: 051-405 4753
URL: www.sa-venues.com/game-reserves

Soetdoring Dam Reserve
Tel: 051-433 9002
URL: www.sa-venues.com/game-reserves

Sterkfontein Dam Reserve
Tel: 058-622 3520
URL: www.freestatetourism.org

Tussen-die-Riviere Reserve
URL: www.places.co.za/html/tussen_die_
riviere.html

Willem Pretorius Game Reserve
Tel: 057-651 4003
URL: www.places.co.za/html/wpretorius_
gr.html

Entertainment

Frontier Inn & Casino
casino
Tel: 058-307 6000
Email: info@frontiercasino.co.za
URL: www.frontierinn.co.za
Address: Johan Blignaut Drive,
Bloemfontein

Goldfields Casino & Entertainment Centre
casino
Tel: 057-391 5700
Email: info@goldfieldscasino.co.za
URL: www.goldfieldscasino.co.za
Address: cnr Stateway &
Buiten Road, Welkom

Naledi Sun
casino
Tel: 051-875 1060
URL: www.suninternational.com
Address: 3 Bridge Street, Thaba Nchu

Shoelaces
club
Tel: 051-448 6941
Address: 18 Loop Street, Bloemfontein

Windmill Casino
casino
Tel: 051-410 2000
URL: www.suninternational.com
Address: cnr Jan Pierewiet Avenue &
N1 Highway, Bloemfontein

Annual Events

Bergbohaai
Tel: 072-609 0857
URL: www.bergbohaai.co.za
Held in Harrismith every August

Bethlehem Air Show
Tel: 082-881 8534
Held in Bethlehem every August

Bethlehem Show
Tel: 015-296 3074
Held in Bethlehem every December

Bloemfontein Bridal Show
Tel: 083-262 2918
Held in Bloemfontein every August

Bloemfontein Rose Festival
Tel: 082-416 7837
Held in Bloemfontein every October

Bloemfontein Show
Tel: 051-448 9894
Held in Bloemfontein every April

Boertjie Kontreifees
Tel: 051-853 2671
Held in Bultfontein every September

Bridal & Fashion Extravaganza
Tel: 051-448 5775
Held in Bloemfontein every July

Cherry Festival
Tel: 051-933 6486
URL: www.cherryfestival.co.za
Held in Ficksburg every November

Clarens MTB Challenge
Tel: 082-330 5548
Held in Clarens every August

Dome Adventure Festival
Tel: 056-811 4000
Held in Parys every November

Erfenis Dam Mile
Tel: 057-733 0164
URL: www.erfenisdammile.co.za
Held in Theunissen every November

Fly Fishing Film Festival
Tel: 086-110 0220
Held in Bloemfontein every December

Fouriesburg Spring Fair
Tel: 058-223 0429
Held in Fouriesburg every September

Free State Food Fair
Tel: 051-448 5775
Held in Bloemfontein every October

KTV Market Day
Tel: 051-430 3027
Held in Bloemfontein every September

Ladybrand Veteran Motor Show
Tel: 051-924 2141
Held in Ladybrand every May

Macufe Mangaung African Cultural Festival
Tel: 051-447 8169
Held in Bloemfontein every October

N3TC Dirty Harry MTB
Tel: 083-275 2123
Held in Harrismith every August

OFM Wheels Expo
Tel: 051-448 5775
Held in Bloemfontein every July

Phillipolis Witblits Festival
Tel: 082-770 0101
Held in Philippolis every April

Ride MTB Expo
Email: cruise@cratercruise.co.za
Held in Parys every October

SA Duathlon Champs
Tel: 051-441 4300
Held in Bloemfontein every July

Surrender Hill Marathon
Tel: 058-223 1042
Held in Clarens every March

Vintage Tractor Fair
Tel: 051-943 1929
Held in Clocolan every March

Voedsel & Witblits Fees
Tel: 051-515 3042
Held in Bothavilla every October

Volksblad Arts Festival
Tel: 051-404 7711
Held in Bloemfontein every July

Vrede Paddadors
Tel: 082-374 2476
Held in Vrede every September

This festival's full name is the Paddadors Rooivleis en Kultuur Fees, which translates literally as the Frog Thirsty Red Meat and Culture Festival...

Shopping www.mallguide.co.za

Central Park
Tel: 051-447 2850
Situated in Bloemfontein

Middestad Centre
Tel: 051-447 6202
Situated in Bloemfontein

College Square
Tel: 051-406 4950
Situated in Bloemfontein

Palm Gate Shopping Centre
Tel: 056-817 7786
Situated in Parys

Loch Logan Waterfront
Tel: 051-448 3607
Situated in Bloemfontein

Sanlam Plaza
Tel: 051-430 2341
Situated in Bloemfontein

Restaurants

Bloemfontein
Barba's Café
Cuisine: Greek
Tel: 051-430 2542
Address: 16 2nd Avenue

Butcher's Prime Cut Steakhouse
Cuisine: Steakhouse
Tel: 051-447 7997
Address: Victorian Square, 2nd Avenue

Cantina Tequila
Cuisine: Cosmopolitan
Tel: 051-430 8697
Address: 22 College Crossing, Zastron Street

Catch 22 Seafood Restaurant
Cuisine: Seafood
Tel: 051-444 6877
Address: Shop U30, 1st Floor, Mimosa
    Mall, Nelson Mandela Drive

De Oude Kraal Restaurant
Cuisine: South African
Tel: 051-564 0636
Address: 40km south of Bloemfontein
    on the N1

Die Mystic Boer
Cuisine: Pub
Tel: 051-430 2206
Address: 84 Kellner Street

Die Stalle
Cuisine: South African
Tel: 051-430 3423
Address: President Brand Street

Fishpaste
Cuisine: Mediterranean
Tel: 051-430 2662
Address: 31 President Steyn Street

Get Together @ Pretty Gardens
Cuisine: South African
Tel: 051-451 1011
Address: Du Plessis Road, Langehoven Park

Glen Pub & Grill
Cuisine: Pub
Tel: 051-430 5724
Address: 68 Glen Road, Hilton

Kalahari Fish
Cuisine: Seafood
Tel: 051-444 6274
Address: Mimosa Mall, Kellner Street

Kerdoni's Pizza and Pasta
Cuisine: Italian
Tel: 051-446 3898
Address: Spar Centre, cnr Baekos Blvd &
    Dirk Opperman Street.

La Galette
Cuisine: Cosmopolitan
Tel: 051-475 8201
Address: Middestad Centre

Margaritas
Cuisine: Cosmopolitan
Tel: 051-436 3729
Address: 59 Milner Road

Mediterranean
Cuisine: Cosmopolitan
Tel: 051-448 6194
Address: Loch Logan Waterfront

Meel
Cuisine: Deli
Tel: 051-448 8836
Address: 87A Kellner Street

New York Restaurant
Cuisine: Cosmopolitan
Tel: 051-447 7279
Address: 60 Medene Centre, 2nd Avenue

Oolong Lounge
Cuisine: Indian
Tel: 051-448 7244
Address: 16A, 2nd Avenue

Red Peppa
Cuisine: Asian
Tel: 051-444 5287
Address: Shop24, Mimosa Mall

Second Avenue Café
Cuisine: Cosmopolitan
Tel: 051-448 3088
Address: cnr Second & Kellner Ave

The Raj
Cuisine: Indian
Tel: 051-421 0034
Address: Shop 10, Windmill Casino

Vida and Arte
Cuisine: Spanish
Tel: 084-509 8591
Address: 67 President Reitz Avenue

Villa Toscana
Cuisine: Italian
Tel: 051-447 7982
Address: 7 Kellner Street

Harrismith
De Oude Huize Yard
Cuisine: African
Tel: 058-623 0483
Address: 17A Stuart Street

Chains and Franchises

Cape Town Fish Market
URL: www.ctfm.co.za

Cappuccino's
URL: www.cappuccinos.co.za

Cattle Baron
URL: www.cattlebaron.co.za

Dros
URL: www.dros.co.za

Mugg & Bean
URL: www.themugg.com

Ocean Basket
URL: www.oceanbasket.co.za

Panarotti's
URL: www.panarottis.com

Spur
URL: www.spur.co.za

The Famous Butcher's Grill
URL: www.butchersgrill.com

Wimpy
URL: www.wimpy.co.za

Accommodation

www.freestate-venues.co.za
www.safarinow.com/destinations/free-state/hub.aspx
www.sa-venues.com/free_state_hotels.htm
www.wheretostay.co.za/fs
www.freestatehotels.co.za
www.aatravel.co.za

Bloemfontein
Hotels

Halevy Heritage Hotel
Tel: 051-403 0600
Email: info@halevyheritage.com
URL: www.halevyheritage.com
Situated in Bloemfontein

Hobbit Boutique Hotel
Tel: 051-447 0663
URL: www.hobbit.co.za
Situated in Bloemfontein

Hotel President
Tel: 051-430 1111
Email: reservations.preshot@rhg.co.za
URL: www.hotelpresident.co.za
Situated in Bloemfontein

Lodges

College Lodge
Tel: 051-444 3837
Email: carli@collegelodge.co.za
URL: www.collegelodge.co.za
Situated in Bloemfontein

Glen Country Lodge
Tel: 051-861 2042
Email: glenlodg@mweb.co.za
URL: www.glencountrylodge.co.za
Situated in Bloemfontein

B&Bs, Guest Houses, Self-catering

A Steward Guest House
Tel: 051-448 4828
Situated in Bloemfontein

Dias Guest House
Tel: 051-436 6225
Situated in Bloemfontein

Florentia Guest House
Tel: 051-436 7847
Email: florentia@internext.co.za
URL: www.florentia.co.za
Situated in Bloemfontein

Gracefalls Exclusive Manor
Tel: 082-825 9056
Situated in Bloemfontein

Horizon Stables Guest House
Tel: 051-451 1057
Situated in Bloemfontein

Hydro Guest House
Tel: 051-448 0523
Situated in Bloemfontein

Kiepersol Accommodation
Tel: 051-436 1721
Situated in Bloemfontein

Lily Guest House
Tel: 051-436 9446
Email: info@lilyhouse.co.za
URL: www.lilyhouse.co.za
Situated in Bloemfontein

Petal Place
Tel: 051-451 1541
Email: info@petalplace.co.za
URL: www.petalplace.co.za
Situated in Bloemfontein

Plover Cottage Bed & Breakfast
Tel: 083-262 0861
Situated in Bloemfontein

Reyneke Park
Tel: 051-523 3888
Email: mreyneke@internext.co.za
URL: www.reynekepark.co.za
Situated in Bloemfontein

Solo Gracia Guest House
Tel: 051-444 2358
Email: sologuesthouse@telkomsa.net
URL: www.sologracia.co.za
Situated in Bloemfontein

Other
Hotels

De Stijl Gariep Hotel
Tel: 051-754 0060
Situated near the Gariep Dam

Green Lantern Inn
Tel: 058-671 0027
Situated in Van Reenen

Mont D'Or
Tel: 058-256 1272
Email: reservations@montdor.co.za
URL: www.montdorhotel.co.za
Situated in Clarens

Lodges

Dome Inn
Tel: 056-818 1577
Email: lodge@domeinn.co.za
URL: www.domeinn.co.za
Situated in Parys

Franshoek Mountain Lodge
Tel: 051-933 2828
Email: lodge@franshoek.co.za
URL: www.franshoek.co.za
Situated in Ficksburg

Inkwe Lodge
Tel: 058-303 9377
URL: www.inkwelodgebeth.co.za
Situated in Bethlehem

Kukuzans Game Lodge
Tel: 058-304 3373
Email: hunt@kukuzans.co.za
URL: www.kukuzans.co.za
Situated in Bethlehem

Letsatsi Private Game Reserve
Tel: 051-444 5716
Email: letsatsireservations@intekom.co.za
URL: www.letsatsigamelodge.co.za
Situated in Smithfield

Orange River Tented Camp
Tel: 051-755 5055
Email: ivansinclair@intekom.co.za
URL: www.orangerivertentscamp.com
Situated near the Gariep Dam

Otavi Game Lodge
Tel: 083-421 7598
Email: otavi@lantic.net
URL: www.otavigamelodge.co.za
Situated in Parys

Schoemanshof
Tel: 018-291 1649
URL: www.schoemanshof.co.za
Situated in Vredefort

The Royal Terrace Guest Lodge
Tel: 058-303 9536
Email: royalt@telkomsa.net
URL: www.royalterrace.co.za
Situated in Bethlehem

The Stables
Tel: 058-622 3020
Situated in Harrismith

Wild Horses Lodge
Tel: 058-622 7000
Email: info@wildhorses.co.za
URL: www.wildhorses.co.za
Situated in Harrismith

B&Bs, Guest Houses & Self-catering

Acacia Hof Guest House
Tel: 057-388 1715
Email: scha.schanel@mweb.co.za
URL: www.acaciaguest.co.za
Situated in Welkom

Agape Guest House B&B
Tel: 057-352 2549
Situated in Welkom

Blue Crane Guest House
Tel: 057-352 7511
Situated in Welkom

Die Nes Guest House
Tel: 058-303 4073
Email: dienes@dienesguesthouse.co.za
URL: www.dienesguesthouse.co.za
Situated in Bethlehem

Farm Yard Self Catering
Tel: 082-415 9374
Situated in Harrismith

Fisant, Bokmakierie en Hoephoep
  Guest House
Tel: 058-303 7144
URL: www.fisant.co.za
Situated in Bethlehem

GooseBerry Lodge Guest House
Tel: 058-303 6319
Email: reservations@gooseberry-lodge.co.za
URL: www.gooseberrylodge.co.za
Situated in Bethlehem

Petronella Guest House & Conference
  Centre
Tel: 058-303 4306
Situated in Bethlehem

Shady Pines Guest House
Tel: 058-622 3020
Situated in Harrismith

Summit Legacy Manor
Tel: 058-623 1834
Situated in Harrismith

The Gem's B&B
Tel: 058-622 1389
Situated in Harrismith

Tom's Place
Tel: 058-623 0006
Situated in Harrismith

Tours

Frontline Africa Travel
tailor-made tours
Tel: 012-991 3822

Jumanji Tours
arranged tours
Tel: 051-451 1789
Email: info@jumanjitours.co.za
URL: www.jumanjitours.co.za

Outlook Africa
tailor-made tours
Tel: 012-809 2784
Email: info@outlookafrica.co.za
URL: www.outlookafrica.co.za

Panorama Tours
tailor-made tours
Tel: 021-426 1634

South Africa Vacation
tailor-made tours
Tel: 021-786 4808

Wimberger SA Tours
tailor-made tours
Tel: 021-913 0801
Email: gisela@wimbergertours.co.za
URL: www.wimbergertours.co.za

Car Rentals

Avis
Tel: 0861-021 111
URL: www.avis.co.za

Budget
Tel: 0861-016 622
URL: www.budget.co.za

Click Car Hire
Tel: 021-551 9515
URL: www.sa-venues.com/explore/clickcarhire/

Drive South Africa
Tel: 0860-000 060
URL: www.drivesouthafrica.co.za

Europcar
Tel: 0861-131 000
URL: www.europcar.co.za

First
Tel: 0861-011 323
URL: www.firstcarrental.co.za

Hertz
Tel: 0861-600 136
URL: www.hertz.co.za

Tempest Car Hire
Tel: 0861-836 7378
URL: www.tempestcarhire.co.za

Emergency Numbers

Ambulance / Fire
10177

Cell phone Emergency Number
112

National Tourism Information & Safety Line
083-113 2345

Police Emergency number
10111

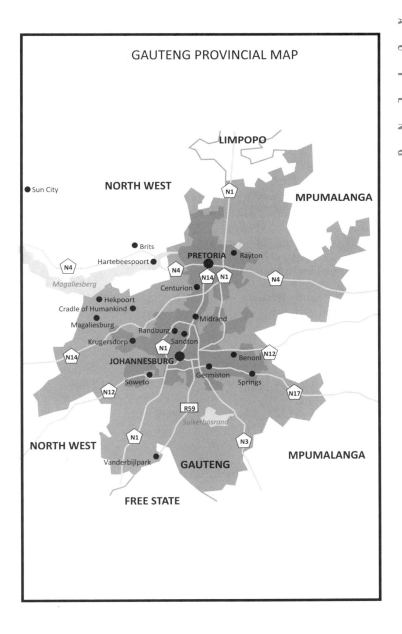

Gauteng

Tourism Information Offices

Alberton Tourism Bureau
Tel: 011-861 2519

Benoni Publicity Association
Tel: 011-422 3651

Boksburg Tourism Bureau
Tel: 011-917 1042

Brakpan Tourism Bureau
Tel: 011-741 2038

Bronkhorstspruit Tourist Information
Tel: 013-932 0061
Email: bronkhorstspruit@citizens.csir.co.za

Edenvale Tourism Bureau
Tel: 011-456 0216

Gauteng Tourism Authority
Tel: 011-639 1600
URL: www.gauteng.net

Germiston Tourism Bureau
Tel: 011-871 7027

Heidelberg Tourism Bureau
Tel: 016-349 1261

Johannesburg Metropolitan Tourism Association
Tel: 011-336 4961
URL: www.joburg.org.za

Johannesburg Tourism Bureau
Tel: 011-883 4033
Email: marketing@tourismjohannesburg.co.za

Johannesburg Tourism Company
Tel: 011-214 0715
Email: info@joburgtourism.com
URL: www.joburg.org.za

Kempton Park Tourism Bureau
Tel: 011-921 2211

Krugersdorp Tourism Bureau
Tel: 011-953 3727

Meyerton Tourism Bureau
Tel: 016-362 0060

Midrand Tourist Association
Tel: 011-266 3316

Nigel Tourism Bureau
Tel: 011-360 6000

OR Tambo International Airport
Tel: 011-390 3614

Pretoria Tourism Office
Tel: 012-337 4430
Email: satour@is.co.za

Randfontein Tourism Bureau
Tel: 011-692 2128

Roodepoort People's Centre
Tel: 011-761 0144
Email: region5@joburg.org.za

Sandton City Tourism Office
Tel: 011-784 9597

Springs Tourism Bureau
Tel: 011-360 2222

Tshwane Tourism Information Bureau
Tel: 012-358 1430
URL: www.tshwane.gov.za

Vanderbijlpark Tourism Bureau
Tel: 016-950 5331

Top 10

Apartheid Museum
Tel: 011-309 4700
Email: info@apartheidmuseum.org
URL: www.apartheidmuseum.org
Tariffs: Adults: R30; pensioners, students, children: R15

In 1995 the South African government allowed the private sector to tender for gambling licenses. The tender documents stated that the bidders should indicate how they would stimulate tourism, grow the economy and create employment. The consortium that proposed the Gold Reef City Casino conceptualized and built the Apartheid Museum in accordance with the tender regulations. It opened in 2001 and is acknowledged as the pre-eminent museum in the world dealing with 20th century South Africa, at the heart of which is the apartheid story.

Constitution Hill
Tel: 011-381 3100
Email: visitorcentre@constitutionhill.org.za
URL: www.constitutionhill.org.za

Also known as Number 4, Constitution Hill is the site of Johannesburg's notorious Old Fort Prison complex, which held many political activists in the years prior to 1994. Both Nelson Mandela and Mahatma Ghandi were imprisoned here. It is now the site of an intriguing museum and the South African Constitutional Court, established to protect our basic human rights. The original prison was built in 1892 to house white male prisoners. The Old Fort was built around the prison by Paul Kruger between 1896 and 1899 to protect the South African Republic from the threat of British invasion. Later, Boer military leaders of the Anglo-Boer War were imprisoned here by the British.

Gauteng Top 10

Hammanskraal

N1

To Limpopo Province

To Sun City

Brits

Boekenhoutskloof

Union Buildings

To Rustenburg

Hartbeespoort

PRETORIA

MAGALIESBERG

N4

N14

To Witbank, Nelspruit

Renosterspruit

Centurion

Walter Sisulu National Botanical Gardens

Hennops River

Lanseria

Cradle of Humankind

N1

To Magaliesburg

Lion Park

Fourways

Midrand

N14

Kromdraai

Randburg

Kempton Park

OR Tambo International

Ruimsig

Sandton

Krugersdorp

N1

Randfontein

N12

JOHANNESBURG

Benoni

Gold Reef City

Boksburg

Ormonde

N17

Soweto

Alberton

To Springs

N12

Nelson Mandela Bridge

Apartheid Museum

Constitution Hill

N3

Hector Pieterson Museum

R59

To Heidelberg

N1

To Meyerton, Vanderbijlpark

Cradle of Humankind
Tel: 011-956 6342
Email: info@maropeng.co.za
URL: www.cradleofhumankind.co.za /
www.maropeng.co.za

The Cradle of Humankind was first inducted onto the World Heritage List as a site of cultural significance in 1999. Initially, it incorporated about 20 caves within an area measuring 47,000 hectares (plus an additional 80,000 hectares of additional land which act as a buffer zone against predatory development). The site is focused around the caves of Sterkfontein, Kromdraai and Swartkrans, situated about 45 kilometres northwest of Johannesburg. Unusually for a World Heritage Site, most of the land in the Cradle is still in private hands, but the Sterkfontein Caves themselves are owned by the University of the Witwatersrand, after the land was donated by the farm's original owners. This group of sites is one of the most important in the world for an understanding of the evolution of modern man (*Homo sapiens sapiens*) from his ancestors. They have produced a wealth of hominid fossils, the oldest dating back some 3.5 million years, along with their tools and with fossils of the contemporary fauna. In 2005, the appellation 'Cradle of Humankind' was extended to include two additional locations related to the Sterkfontein area but not geographically contiguous—the Taung Quarry near Kimberley and Makapansgat near Polokwane (formerly Pietersburg). Both consist of the same kind of rock deposits as Sterkfontein (classified as part of the Transvaal Supergroup), and both contain valuable fossil specimens which confirm that hominids lived in the area for an unbroken stretch of nearly 3.5 million years, if not longer. The really exciting thing about the Cradle is that it is still very much a working site, and many ancient secrets still lie buried just waiting to be discovered. Literally dozens of scientists, archaeologists and palaeoanthropologists are constantly excavating, uncovering rare and mysterious fossils (both hominid and mammalian) that add to our incomplete understanding of the origins of life on Earth. (*David Fleminger, World Heritage Sites of South Africa—The Cradle of Humankind, 2006*)

Freedom Park
Tel: 079 873 9092
Email: info@freedompark.co.za
URL: www.freedompark.co.za
Open daily and can be visited at any time.

All countries pay hommage to their fallen and Feedom Park is South Africa's memorial. The names of fallen soldiers from the Boer War, the First and Second World Wars as well as whose who died during the apartheid era are engraved on the walls, set in beautiful gardens to the east of the N1 highway when entering Pretoria from Johannesburg. There's a fair amount of quibbling over whose names should and should not embellish the wall. Let's hope that the parties involved sort it out. A wall of rememberance should not be about politics.

Gold Reef City
Tel: 011-248 6800
Email: info@goldreefcity.co.za
URL: www.goldreefcity.co.za
Tariffs: Weekends, school holidays: Adults: R120;
 Pensioners: R80; Toddlers under 1.2m: R70
 Weekdays, out of school holidays: Adults: R90;
 Pensioners: R80; Toddlers under 1.2m: R70

A theme park created around an authentic 19th-century gold mine with underground tours where visitors can see the reef that gave birth to the city of Johannesburg. Packed with hotels, bars, restaurants and museums, this theme park has developed rapidly over the last few years. The gut-churning rides are bigger and better, faster and scarier with new additions all the time. Gold Reef City now also boasts a massive casino complex with its own hotel, theatres and restaurants. It is a gambler's paradise in terms of slot machines, tables and numerous other pocket-sapping activities. It is a great day out for families or adrenalin junkies. The night-time vibe is somewhat surreal what with the can-can girls of Rosie O'Grady's.

Hector Pieterson Memorial / Museum
The memorial site can be visited at any time and is one of the main attractions on the Soweto tour.
URL: www.soweto.co.za/html/p_hector.htm

On 16 June 1976 Soweto school children took to the streets to protest the imposition of Afrikaans as the medium for instruction in black schools. Of the 20-odd children who died after the order to shoot was given, Hector Pieterson has become somewhat of an iconic figure, due in large part to the world-renowned photograph of a fellow student carrying his limp body with his sister running alongside, her arms outstretched in panic. Sam Nzima's photograph of Hector Pieterson and the 13-year-old boy himself are seen as the symbol of youth resistance to the brutality of the apartheid government. A memorial was erected in the early 1990s and is situated in Khumalo Street, a few hundred metres from where Pieterson was shot. A new museum opened in 2002 and houses photographic and audio-visual displays of the struggle of the youth against the injustices of apartheid.

Nelson Mandela Bridge
Situated in Johannesburg and can be viewed at any time.
URL: www.sa-venues.com/attractionsga/nelson-mandela-bridge.htm

The largest cable-stayed bridge in southern Africa, the Nelson Mandela Bridge symbolizes the crossing of the apartheid divide as its namesake did in the flesh. Practically, it is a vital link to the rejuvenation of the inner city. This landmark bridge will take you directly into the Newtown Precinct: home to the Market Theatre, Museum Africa, a plethora of traditional and hip bars and restaurants, jazz clubs etc. The Newtown Precinct is situated around the Mary Fitzgerald Square where regular music concerts are held. The atmosphere here is electric, especially at night. It is safe, but put away your bling before paying it a visit. This is the real Jozi (what we natives of the city call it).

The Lion Park
Tel: 011-691 9905
Email: lionpark@cknet.co.za
URL: www.lion-park.com
Tariffs: Adults: R100; Children 4–12: R70;
   Children under 4 free
Opening Times: 08h30
Closing Times: Weekdays: 17:00; Public Holidays, Weekends
1 September–30 April: 18:00; 1 May–31 August: 17h00

So you're in Jo'burg and you're cultured-out, the weight of the apartheid ear is bearing down on you and you need something a little more mindless but no less entertaining. The Lion Park, situated to the northwest of Johannesburg, near Lanseria Airport is a great family day out. It is home to over 80 lions including the rare white lions and many other carnivores such as cheetah, wild dog, brown hyena, striped hyena, spotted hyena, black-backed jackal, side-striped jackal, and a wide variety of buck which roam freely in the antelope area. Visitors have an opportunity to interact with some of the animals in the Cub World area which has a giraffe-feeding platform that puts you at eye level with the tame resident giraffe, creating a fun experience for all ages. Then there is the popular cub interaction which allows you to touch the cubs and take photographs.

Union Buildings
Situated in Pretoria and can be visited at any time.
URL: www.visitpretoria.co.za/history/union-buildings

An architectural masterpiece! The Union Buildings form the official seat of the South African government and the office of the the president. Designed by Sir Herbert Baker in the English Monumental style this semi-circular sandstone building, completed in 1913, is 285m long. The east and west wings are said to represent the languages of English and Afrikaans, another fissure in the country's history sorely needing unity at the time of its conception. Notable are the terraced gardens, planted exclusively with indigenous plants, surrounding the buildings as well as the 9,000-seat amphitheatre. Within the grounds are various monuments, statues and memorials. Starting at the bottom of the gardens, a large statue of General Louis Botha (first prime minister of the Union of South Africa) on horseback dominates the lawn. About half way up the terraces, the Delville Wood War Memorial is a tribute to South African troops who died during the First World War as well as a plaque in memory of those who died during the Korean War. Two levels above that is a statue of prime minister J.B.M. Hertzog. To the right of the gardens stands the South African Police Memorial.

Walter Sisulu National Botanical Gardens
Tel: 011-958 1750
Email: SisuluGarden@sanbi.org
URL: www.sanbi.org/frames/sisulufram.htm
Tariffs: Adults: R23; Students: R13; Scholars: R7; fees vary
    for entrance to events held each year during winter
Opening Time: 08h00
Closing Time: 18h00

The gardens were founded in 1982, but with the dramatic Witpoortjie waterfall as the main feature the area has enjoyed visitors since the 1800s. The natural vegetation of the area is known as 'Rocky Highveld Grassland' and consists of a mosaic of grassland and savannah, with dense bush in the kloofs and along the streams. A list of naturally occuring trees is available. The variety of habitats accommodates over 600 naturally occurring plant species. A breeding pair of majestic Verreaux's eagles nests on the cliffs alongside the waterfall. The gardens are home to an abundance of wildlife. Together with the other 220 bird species, there are also a number of reptile and small mammals, including small antelope and jackal, which occur naturally here.

Activities

Adventure Activities

@ Point Blank
Tel: 082-330 9070
URL: www.point-blank-paintball.co.za

Adventure Projects
Tel: 076-410 6079
Email: info@adventureprojects.co.za
URL: www.adventureprojects.co.za

Airventures Hot Air Ballooning
Tel: 011-793 5782
Email: info@air-ventures.co.za
URL: www.air-ventures.co.za

Balloons over Dinokeng
Tel: 012-711 0098
URL: www.adventurezone.co.za/
    what_to_do_detail/Cullinan/
    BalloonsOverDinokeng/313

Bass Lake Adventures
Tel: 016-366 1127
Email: basslake@basslake.co.za
URL: www.basslake.co.za

Bungee Mogale Bungee Jumping
Tel: 0861-286 433
Email: info@bungeemogale.co.za
URL: www.bungeemogale.co.za

Dragon Boat Racing
Tel: 083-779 9659
Email: george@dragonboatracing.co.za
URL: www.dirtyboots.co.za/ad-
    actiondragon.php

Go Vertical Mountaineering
Tel: 082-731 4696
Email: info@govertical.co.za
URL: www.gotrekking.co.za

Magaliesberg Canopy Tours
Tel: 014-535 0150
Email: info@magaliescanopytour.co.za
URL: www.magaliescanopytour.co.za

Orlando Towers
Tel: 012-345 5114
URL: encounter.co.za/orlando-towers.html

Paddle Power Adventures
Tel: 012-205 1278
Email: padpower@lantic.net
URL: www.paddlepower.co.za

Pure Rush Industries
Tel: 082-605 1150
Email: marco@purerush.co.za
URL: www.purerush.co.za

SA Trails
Tel: 082-533 4545
Email: info@satrails.co.za
URL: www.satrails.co.za

Sundowner Adventures
Tel: 011-315 4503
Email: sundown@iafrica.com
URL: www.sundowner.co.za

Wild Cave Adventures
Tel: 011-956 6197
Email: info@wildcaves.co.za
URL: www.wildcaves.co.za

GAUTENG

Outdoor Activities

Astronomy Africa Stargazing
Tel: 082-901 3796
Email: info@astronomyafrica.com
URL: www.astronomyafrica.com

Clay Pigeon Shooting
Tel: 082-566 6708
Email: info@danielsrust.co.za

Danielsrust Horse Trails
Tel: 082-891 8365
Sitauted in the Cradle of Humankind
   Heritage Site

Elephant Experience
Tel: 012-258 0423
Email: elephantsanctuary@mweb.co.za
URL: www.elephantsanctuary.co.za/
   hartiescontact.htm

Follow Me Through Africa 4X4 Tours
Tel: 012-345 4686
Email: blackie@followmethroughafrica.com
URL: www.followmethroughafrica.com

Land Rover Centurion Adventures
Tel: 082-258 9880
Email: lrca@webmail.co.za
Situated in Centurion

Old Willow No.7 Houseboat Charters
Tel: 083-391 4884
Email: info@oldwillow.co.za
URL: www.oldwillow.co.za
Situated on the Vaal River

SA Horse Trails
Tel: 082-533 4545
URL: www.uncoversouthafrica.com/gauteng/
   outdoors/horse-riding/sa-trails/index.htm
Situated in the Northern Farm
   Nature Reserve

Saddle Creek Ranch
Tel: 079-467 9906
Email: horseridingsa@hotmail.com
URL: www.horseridingsa.co.za
Situated in Hekpoort

Tangaroa The Strawberry Farm
Tel: 012-207 1116
Email: info@tangaroa.co.za
URL: www.tangaroa.co.za
Situated at Hartbeespoort Dam

Sport

Pretoria
www.sa-venues.com/golf/ga-
   pretoria-golf-courses.htm

Centurion Country Club
Tel: 012-665 0279

Irene Country Club
Tel: 012-667 1081

Monument Golf Course
Tel: 012-460 2542

Pretoria Country Club
Tel: 012-460 6241

Pretoria Golf Club
Tel: 012-386 6836

Silver Lakes Golf Course
Tel: 012-809 0281

Wingate Park Golf Course
Tel: 012-997 1312

Woodhill Golf Course
Tel: 012-998 0011

Zwartkop Country Club
Tel: 012-654 1144

Johannesburg
www.sa-venues.com/golf/ga-
 johannesburg-golf-courses.htm

Bryanston Golf Course
Tel: 011-706 1361

Dainfern Golf Course
Tel: 011-469 0101

Glendower Golf Course
Tel: 011-453 1013

Houghton Golf Course
Tel: 011-728 7337

Killarney Golf Course
Tel: 011-442 3880

Kyalami Country Club
Tel: 011-702 1610

Observatory Golf Course
Tel: 011-648 8402

Parkview Golf Course
Tel: 011-646 5400

Randpark Golf Club
Tel: 011-476 1691

Royal Johannesburg Golf Club
Tel: 011-640 3021

The River Club Golf Club
Tel: 011-783 1166

Wanderers Golf Club
Tel: 011-447 3311

Woodmead Golf Course
Tel: 011-202 1600

Stadiums

Coca-Cola Park
(formerly Ellis Park)
Tel: 011-402 8644
Email: susan@ellispark.co.za
URL: www.ellispark.co.za
Situated in Johannesburg

To Gautengers and Jozi locals this stadium will always be Ellis Park, home of the Golden Lions and Orlando Pirates. Who can ever forget South Africa's 1995 World Cup victory against the All Blacks here with Madiba clad in a Springbok jersey. Upgraded in the early '80s this stadium needs very little refurbishment for the 2010 World Cup, although it is seeing a capacity increase on its northern side, bringing the total number of seats to over 65,000.

Loftus Versfeld
Tel: 012-420 0700
URL: www.bluebulls.co.za
Situated in Pretoria

Loftus also changed names, much to the chagrin of all those whose blood is blue, but in 2005 when Vodacom took over the sponsorship of the Blue Bulls and the stadium the name Loftus Versfeld was given back to its home teams and fans alike. Minimal upgrading was necessary aside from some additional floodlighting, scoreboards and roofing. When the Bulls play at Loftus you are guaranteed bums on all 51,762 seats.

Soccer City
URL: www.soccercity2010.co.za
Situated in Johannesburg

Soccer City is a new addition to the Johannesburg landscape, built from scratch, at the location of the former FNB Stadium, for the 2010 World Cup. At capacity fans will be cheered by a massive 94,000 voices. The Calabash as it's known locally takes its design from a series of concepts and is steeped in symbolism. On various levels, whether from an aerial look at the roof or a horizontal depiction of the gardens, Soccer City represents the continent of Africa, the country's mineral wealth, deserts, the protea (our national flower) and a host of other intrigues.

Centurion Cricket Stadium /
  SuperSport Park
Tel: 012-663 1005
URL: www.titans.co.za/content/view/19/40/

Johannesburg Stadiun
Tel: 011-402 8644
Email: susan@ellispark.co.za
URL: www.ellispark.co.za

Liberty Life Wanderers Stadium
Tel: 011-340 1500
Email: general@cricketgauteng.co.za
URL: www.wanderers.co.za
Situated in Johannesburg

Culture

Museums

Adler Museum of Medicine
Tel: 011-717 2081
Email: adler.museum@wits.ac.za
URL: http://web.wits.ac.za/Academic/Health/Museums/AdlerMuseum
Opening Time: Monday to Friday: 09h30
Closing Time: Monday to Friday : 16h00
Situated in Johannesburg

Bensusan Museum of Photography
Tel: 011-833 5624
URL: www.sa-venues.com/things-to-do/gauteng/details.php?id=373
Opening Time: Tuesday to Sunday: 09h00
Closing Time: Tuesday to Sunday: 17h00
Situated in Johannesburg

Bleloch Geological Museum
Tel: 011-717 6665
Email: ian.mckay@wits.ac.za
URL: http://web.wits.ac.za/Academic/Science/GeoSciences/BlelochGeologicalMuseum
Situated in Johannesburg

Department of Historical Papers
Tel: 011-717 1940
Email: michele.pickover@wits.ac.za
URL: www.historicalpapers.wits.ac.za
Opening Times: Weekdays:08h00
Closing Times: Weekdays: 17h00
Situated in Johannesburg

James Hall Museum of Transport
Tel: 011-435 9718
Email: peterh@joburg.org.za
URL: www.jhmt.org.za
Tariffs: Entrance is free
Opening Time: Tuesday to Sunday 09h00
Closing Time: Tuesday to Sunday 17h00
Situated in Johannesburg

Kruger House Museum
Tel: 012-326 9172
URL: www.sa-venues.com/attractionsga/kruger-house.htm
Opening Time: Monday to Friday 08h30, Weekends and Public Holidays 08h30
Closing Time: Monday to Friday 17h30, Weekends and Public Holidays 17h00
Situated in Pretoria

Melrose House Museum
Tel: 012-322 0420
URL: www.melrosehouse.co.za
Opening Time: Tuesday to Sunday 10h00
Closing Time: Tuesday to Sunday 17h00
Tariffs: Adults: R8; Scholars: R5
Situated in Pretoria

Museum Africa
Tel: 011-833 5624
URL: www.sa-venues.com/things-to-do/gauteng/detail.php?id=371
Opening Time: Tuesday to Sunday 09h00
Closing Time: Tuesday to Sunday 17h00
Situated in Johannesburg

Museum of Military History
Tel: 011-646 5513
Email: milmus@icon.co.za
URL: www.militarymuseum.co.za
Situated in Johannesburg

Pretoria Art Museum
Tel: 012-344 1807
Email: arthurk@tshwane.gov.za
URL: www.pretoriaartmuseum.co.za
Tariffs: Adults: R6; Children: R4
Opening Time: Tuesday to Sunday 10h00
Closing Time: Tuesday to Sunday 17h00

Porcinarium
Tel: 012-672 9076
Situated in Pretoria

Roodepoort Museum
Tel: 011-761 0225
Email: albal@joburg.org.za
URL: www.museums.org.za/roodepoortmuseum/info.htm
Tariffs: Adults: R5.25, Children: R0.55; Students and pensioners: R2.10; Teachers: R1.05
Opening Times: Tuesday to Friday: 09h30; Sunday: 14h00
Closing Times: Tuesday to Friday: 16h30; Sunday: 17h00
Situated in Florida, Roodepoort

Transvaal Museum
Tel: 012-322 7632
URL: www.gauteng.com/content.php?page=Transvaal%20Museum
Tariffs: Adults: R10; Students, pensioners and scholars: R8
Opening Time: 08h00
Closing Time: 16h00
Situated in Pretoria

Tswaing Crater Museum
Tel: 012-790 2302
URL: www.southafrica.info/travel/cultural/tswaingcrater.htm
Situated in Pretoria

Voortrekker Monument
Tel: 012-326 6770
Email: marketing@voortrekkermon.org.za
URL: www.voortrekkermon.org.za
Tariffs: Adults: R32; Scholars: R10
Opening Time: 08h00
Closing Times: 1May-31August 17h00; 1 September-31April 18h00
Situated in Pretoria

Theatres

Johannesburg
Emperor's Palace
Tel: 011-928 1000
Email: info@emperorspalace.com
URL: www.emperorspalace.com

Johannesburg Civic Theatre
Tel: 011- 877 6800
Email; justine@showbusiness.co.za
URL: www.showbusiness.co.za

Liberty Theatre on The Square
Tel: 011-883 8606
Email: theatreonthesquare@gmail.com
URL: www.at.artslink.co.za/~tots/

Linder Auditorium
Tel: 011-717 3223
Email: facilities.wec@wits.ac.za
URL: http://web.wits.ac.za/
  placesofinterest/linder

Market Theatre
Tel: 011-832 1641
Email: anthony@markettheatre.co.za
URL: www.markettheatre.co.za

Montecasino Theatre
Tel: 011-511 1988
Email: mark@montetheatre.co.za
URL: www.montecasinotheatre.co.za

University of Johannesburg Arts Centre
Tel: 011-559 3058
URL: www.uj.ac.za/artsacademy

Pretoria
Aula Theatre
Tel: 012-420 2033
Email: moses.rakau@up.ac.za

Breytenbach Theatre
Tel: 012-440 4834
Email: breytie@tut.ac.za
URL: www.tut.ac.za/other/breytie/pages/
  default.aspx

Centurion Theatre
Tel: 012-664 5978
Email: info@centurionteater.co.za
URL: www.centurionteater.co.za

Little Theatre
Tel: 012-322 7676
Email: little_theatre@hotmail.com
URL: www.unisa.ac.za

Masker Theatre
Tel: 012-420 2033
Email: moses.rakau@up.ac.za

Musaion
Tel: 012-420 2033
Email: moses.rakau@up.ac.za

State Theatre
Tel: 012-392 4000
Email: christine@statetheatre.co.za
URL: www.statetheatre.co.za

The Barnyard Theatres
URL: www.barnyardtheatre.co.za
Please visit the website for details on venues
   as there are several Barnyard theatres
   throughout Gauteng

The Performer Theatre
Tel: 012-346 0801
Email: boxoffice@theperformer.co.za
URL: www.theperformer.co.za

West End Theatre
Tel: 012-327 1487

Galleries

ABSA Gallery
Tel: 011-888 8548
Situated in Johannesburg

African Feelings Gallery
Tel: 011-884 1148
Situated in Sandton, Johannesburg

Afronova Art Gallery
Tel: 083-726 5906
Email: afronova@tiscali.co.za
URL: www.afronova.com
Opening Time: Tuesday to Saturday 13h00
Closing Times: Tuesday to Friday 19h00;
   Saturday 17h00
Situated in Newtown, Johannesburg

Alliance Française
Tel: 011-646 1169
Email: culture.jhb@alliance.og.za
URL: www.alliance.org.za
Situated in Parkview, Johannesburg

Alice Art Gallery
Tel: 011-958 1392
Email: aliceart@global.co.za
URL: www.aliceart.co.za
Situated in Roodepoort, Johannesburg

ArtCase Inc
Tel: 012-803 8765
Email: artcase@global.co.za
URL: www.artcase.co.za
Gallery can be visited by appointment
Situated in La Montagne, Pretoria

Art on Paper
Tel: 011-726 2234
Email: info@artonpaper.co.za
URL: www.artonpaper.co.za
Situated in Braamfontein, Johannesburg

Artist Proof Studio
Tel: 011-492 1278
Email: artistp@mweb.co.za
URL: www.artistproofstudio.org.za
Situated in Newtown, Johannesburg

Association Of Arts Pretoria
Tel; 012-346 3100
Email: artspta@mweb.co.za
URL: www.art.co.za/artspta
Opening Time: Tuesday to Saturday 09h30
Closing Time: Tuesday to Friday 17h30;
   Saturday 13h00
Situated in Nieuw Muckleneuk, Pretoria

Centurion Art Gallery
Tel: 012-358 3477
Email: artg@tshwane.gov.za
URL: www.pretoriaartmuseum.co.za/
   centurion/default.htm
Opening Time: Monday to Friday 10h00
Closing Time: 17h00
Situated in Lyttleton Manor, Pretoria

Chapungu Garden Gallery
Tel: 011-447 2476
Situated in Sandton, Johannesburg

Cherie de Villiers Fine Art Gallery
Tel: 011-788 9949
Email: cheart@global.co.za
URL: www.gallery.co.za
Situated in Rivonia, Johannesburg

Engelenburghuis Art Collection
Tel: 012-328 5082
Situated in Arcadia, Pretoria

Everard Read Gallery
Tel: 011-788 4805
Email: gallery@everard.co.za
URL: www.everard-read.co.za
Opening Time: Monday to Saturday 09h00
Closing Time: Monday to Friday 18h00;
    Saturday 13h00
Situated in Rosebank, Johannesburg

Gallery On The Side
Tel: 011-467 2475
Email: info@fineartportfolio.co.za
URL: www.fineartportfolio.co.za
Situated in Fourways, Johannesburg

Gallery On The Square
Tel: 011-784 2847
Email: gots@mweb.co.za
URL: www.galleryonthesquare.co.za
Opening Time: Monday to Saturday 09h00
Closing Time: 18h00
Situated on Nelson Mandela Square,
    Sandton City, Johannesburg

Goodman Gallery
Tel: 011-788 1113
Email: jhb@goodman-gallery.com
URL: www.goodman-gallery.com
Opening Time: Tuesday to Saturday 09h30
Closing Time: Tuesday to Friday 17h30;
Saturday 16h00
Situated in: Parkwood, Johannesburg

Johannesburg Art Gallery
Tel: 011-725 3130
URL: www.joburg.org.za
Situated in Joubert Park, Johannesburg

Hyde Park Gallery
Tel: 011-325 5352
Email: info@fineartportfolio.co.za
URL: www.fineartportfolio.co.za/galleries
Situated in Hyde Park, Johannesburg

Kim Sacks Gallery
Tel: 011-447 5804
Situated in Parkwood, Johannesburg

Ngwenya Gallery
Tel: 011-796 3000
URL: www.amethyst.co.za/jhbguide/
    ngwenya.htm
Situated in Muldersdrift, Johannesburg

Open Window Contemporary Art Gallery
Tel: 012-470 8680
Email: info@openwindow.co.za
URL: www.openwindow.co.za
Situated in Lynnwood, Pretoria

Thompson Gallery
Tel: 011-482 2039
Email: info@thompsongallery.co.za
URL: www.thompsongallery.co.za
Opening Time: Tuesday to Saturday 10h30
Closing Time: Tuesday to Saturday 17h00
Situated in Melville, Johannesburg

Suburbs of Johannesburg

Game and Nature Reserves (including National Parks)

Bird Gardens at Montecasino
Tel: 011-511 1864
URL: http://montecasino.tsogosun.co.za

De Wildt Cheetah & Wildlife Research Centre
Tel: 012- 504 1921
URL: www.dewildt.co.za
Situated at Hartbeespoort Dam

Groenkloof Nature Reserve
Tel: 012-440 8316
Email: groenkloofnaturereserve@tshwane.gov.za
URL: www.tshwane.gov.za/groenkloof.cfm
Tariffs: Please refer to website as tariffs differ for each activity
Opening Time: September-April 05h30; May-August 07h00
Closing Time: September-April 19h00; May-August 18h00

Krugersdorp Game Reserve
Tel: 011-950 9900
Email: info@afribush.co.za
URL: www.afribush.co.za
Opening Time: Daily 08h00
Closing Time: Daily 17h00

Lion & Rhino Park
Tel: 011-957 0349
Email: trs@iafrica.com
URL: www.rhinolion.co.za
Tariffs: Please refer to the website as there are various offers available
Opening Time: Main entrance gate and hippo walkway: Daily 08h00; Lion and predator
    camp: Daily 08h30; Croc Pub: Daily 10h00; Curio Shop, Restaurant and Kiosk:
    Daily 08h30
Closing Time: Main entrance gate and hippo walkway: Weekdays 17h00, Weekends &
    Public Holidays 18h00; Lion and predator camp: Daily 16h30; Croc Pub: Daily 16h00;
    Curio Shop, Restaurant and Kiosk: Daily 16h00

Rietvlei Nature Reserve
Tel: 012-345 2274
URL: footprint.co.za/rietvlei.htm
Opening Time: Weekdays 08h00; Weekends and Public Holidays 06h00
Closing Time: Daily 18h00

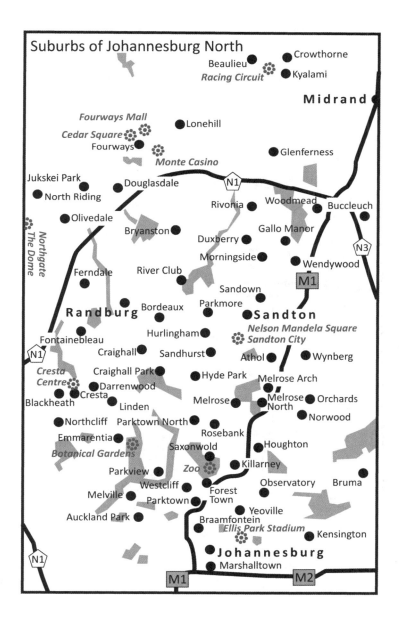

Suburbs of Johannesburg North

Crowthorne

Beaulieu
Racing Circuit
Kyalami

Midrand

Fourways Mall
Lonehill
Cedar Square
Fourways
Monte Casino

Glenferness

Jukskei Park
Douglasdale
N1

North Riding
Rivonia
Woodmead
Buccleuch

Olivedale
Gallo Manor

Northgate The Dome
Bryanston
Duxberry
N3

Morningside
Wendywood

Ferndale
River Club
M1

Sandown

Randburg
Bordeaux
Parkmore
Sandton

Fontainebleau
Hurlingham
Nelson Mandela Square
Sandton City

N1
Craighall
Sandhurst
Athol
Wynberg

Cresta Centre
Craighall Park
Hyde Park
Melrose Arch

Darrenwood
Melrose
Melrose
North
Orchards

Blackheath
Cresta
Linden
Norwood

Northcliff
Parktown North
Rosebank

Emmarentia
Saxonwold
Houghton

Botanical Gardens
Zoo
Killarney

Parkview
Observatory
Bruma

Westcliff
Forest
Town

Melville
Parktown
Yeoville

Auckland Park
Braamfontein
Ellis Park Stadium
Kensington

N1
Johannesburg

Marshalltown
M1
M2

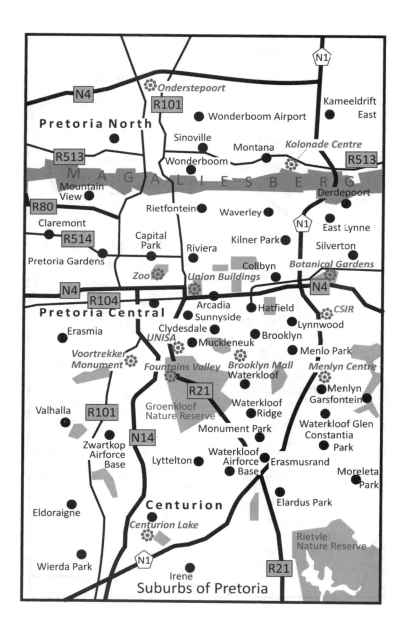

Entertainment www.what2night.co.za

Amber's Music Café
chill lounge
Tel: 011-463 0977
Situated in Bryanston, Johannesburg

Bassline
club
Tel: 011-838 9145
Situated in Newtown, Johannesburg

Buzz 9
cocktail bar
Tel: 011-726 2019
Situated in Melville, Johannesburg

Carnival City
casino
Tel: 011-898 7000
Situated in Brakpan, Johannesburg

Café Vacca Matta
cocktail bar
Tel: 011-511 0511
Situated in Fourways, Johannesburg

Carfax
chill lounge & live entertainment
Tel: 011-834 9187
Situated in Newtown, Johannesburg

Club Globe
club
Tel: 082-883 4553
Situated in Alberton, Johannesburg

Club Recess
club
Tel: 012-663 7863
Situated in Centurion, Pretoria

Chilli's
pub
Tel: 012-362 9999
Situated in Hatfield, Pretoria

Diva's and Don's
cocktail bar
Tel: 012-362 6074
Situated in Hatfield, Pretoria

Emerald Casino
casino
Tel: 016-982 8065
Situated in Vanderbijlpark,
  south of Johannesburg

Emperor's Palace
casino
Tel: 011-928 1000
Situated in Kempton Park, Johannesburg

ETC Lounge
chill lounge
Tel: 012-362 1144
Situated in Hatfield, Pretoria

Gold Reef City
theme park & casino
Tel: 011-248 6800
Situated in Ormonde, Johannesburg

Gorgeous
cocktail lounge
Tel: 012-415 9487
Situated in Irene, Pretoria

Just Friends
chill lounge
Tel: 012-362 2177
Situated in Hatfield, Pretoria

Katzy's
piano bar
Tel: 011-880 3945
Situated in Rosebank, Johanesburg

Legends
club (gay)
Tel: 082-567 8894
Situated in Brooklyn, Pretoria

Mama Tembo's Café
cocktail bar
Tel: 011-646 7302
Situated in Greenside, Johannesburg

Monsoon Lagoon
club
Tel: 011-928 1280
Situated in Kempton Park, Johannesburg

Monte Casino
casino
Tel: 011-510 7000
Situated in Fourways

Radium Beer Hall
jazz club
Tel: 011-728 3866
Situated in Orange Grove, Johannesburg

Rat'z Bar
cocktail bar
Tel: 011-726 2019
Situated in Melville, Johannesburg

Salvatore
cocktail lounge
Tel: 011-675 5800
Situated in Weltevreden Park,
   Johannesburg

Silverstar Casino
Tel: 011-662 7300
Situated in Mogale City, Krugersdorp

Six Restaurant & Cocktail Bar
cocktail bar
Tel: 011-482 8306
Situated in Melville, Johannesburg

Sudada
cocktail bar
Tel: 011-884 1980
Situated in Sandton, Johannesburg

The Godfather
cocktail bar
Tel: 012-663 3302
Situated in Centurion, Pretoria

Tings an' Times
dining lounge & live entertainment
Tel: 012-430 3176
Situated in Hatfield, Pretoria

Zeplin's
club
Tel: 082-787 9532
Situated in Wonderboom, Pretoria

Annual Events

Arts Alive
URL: www.artsalive.co.za
Held in Johannesburg every September

Capital Arts Festival
URL: www.sa-venues.com
Held in Pretoria every August

Cars in the Park
URL: www.sa-venues.com/events
Held in Pretoria every August

Cellar Rats Wine Festival
URL: www.cellarrats.co.za
Held in Magaliesburg every July and
   September

Chocolate Festival
URL: www.sa-venues.com/events
Held in Midrand every March

Frontier Fly-fishing Open Day
URL: www.sa-venues.com/events
Held in Muldersdrift every September

FNB Dance Umbrella
URL: www.fnb.co.za
Held in Johannesburg every March

Good Life Fine Brandy festival
URL: www.sa-venues.com/events
Held in Sandton every May

Hazel Food Christmas Market
URL: www.sa-venues.com/events
Held in Pretoria every December

Joburg Art Fair
URL: www.sa-venues.com/events
Held in Sandton every April

Joburg Day!
URL: www.highveld.co.za
Held in Fourways every October

Joy of Jazz
URL: www.joyofjazz.co.za
Held in Johannesburg every August

Jozi Spoken Wordfest
URL: www.sa-venues.com/events
Held in Braamfontein every July

Lucky Fish Music Festival
URL: www.sa-venues.com/events
Held in Johannesburg every September

National Marimba Festival
URL: www.sa-venues.com/events
Held in Boksburg every July

Newtown Diwali Festival
URL: www.sa-venues.com/events
Held in Newtown every October

Rocking the Gardens
URL: www.rockingthegardens.com
Held in Emmerentia every October

SANCTA One Act Play Festival
URL: www.sa-venues.com/events
Held in Braamfontein every July

Sibikwa Story Telling Festival
URL: www.sa-venues.com/events
Held in Benoni every May

Sisters with Blisters
URL: www.sa-venues.com/events
Held in Sandton every November

South African Tattoo
URL: www.sa-venues.com/events
Held in Fourways every September

Soweto Festival
URL: www.sa-venues.com/events
Held in Soweto every September

Soweto Food Festival
URL: www.sa-venues.com/events
Held in Soweto every October

Soweto Mushroom Festival
URL: www.sa-venues.com/events
Held in Soweto every October

Soweto Wine Festival
URL: www.sa-venues.com/events
Held in Soweto every September

Summer Festival
URL: www.sa-venues.com/events
Johannesburg's East Rand every September

Taste of Joburg
URL: www.sa-venues.com/events
Held in Fourways every September

The Rand Show
URL: www.randshow.co.za
Held in Johannesburg every March

The Rockford Big City Bash
URL: www.sa-venues.com/events
Held in Braamfontein every October

Total Sibikwa Play Competition
URL: www.sa-venues.com/events
Held in Benoni every July

The Windybrow Arts Festival
URL: www.windybrowarts.co.za
Held in Johannesburg every March

Vaal River Meander Wine Route
URL: www.sa-venues.com/events
Held on the Vaal Meander every July

Vodacom Jazz Picnic
URL: www.sa-venues.com/events
Held in Kempton Park every December

Woodstock
URL: www.sa-venues.com/events
Held in Fourways every November

Kids

Babbelbox Children's Theatre
Tel: 012-997 7907
Email: babbelbox@stof.co.za
URL: www.babbelbox.co.za
Situated in Moreleta Park, Pretoria

Bester Birds & Animals Zoo Park
Tel: 012-807 2574
Email: zoo@besterbirdsanimals.co.za
URL: www.besterbirdsanimals.co.za
Situated in Wollow Glen, Pretoria

Croc City Crocodile Farm
Tel: 083 321 1016
Email: info@croccity.co.za
URL: www.croccity.co.za
Situated in Fourways, Johannesburg

Earth Kids Play Patch
Tel: 083 233 7806
Email: info@earthkids.co.za
URL: www.earthkids.co.za
Situated in Midrand

Jimmy Jungles
Tel: 011 467 8652
Email: fourways@jimmyjungles.co.za
URL: www.jimmyjungles.co.za
Situated in Fourways, Johannesburg

KidzWorld
Visit this exciting website
URL: www.kidzworld.co.za

Kolonnade Ice Rink
Tel: 012-548 1902
URL: www.kolonnadecentre.co.za
Situated in Montana Park, Pretoria

Pretoria Zoo
Tel: 012-328 3265
Email: info@nzg.ac.za
URL: www.nzg.ac.za

Smudge Art
Tel: 011-501 0234
Email: sandra@smudgeart.co.za
URL: www.smudgeart.co.za
Situated in Craighall Park, Johannesburg

The Secret Garden
Tel: 011-467 1191
Email: secretteagar@mweb.co.za
Situated in Fourways, Johannesburg

Très Jolie Restaurant
Tel: 011-794 2473
Email: info@tresjolie.co.za
URL: www.tresjolie.co.za
Situated in Ruimsig, Johannesburg

Wacki Warehouse Kiddies Play Park
Tel: 012-665 5211
URL: www.wackiwarehouse.co.za
Situated in Centurion, Pretoria

Yeesh!
Tel: 083 923 2306
Email: yeesh@mweb.co.za
URL: www.yeesh.co.za
Situated in Woodmead, Johannesburg

Shopping www.mallguide.co.za

Bedford Centre
Tel: 011-622 1840
URL: www.bedfordcentre.com
Situated in Bedfordview, Johannesburg

Lakeside Mall
Tel: 011-427 1801
URL: www.lakesidemall.co.za
Situated in Benoni, Johannesburg

Brooklyn Mall
Tel: 012- 346 1063
URL: www.brooklynmall.co.za
Situated in New Muckleneuk, Pretoria

Market Theatre Flea Market
Tel: 083-586 8687
Situated in Newtown, Johannesburg

Bruma Market World
Tel: 011-622 9648
Situated in Edenvale, Johannesburg

Menlyn Park Shopping Centre
Tel: 012-348 8766
URL: www.menlynpark.co.za
Situated in Menlo Park, Pretoria

Bryanston Shopping Centre
Tel: 011-706 3519
URL: www.bryanstoncentre.co.za
Situated in Bryanston, Johannesburg

Norwood Mall
Tel: 011-728 6640
URL: www.norwoodmall.co.za
Situated in Norwood, Johannesburg

Fourways Mall
Tel: 011-465 6095
URL: www.fourwaysmall.com
Situated in Fourways, Johannesburg

Sandton City Shopping Centre
Tel: 011-217 6000
URL: www.sandton-city.co.za
Situated in Sandton, Johannesburg

Greenstone Shopping Centre
Tel: 011-524 0445
URL: www.greenstoneshoppingcentre.co.za
Situated in Edenvale, Johannesburg

Westgate Shopping Centre
Tel: 011-768 0616
URL: www.westgate.co.za
Situated in Roodepoort, Johannesburg

Johannesburg Craft Markets
URL: www.joburg.org.za
Visit the website for detailed information on
  their various markets

Restaurants

Arcadia
Eastwoods Tavern
Cuisine: Fusion
Tel: 012-344 0243
Address: cnr Eastwood & Park Streets

Bedfordview
Dinos Restaurant
Cuisine: Global/ International
Tel: 011-622 3007
Address: Bedford Centre, Smith Street

Harbour Fish Market
Cuisine: Seafood
Tel: 087-805 9088
Address: Shop 456, Bedford Centre

Macedonia
Cuisine: Greek
Tel: 011-616 8231
Address: Upper Level, Bedford Centre

Olive's Bistro
Cuisine: Mediterranean
Tel: 011-455 2000
Address: Bedfordview Arcade,
    cnr Van Buuren & Hawley Streets

OYO
Cuisine: Asian
Tel: 011-615 3600
Address: Shop 10, Bedford Square,
    Kirby Road

Birnam
Bellagio
Cuisine: Italian
Tel: 011-885 3938
Address: Blubird Shopping Centre, cnr
    Athol Oaklands Road & Fort Street

The Gypsy Lounge
Cuisine: Tapas
Tel: 011-887 7247
Address: Shop 22, Blubird Centre, cnr
    Athol Oaklands Road & Fort Street

Boksburg
Il Gusto
Cuisine: Italian
Tel: 011-894 7847
Address: Key Largo Centre, cnr North
    Rand & Trichardt Roads

La Campana
Cuisine: Portuguese
Tel: 011-913 2505
Address: 261 Kingfisher Avenue,
    Sunward Park

Tribes
Cuisine: African
Tel: 011-397 6512
Address: 64 Jones Road, Shop 23.
    Emperor's Palace Retail Centre

Brooklyn
Capeesh
Cuisine: Italian
Tel: 012-346 1932
Address: Cherry Lane Centre, cnr
    Fehrsen & Middel Streets

Ciao!
Cuisine: Italian
Tel: 012-346 0911
Address: Shop 35, Brooklyn Mall,
    Bronkhorst Street

Daruma
Cuisine: Japanese
Tel: 012-346 7757
Address: cnr Bronkhorst & Tram Roads

Geet Indian Restaurant
Cuisine: Indian
Tel: 012-460 3199
Address: 541 Fehrsen Street

Kream
Cuisine: Fine Dining
Tel: 012-346 4642
Address: 570 Fehrsen Street

Little Durban Food & Spices
Cuisine: Indian
Tel: 012-460 8838
Address: Shop 1, Bronkhorst Street

Bryanston
Bistro 277 on Main
Cuisine: French
Tel: 011-706 2837
Address: 277 Main Road, Cramerview
    Shopping Centre

La Campagnola
Cuisine: Italian
Tel: 011-463 4199
Address: Shop 9&10, Hobart Centre,
    cnr Hobart & Grosvenor Roads

Maharaja
Cuisine: Indian
Tel: 011-463 1651
Address: Sloane Centre, Sloane Street

Centurion
Al Fiume
Cuisine: Italian
Tel: 012-659 0052
Address: 18 River Place, R511,
   Hennops River

Bruno's Restaurant, Bar & Deli
Cuisine: Contemporary
Tel: 0861-278 667
Address: 1001 Lenchen Avenue North

The Godfather
Cuisine: Steakhouse
Tel: 012-663 1859
Address: Shop 2, Biella Centre,
   cnr Heuwel & Mike Crawford Roads

Craighall Park
Bushveld Pub & Diner
Cuisine: South African
Tel: 011-326 0170
Address: Valley Shopping Centre,
   396 Jan Smuts Avenue

Giles Restaurant
Cuisine: Global
Tel: 011-442 4056
Address: 9 Grafton Avenue

Osteria Tre Nonni
Cuisine: Italian
Tel: 0861-222 532
Address: 9 Grafton Avenue

Sides Restaurant
Cuisine: International
Tel: 011-325 2442
Address: 10 Bompas Road, Dunkeld West

Douglasdale
Ciro Umberto
Cuisine: Italian
Tel: 011-658 1015
Address: Shop 14, Waterford Shopping
   Centre, cnr Witkoppen & Douglas Roads

Throbbing Strawberry
Cuisine: Grills
Tel: 011-704 6982
Address: Shop 1, Douglasdale Village,
   Leslie Road

Edenvale
Fahrenheit Seafood & Grill
Cuisine: Grills
Tel: 011-452 9704
Address: 1 Hudson Street

Elandsdrift
Toadbury Hall
Cuisine: International
Tel: 079-512 0554
Address: Beyers Naudé Drive Ext

Equestria
Urban Bar & Grill
Cuisine: Steakhouse
Tel: 012-807 5512
Address: Equestria Gateway Centre,
   cnr Simon Vermooten & Furrow Streets

Faerie Glen
Nuvo Cuisine
Cuisine: Inernational
Tel: 012-991 3396
Address: 823 Old Farm Centre

Pascali's Trattoria
Cuisine: Italian
Tel: 012-991 7121
Address: Faeriedale Centre,
   Cliffendale Street

Steak-Inn Grill & Butcher
Cuisine: Steakhouse
Tel: 012-991 4733
Address: 107 Haymeadow,
   Boardwalk Lakeside

The Greek Easy Ouzaria
Cuisine: Greek
Tel: 012-991 7963
Address: Block F, Boardwalk Centre,
   cnr Haymeadow & Hans Strijdom Roads

Fourways
@Monte Winebar & Restaurant
Cuisine: Continental
Tel: 011-510 7471
Address: Monte Casino

Café Maude
Cuisine: French
Tel: 011-269 7451
Address: Garden Court, Maude Street,
   Sandton City

Central Grill Cocktail House
Cuisine: Grills
Tel: 011-465 3683
Address: Shop U3 13, Cedar Square,
   Cedar Lane

Karma Nirvana
Cuisine: Contemporary
Tel: 011-465 0856
Address: Pineslopes Shopping Centre,
   cnr Witkoppen & The Straight

Kitchen Bar
Cuisine: Fusion
Tel: 011-465 5011
Address: No. 6 Design Quarter,
   cnr William Nicol & Leslie Avenue

Medeo
Cuisine: Mediterranean
Tel: 011-510 3000
Address: The Palazzo Hotel, Monte Casino

Greenside
Addictions
Cuisine: Contemporary
Tel: 011- 646 8981
Address: 137 Greenway Road

Fratelli
Cuisine: Italian
Tel: 011-646 9573
Address: 12 Gleneagles Road

Hanna B
Cuisine: Bistro
Tel: 011-486 1000
Address: 10 Gleneagles Road

Karma
Cuisine: Indian (Halaal)
Tel: 011-646 8555
Address: cnr Gleneagles & Greenfields Roads

Groenkloof
Il Bar Italiano
Cuisine: Italian
Tel: 012-346 4040
Address: 78 George Storrar Drive

Pride of India
Cuisine: Indian
Tel: 012-346 3684
Address: 22 Groenkloof Plaza,
   43 George Storrar Drive

Smoke Café & Grill Lounge
Cuisine: Grills
Tel: 012-346 0916
Address: Shop 21, Groenkloof Plaza,
   George Storrar Drive

Hatfield
Crystal Restaurant
Cuisine: Middle Eastern
Tel: 012-362 8888
Address: 525 Duncan Street

Just Cuban
Cuisine: Cuban
Tel: 012-362 1800
Address: 129 Duxbury Road

Hazelwood
Pachas Restaurant & Cherry Room
Cuisine: Internaitonal
Tel: 012-460 5063
Address: Club 2 Centre, 22 Dely Road

Hekpoort
Barton's Folly Restaurant
Cuisine: Fine Dining
Tel: 082-901 1382
Address: Rem Ext 158, Farm Hekpoort 504

Houghton
La Rustica
Cuisine: Mediterranean
Tel: 011-728 2092
Address: 103 Houghton Drive

Hyde Park
Santorini
Cuisine: Mediterranean
Tel: 011-325 5008
Address: Shop U29, Hyde Park Mall, cnr
    William Nicol, Jan Smuts & 6th Road

Illovo
2 Thai 4
Cuisine: Thai
Tel: 011-440 3000
Address: 59 Corlett Drive

Firehouse
Cuisine: Steakhouse
Tel: 011-268 6622
Address: Illovo Square, 3 Rivonia Road

Yamato
Cuisine: Japanese
Tel: 011-268 0511
Address: 196 Oxford Road

Irene
A'la Turka
Cuisine: Turkish
Tel: 012- 662 4314
Address: Shop 121, Irene Village Mall,
    Nellmapius Drive

Karoo Cattle & Land
Cuisine: Steakhouse
Tel: 012-662 1111
Address: Shop 176, Irene Village Mall,
    Nellmapius Drive

Meadow Green & Lakeside Country
    Kitchen
Cuisine: Country
Tel: 012-667 6464
Address: 391 Nellmapius Drive

Kempton Park
Queen of the Nile
Cuisine: Greek
Tel: 011-928 1367
Address: Emperor's Palace, 64 Jones Road

Kensington
The Bell Pepper
Cuisine: French
Tel: 011-615 7531
Address: 176 Queen Street

Kyalami
Da Vincenzo
Cuisine: Italian
Tel: 011-466 2618
Address: 29 Montrose Road,
    Barbeque Downs

Linden
Satori
Cuisine: Italian
Tel: 011-888 7452
Address: 61 4th Avenue

Linksfield
Afrodisiac and Voodoo Lounge
Cuisine: African
Tel: 011-443 9990
Address: cnr Civin &
    Linksfield Drives

Lonehill
Byzance Restaurant
Cuisine: Mediterranean
Tel: 011-465 5735
Address: 22 Lonehill Boulevard,
    Lonehill Shopping Centre

Lynnwood Ridge
La Madeleine
Cuisine: French
Tel: 012-361 3667
Address: 122 Priory Road

Melrose Arch
Giovanni's Melrose Arch
Cuisine: Italian
Tel: 011-684 1007
Address: Shop 2, Melrose Square,
    Melrose High Street

Orient
Cuisine: Asian
Tel: 011-684 1616
Address: 4 The High Street

Melville
Café Picobella
Cuisine: Italian
Tel: 011-482 4309
Address: 66 4th Avenue

Cool Runnings
Cuisine: Caribbean
Tel: 011-482 4786
Address: 27A 4th Avenue

Menlo Park
BOER'geoisie
Cuisine: South African
Tel: 012-460 0264
Address: Greenlyn Village, 13th Street

Midrand
Viva Espana Restaurant & Tapas Bar
Cuisine: Spanish
Tel: 011-805 2720
Address: 546 16th Road

Modderfontein
33 High Street Restaurant & Cellar Bar
Cuisine: International
Tel: 011-606 3574
Address: 33 High Street

Mooiplaats
Villa Francesco
Cuisine: Italian
Tel: 082-441 4909
Address: Plot 198, Mooiplaats Road

Morningside
Al Dente
Cuisine: Italian
Tel: 011-783 9989
Address: 173 Rochester Place, Rivonia Road

Muldersdrift
Pangea
Cuisine: African
Tel: 011-659 0466
Address: Elandsdrift Road

New Muckleneuk
Cynthia's Indigo Moon
Cuisine: International
Tel: 012-346 8926
Address: 283 Dey Street

The Blue Crane Restaurant
Cuisine: International
Tel: 012-460 7615
Address: 156 Melk Street

Northcliff
Alex del Mar
Cuisine: Seafood
Tel: 011-678 4790
Address: cnr Weltevreden & 14th Avenue

Eat Bistro
Cuisine: Contemporary
Tel: 011-476 3749
Address: 'L Corro Centre, 14th Avenue

Norwood
Alexander's Deli
Cuisine: Light Meals
Tel: 011-728 5901
Address: 48 The Avenue

Oakdene
Ribs & Rumps
Cuisine: Steakhouse
Tel: 012-436 2269
Address: The Glen Centre,
    cnr Orpen & Letaba Roads

Ormonde
Back of the Moon
Cuisine:International
Tel: 011-496 1423
Address: Shop 17, Gold Reef City Casino,
    Nothern Parkway Road

Parkhurst
Cilantro
Cuisine: Mediterranean
Tel: 011-327 4558
Address: Shop 24 E, 4th Avenue

George's on 4th
Cuisine: International
Tel: 011-447 7705
Address: 21 4th Avenue

The Attic
Cuisine: Fusion
Tel: 011-880 6102
Address: 24 4th Avenue

Parkmore
Canto Latino
Cuisine: Spanish
Tel: 011-883 3925
Address: 136 11th Street

Thomas Maxwell Bistro
Cuisine: Bistro
Tel: 011- 784 1575
Address: 140 11th street

Parktown North
Fino Bar & Restaurant
Cuisine: Spanish
Tel: 011-447 4608
Address: 19 4th Avenue

La Cucina di Ciro
Cuisine: Italian
Tel: 011-442 5187
Address: 17 4th Avenue

Pretoria
Café Riche
Cuisine: Continental
Tel: 012-328 3173
Address: 2 Church Square, cnr Church &
    Paul Kruger Streets

Queenswood
Namaskar
Cuisine: Indian
Tel: 012-342 9081
Address: 1270 Church Street

Rivonia
Rocket Restaurant
Cuisine: Contemporary
Tel: 011-234 8807
Address: Shop 7, Rivonia Corner,
    362 Rivonia Boulevard

Saigon Rivonia
Cuisine: Vietnamese
Tel: 011-807 5272
Address: Shop F2, 2nd Floor,
    Rivonia Junction

Zenatude
Cuisine: Contemporary
Tel: 011-234 3343
Address: Rivonia Crossing West Shopping
    Centre, cnr Witkoppen & Achter Roads

Roodepoort
Angie's Restaurant
Cuisine: Fine Cuisine
Tel: 082-554 3359
Address: 39 Pierre Road, Honeydew

Rusty Hook
Cuisine: Country
Tel: 072-312 0536
Address: 22 Wilge Street, Honeydew

Rosebank
Barry's Grill Room
Cuisine: Steakhouse
Tel: 011-447 2200
Address: Shop 8&9, The Mall at Rosebank

Bombay Blues
Cuisine: Indian
Tel: 011-447 3210
Address: Standard Bank Building, cnr
    Cradock & Tyrwhitt Avenues

F!sh Restaurant
Cuisine: Sushi
Tel: 011-447 9188
Address: Shop 2, Rosebank Arena,
    cnr Cradock & Baker Avenues

Louis XVI
Cuisine: French
Tel: 011-447 6244
Address: 160 Jan Smuts Avenue

Tsunami
Cuisine: Seafood
Tel: 011-880 8409
Address: Shop 304-308, The Mall
    at Rosebank

Ruimsig
Très Jolie Restaurant
Cuisine: International
Tel: 011-794 2473
Address: 22 Peter Road

Sandhurst
Saxon
Cuisine: Fine Dining
Tel: 011-292 6000
Address: 36 Saxon Road

117

Sandown
Filakia
Cuisine: Greek
Tel: 011-783 5805
Address: 24 Central Fredman Drive

Sandton
8 at the Towers
Cuisine: International
Tel: 011-884 1333
Address: Lobby of Michelangelo Towers,
    Maude Street

Faff Restaurant
Cuisine: International
Tel: 011-728 2434
Address: 44 The Avenue

Koi Restaurant & Sushi Bar
Cuisine: Sushi
Tel: 011-883 7247
Address: 24 Central, Shop 3, cnr
    Fredman Drive & Gwen Lane

Lekgotla
Cuisine: South African
Tel: 011-884 9555
Address: Nelson Mandela Square

Montego Bay
Cuisine: Seafood
Tel: 011-883 6407
Address: Shop 31, Square Level,
    Nelson Mandela Square

Piccolo Mondo
Cuisine: International
Tel: 011-282 7067
Address: Nelson Mandela Square

The Gourmet Garage
Cuisine: Steakhouse
Tel: 011-883 2226
Address: 24 Central, cnr Fredman Drive
    & Gwen Lane

The White Boy Shebeen
Cuisine: South African
Tel: 011-444 8850
Address: City Lodge, cnr Katherine Street
    & Grayston Drive

Wang Thai
Cuisine; Thai
Tel: 011-784 8484
Address: Shop 120, 1st Floor,
    Nelson Mandela Square

Saxonwold
The Birdcage
Cuisine: International
Tel: 011-646 6315
Address: 82 Jan Smuts Avenue

Sterkfontein / Cradle of Humankind
Greensleeves Medieval Kingdom
Cuisine: Medieval
Tel: 083-229 5677
Address: Hekpoort Road, R563

The Cradle Restaurant
Cuisine: South African
Tel: 011-659 1622
Address: Route T9, Kromdraai Road

Sunninghill
Beach Blanket Bohemia
Cuisine: Mediterranean
Tel: 011-234 2714
Address: Sunninghill Village Centre,
    cnr Maxwell Drive and Edison Street

Juniper
Cuisine: International
Tel: 011-803 3279
Situated in Sunninghill

Waterkloof & Surrounds
Al Dente Ristorante & Pizzeria
Cuisine: Italian
Tel: 012-460 9686
Address: 103 Club Avenue

Brasserie de Paris
Cuisine: French
Tel: 012-460 3583
Address: 381 Aries Street

Magenta
Cuisine: Mediterranean
Tel: 012-460 8840
Address: Waterkloof Tower,
    cnr Milner & Long Streets

Red Tomato @ Home
Cuisine: Bistro
Tel: 012-346 6309
Address: 421 Main Street

Ritrovo Ristorante
Cuisine: Italian
Tel: 012-460 5173
Address: Shop 2, Waterkloof Heights
   Shopping Centre, 103 Club Avenue

Wierda Valley
Linger Longer
Cuisine: Fine Dining
Tel: 011-884 0465
Address: 58 Wierda Road

Wonderboom
Villa San Giovanni Ristorante
Cuisine: Fine Dining
Tel: 012-543 0501
Address: Wonderboom Airport, Main
   Terminal Building, Linvelt Road

Wynberg
Zambezi Lounge & Grill
Cuisine: South African
Tel: 011-440 5021
Address: 676 Old Pretoria Main Road

Zwartkops
Hedwig's Fine Dining
Cuisine: Fine Dining
Tel: 011-957 2070
Address: Aloe Ridge Hotel & Game Reserve,
   Beyers Naudé Drive Ext.

Chains and Franchises

Adega
URL: www.adegas.co.za

Allora
URL: www.allora.co.za

Cape Town Fish Market
URL: www.ctfm.co.za

Cattle Baron
URL: www.cattlebaron.co.za

Ciao Baby Cucina
URL: www.ciaobabycucina.co.za

Col'Cacchio Pizzeria
URL: www.colcacchio.co.za

Crawdaddy's Restaurant
URL: www.crawdaddys.co.za

Doppio Zero
URL: www.doppio.co.za

Jimmy's Killer Prawns
URL: www.jimmyskillerprawns.com

Mugg & Bean
URL: www.themugg.com

Mythos
URL: www.mythos.co.za

O'Galito
URL: www.ogalito.com

Ocean Basket
URL: www.oceanbasket.co.za

Piatto Mediterranean Kitchen
URL: www.piatto.co.za

Pigalle
URL: www.pigallerestaurants.co.za

Primi Restaurants
URL: www.primi-piatti.com

Rhapsody's
URL: www.rhapsodys.co.za

The Baron
URL: www.thebaron.co.za

The Boma
URL: www.theboma.com

The Brazen Head
URL: www.thebrazenhead.co.za

The Raj
URL: www.therajrestaurant.com

Accommodation

www.sa-venues.com/gauteng_index.htm
www.wheretostay.co.za/g/
www.safarinow.com/destinations/gauteng/hub.aspx
www.sleeping-out.co.za/Gauteng-accommodation.asp
www.countryroads.co.za/.../gauteng-accommodation.html
gauteng.hotelguide.co.za/
www.roomsforafrica.com/dest/south-africa/gauteng.jsp
www.gauteng.com
www.gauteng-africaninvitation.co.za

Johannesburg
Hotels

Africa Centre Airport Leisure Hotel
Tel: 011-894 4857
Email: afrcentr@global.co.za
URL: www.africacentrelodge.co.za
Situated in Benoni

Birchwood Hotel
Tel: 011-897 0000
Email: reservations@birchwoodhotel.co.za
URL: www.birchwoodhotel.co.za
Situated in Boksburg

D'Oreale Grande Hotel (Emperor's Palace)
Tel: 011-928 1770
Email: info@ep.doreale.com
URL: www.doreale.com
Situated in Kempton Park

Garden Court Eastgate
Tel: 011-622 0570
Email: gceastgate@southernsun.com
URL: www.southernsun.com
Situated in Bruma

Garden Court Milpark
Tel: 011-726 5100
Email: gcmilpark@southernsun.com'
URL: www.southernsun.com
Situated in Auckland Park

Garden Court Morningside
Tel: 011-884 1804
Email: gcmorningside@southernsun.com
URL: www.southernsun.com
Situated in Morningside

Garden Court OR Tambo International
  Airport
Tel: 011-392 1062
Email: gcortairport@southernsun.com
URL: www.southernsun.com

Garden Court Sandton
Tel: 011-884 5660
Email: gcsandton@southernsun.com
URL: www.southernsun.com
Situated in Sandton

Garden Court Sandton City
Tel: 011-269 7000
Email: gcsandtoncity@southernsun.com
URL: www.southernsun.com
Situated in Sandown

Gold Reef City Hotel
Tel: 011-248 5152
Email: reservations@grcc.co.za
URL: www.goldreefcitycasinc.co.za
Situated in Johannesburg

Grace Hotel
Tel: 011-280 7200
Email: pacro@africansunhotels.com
URL: www.africansunhotels.com
Situated in Rosebank

Lodges

Kloofzicht Lodge
Tel: 011-317 0600
Email: gm@kloofzicht.co.za
URL: www.kloofzicht.co.za
Situated in Muldersdrift

N'Gomo Safari Lodge
Tel: 011-662 4900
Email: info@ngomolodge.co.za
URL: www.ngomolodge.co.za
Situated in Muldersdrift

Safari Club SA
Tel: 011-979 0321
URL: www.safariclubsa.co.za
Situated in Kempton Park

B&Bs, Guest Houses & Self-catering

28 Vincent
Tel: 011-883 1304
Email: info@28vincent.co.za
URL: www.28vincent.co.za
Situated in Rivonia

Archie's Place
Tel: 011-726 4670
Email: enquiries@archies.co.za
URL: www.archies.co.za
Situated in Mellville

Auberge Le Fleur
Tel: 011-534 3584
Email: leonieb@polka.co.za
URL: www.aubergelefleur.com
Situated in Northcliff

Mi Casa Su Casa
Tel: 011-726 8693
Email: reservation@micasasucasa.co.za
URL: www.micasasucasa.co.za
Situated in Mellville

Renates Heim B&B
Tel: 011-867 5517
Email: info@renatesheim.co.za
URL: www.renatesheim.co.za
Situated in Meyersdal

Camping

Brown Sugar Backpackers
Tel: 011-648 7397
Email: sugarbrown@mweb.co.za
URL: www.brownsugarbackpackers.com
Situated in Observatory

Bushwillow Tented Camp
Tel: 011-668 1600
Email: bushwillow@glenburn.co.za
URL: www.bushwillowtentedcamp.co.za
Situated in Muldersdrift

Gemini Backpackers Lodge
Tel: 011-882 6845
Email: lodge@geminibackpackers.co.za
URL: www.geminibackpackers.co.za
Situated in Crystal Gardens

Rockey's of Fourways
Tel: 011-465 4219
Email: info@backinafrica.com
Situated in Sandton

Pretoria
Hotels

Arcadia Hotel
Tel: 012-326 9311
Email: archot@arcadiahotel.co.za
URL: www.arcadiahotel.co.za
Situated in Arcadia

Centurion Lake Hotel
Tel: 012-643 3800
Email: centurion@legacyhotels.co.za
URL: www.centurionlakehotel.co.za
Situated in Centurion

Garden Court Hatfield
Tel: 012-342 1444
Email: gchatfield@southernsun.com
URL: www.southernsun.com
Situated in Hatfield

Premier Hotel
Tel: 012-441 1400
Email: pretoria@premierhotels.co.za
URL: www.premierhotels.co.za
Situated in Arcadia

Sheraton Hotel & Towers
Tel: 012-429 9999
URL: www.south.african-hotels.com/
 sheraton-pretoria/
Situated in Pretoria

Hoogland Health Hydro
Tel: 012-380 4000
Email: hydro@hoogland.co.za
URL: www.hoogland.co.za
Situated in Erasmia

Lodges

Leriba Lodge
Tel: 012-660 3300
Email: marketing@leriba.co.za
URL: www.leriba.co.za
Situated in Centurion

Leribisi Lodge
Tel: 012-811 0553
Email: leribisi@leribisi.co.za
URL: www.leribisi.co.za
Situated in Pretoria

B&Bs, Guesthouses & Self-catering

All Seasons B&B
Tel: 012-997 0557
Email: info@allseason.co.za
URL: www.allseason.co.za
Situated in Moreleta Park

Blue Periwinkle
Tel: 012-667 1869
Email: blueperiwinkle@netactive.co.za
URL: www.blueperiwinkle.co.za
Situated in Irene

Loerie's Nest B&B
Tel: 012-460 3605
Email: marlene@loeriesnest.co.za
URL: www.loeriesnest.co.za
Situated in Bailey's Muckleneuk

Maribelle's Bed & Breakfast
Tel: 012-361 6970
URL: www.wheretostay.co.za/maribelles
Situated in Lynnwood Ridge

Camping

N'kosi Sana Game Lodge
Tel: 012-735 1018
Email: schachl@global.co.za
URL: www.nkosisana.co.za
Situated in Groenfontein

Phumula Holiday Resort
Tel: 012-722 0072
Situated in Pretoria

Pretoria Backpackers
Tel: 012-343 9754
Email: info@pretoriabackpackers.net
URL: www.pretoriabackpackers.net
Situated in Pretoria

Other
Hotels

City Lodge Hotels
Tel: 0800 113 790
Email: info@citylodge.co.za
URL: www.citylodge.co.za

Court Classique Suite Hotel
Tel: 012-344 4420
Email: pretoria@courtclassique.co.za
URL: www.courtclassique.co.za

Forum Homini
Tel: 011-668 7000
Email: reservations@forumhomini.co.za
URL: www.forumhomini.co.za
Situated in the Cradle of Humankind

Maropeng Boutique Hotel
Tel: 014-577 9100
Email: info@maropeng.co.za
URL: www.maropeng.co.za
Situated on the R400 close to Hekpoort

Protea Hotel Group
Tel: 0861-119 000
Email: info@proteahotels.com
URL: www.proteahotels.com

Southern Sun Hotels
Tel: 011-461 9741
Email: contactus@southernsun.com
URL: www.southernsun.com

Riviera on Vaal
Tel: 0861 967 485
Email: reservations1@zorgvliet.com
URL: www.rivieraonvaal.co.za
Situated in Vereeniging

Velmore Hotel
Tel: 086 538 8417
Email: Heinz@velmore.co.za
URL: www.velmore.co.za
Situated in Hennops Park

Lodges

Bundhu-Rus
Tel: 082 824 9340
Email: louise@bundhurus.co.za
Situated in Doornpoort

Butjani Lodge
Tel: 082 803 8608
Email: penny@butjanilodge.co.za
URL: www.butjanilodge.co.za/events.htm
Situated near Cullinan

iKhaya IamaDube Bushveld Lodge
Tel: 012-711 3558
URL: www.wheretostay.co.za
Situated in Hartebeestfontein

Jabali Game Reserve
Tel: 082-922 8449
Email: info@jabali.co.za
URL: www.jabali.co.za
Situated in Bronkhorstspruit

Tamboti Bush Lodge
Tel: 012-711 0909
Email: info@tamboti.co.za
URL: www.tambotie.co.za
Situated in Dinokeng North

The Nutbush Boma Lodge
Tel: 014-576 2248
Email: kgatours@mweb.co.za
URL: www.kgatours.co.za
Situated in Hekpoort

Zebra Country Lodge
Tel: 012-735 9000
URL: http://legendlodges.co.za/
    bushlodge.htm
Situated at Roodeplaat Dam

B&Bs, Guesthouses & Self-catering

Ted's Place
Tel: 012-807 2803
Email: stay@tedsplace.za.net
URL: www.teds-place.za.net
Situated in Wapadrand

The Country Cottage
Tel: 011-622 1066
Email: bookings@thecountrycottage.co.za
URL: www.thecountrycottage.co.za
Situated in Bedfordview

Camping

Airport En Route
Tel: 011-963 0045
URL: www.sa-venues.com/visit/
    airportenroute

Eastco Magaliesburg Holiday Resort
Tel: 082-855 1994
URL: www.eastcomagalies.co.za
Situated in the Magaliesberg

Goose Bay Canyon Centre
Tel: 016-987 1130
Email: info@goosebayconference.co.za
URL: www.goosebayconference.co.za
Situated on the Vaal River

Hennops Pride Caravan Park
Tel: 012-659 0043
URL: www.hennopspride.caravanparks.co.za
Situated in the Hennops River Valley

Jakkals Asem
Tel: 082-806 4410
Situated in Dinokeng

Kaia Manzi
Tel: 013-932 3140
Email: info@kaiamanzi.co.za
URL: www.kaiamanzi.co.za
Situated just outside Bronkhorstspruit

Koppisol Klub Holiday Resort
Tel: 016-556 1112
Email: koppisol@cyberserv.co.za
URL: www.koppisolklub.co.za
Situated in Vereeniging

Kungwini Resort
Tel: 013-932 2202
Situated in Bronkhorstspruit

Magalies Sleepy River Caravan Park
Tel: 014-577 1524
URL: www.magaliessleepyriver.co.za
Situated on the Magalies River

Monte Metse River Ranch
Tel: 012-346 1326
Situated in Rust de Winter

Riebeeck Lake Caravan Park
Tel: 011-411 0184
Situated in Randfontein

Somabula Nature Reserve
Tel: 082-550 1892
Email: info@somabula.co.za
URL: www.somabula.co.za
Situated in Cullinan

Tours

African Breeze
Tel: 011-516 0001
Email: info@africanbreeze.co.za
URL: www.africanbreeze.co.za

Adventours & Transfers
Tel: 011-828 2791
Email: info@adventours.co.za
URL: www.adventours.co.za

AfriFriends Unique African Journeys
Tel: 011-609 6142
Email: africa@afrifriends.co.za
URL: www.afrifriends.co.za

AfriXplorer
Tel: 012-348 1708
Email: info@afrixplorer.co.za
http://afrixplorer.co.za

Baobab Tourist Services
Tel: 012-341 8967
Email: benjamin@baobabtourism.co.za
URL: www.baobabtourism.co.za

Bizi Bee Tours
Tel: 011-781 2977
Email: bizibee@telkomsa.net

Bono Tours & Safaris
Tel: 073-636 7018
Email: info@bonosafaris.com
URL: www.bonosafaris.co.za

Bushtrackers Africa
Tel: 011-465 5700
Email: bushtrackers@iafrica.com
URL: www.bushtrackers.co.za

Catz Private Tours
Tel: 011-782 5416
Email: info@catztours.co.za
URL: www.catztours.co.za

Charlton Tours & Safaris
Tel: 012-333 6677
Email: charl@charltontours.co.za
URL: www.charltontours.co.za

Deeprift Ventours
Tel: 011-954 1868
Email: info@deeprift.co.za
URL: www.deeprift.co.za

Duto, The Travel Advisors
Tel: 012-460 8382
Email: info3@duto.co.za
URL: www.duto.co.za

GAUTENG

Escape Cycle Tours
Tel: 011-646 9970
Email: chris@escapecycletours.com
URL: www.escapecycletours.com

Exclusive Combi Tours
Tel: 011-672 5738
Email: tailoredtours@airpost.net
URL: www.tailoredtours.itgo.com

Executive Breakaway Tours
Tel: 011-464 3669
Email: ebtours@ebtours.co.za

Frontline Africa Travel
Tel: 012-991 3822
Email: tours@frontlineafrica.co.za
URL: www.frontlineafrica.co.za

Gone Roaming
Tel: 011-314 2829 / 082-355 8806
Email: goneroaming@metroweb.co.za
URL: www.goneroaming.co.za

Green Rhino African Travel
Tel: 012-794 7365
Email: info@greenrhino.co.za
URL: www.greenrhino.co.za

Haywards Luxury Mobile Safari Camps
Tel: 0861-732 583
Email: reservations@secluded.com
URL: www.haywardsafaris.com

Imfuduko African Safaris
Tel: 011-314 3264
Email: info@imfuduko.com
URL: www.imfuduko.com

J & K Tours
Tel: 082-568 1066
Email: jktours@telkomsa.net
URL: www.jktours.co.za

Jumbo Tours & Transfers
Tel: 082-655 4444
Email: henne@netactive.co.za
URL: www.jumbotours.co.za

King & Queen Tours
Tel: 011-412 3407
Email: reservations@kingandqueen.co.za
URL: www.kingandqueen.co.za

Kwanvelo
Tel: 012-348 6972

Kwazukela River Adventures
Tel: 011-708 1079

Moratiwa Tours & Marketing
Tel: 011-869 6629
URL: www.moratiwa.co.za

Moremi Safaris & Tours
Tel: 011-463 3999
Email: info@moremi-safaris.com
URL: www.moremi-safaris.com

Mothoa Tours & Safaris
Tel: 011-945 2530
URL: http://mothoatours.co.za/contacts.htm

Outlook Safaris
Tel: 011-894 5406
Email: safaris@outlook.co.za
URL: www.outlook.co.za

Peregrene Tours
Tel: 011-678 2616
Email: info@peregrinetours.co.za
URL: www.peregrinetours.co.za

Prima Luce Tours & Safaris
Tel: 011-704 2199
Email: info@primalucetours.com
URL: www.primalucetours.com

Shumba Safaris
Email: mwshumba@mweb.co.za
URL: www.shumbasafaris.com

Sun Land Tours & Transfers
Tel: 012-345 5477
Email: sunland@sunlandsouthafrica.co.za
URL: www.sunlandsouthafrica.co.za

Sunrise Africa Tours & Safaris
Tel: 072-463 8334
Email: info@sunriseafrica.com
URL: www.sunriseafrica.com

Tagalong Tours
Tel: 011-975 3293
Email: tagalong@global.co.za
URL: www.tagalong.co.za

Themba Tours & Safaris
Tel: 011-463 3306
Email: nik@global.co.za
URL: www.sowetotour.co.za

Ulysses Tours & Safaris
Tel: 012-653 0018
Email: info@ulysses.co.za
URL: www.ulysses.co.za

Vhupo Tours
Tel: 011-936 0411
Email: info@vhupo-tours.com
URL: www.vhupo-tours.com

Vulamehlo Safaris & Tours
Tel: 012-660 1496
Email: info@vulamehlo.com
URL: www.vulamehlo.com

Car Rentals

Avis
Tel: 0861-021 111
URL: www.avis.co.za

Budget
Tel: 0861-016 622
URL: www.budget.co.za

Click Car Hire
Tel: 021-551 9515
URL: www.sa-venues.com/explore/
   clickcarhire/

Drive South Africa
Tel: 0860-000 060
URL: www.drivesouthafrica.co.za

Europcar
Tel: 0861-131 000
URL: www.europcar.co.za

First
Tel: 0861-011 323
URL: www.firstcarrental.co.za

Hertz
Tel: 0861-600 136
URL: www.hertz.co.za

Leisuremobiles Rent a Car
Tel: 011-475 2902
Email: info@africanleisure.com
URL: www.africanleisure.co.za/
   vehicle_hire.asp

Maximum Car Rentals
Tel: 011-640 6444
Email: maximum@iafrica.com
URL: www.maximum.co.za

ResQ Rent a Car
Tel: 011-867 6552
E-mail: info@resqrentacar.co.za
URL: www.resqrentacar.co.za

Sixt Car Rental
URL: www.sixt.com

Tempest Car Hire
Tel: 0861-836 7378
URL: www.tempestcarhire.co.za

Tony's Car Hire
Tel: 011-975 8081
E-mail: info@sacarhire.co.za
URL: www.sacarhire.co.za

Value Car Hire
Tel: 021-386 7699
URL: www.valuerentalcar.com

Emergency Numbers

Any Emergency
107

Ambulance and Fire Department
10177

Automobile Association Rescue
0800-010 101

Cell Phone Emergency Number
112

Flying Squad – Police
10111

National Tourism Information & Safety Line
083-113 2345

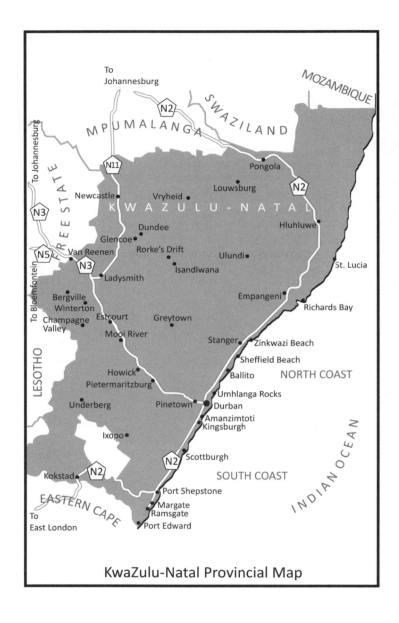

KwaZulu-Natal Provincial Map

KwaZulu-Natal

Tourism Information Offices

Amanzimtoti Tourism Association
Tel: 031-903 7498

Battlefields Route
Tel: 086-565 7727
Email: route@battlefield.org.za

Bergville & Northern Drakensberg
Tel: 036-448 1296 / 1244 / 1557

Cato Manor Tourism
Tel: 031-261 8657

Central Drakensberg Publicity Association
Tel: 036-488 1180
Email: info@drakensberg.co.za

Dannhauser Tourism Office
Tel: 034-621 2666

Durban Central
Tel: 031-304 4934
Email: funinsun@iafrica.com

Ezemvelo KZN Wildlife
Tel: 033-845 1000
Email: webmail@kznwildlife.com
URL: www.kznwildlife.com

Howick Tourism
Tel: 033-330 5305

KZN Tourism Authority
Tel: 0860-101 099 / 031-366 7500
Email: kznta@iafrica.com
URL: www.zulu.org

129

Ladysmith & Surrounds
Tel: 036-637 2992 / 4231
Email: tourism@ladysmith.co.za

Major Adventures
Tel: 033-701 1628

Mkhuze Information Centre
Tel: 035-573 1328

Pietermaritzburg & the Midlands
Tel: 033-345 1348
Email: info@pmbtourism.co.za

South Coast Tourism
Tel: 039-682 7944
Email: info@southcoasttourism.org.za

Southern Berg Escape & Underberg Tourism Bureau
Tel: 033-701 1471

St Lucia & Surrounds
Tel: 035-562 0353 / 0966
Email: res@elephantcoastbookings.co.za

Thousand Hills
Tel: 031-777 1874

Tourism KwaZulu-Natal – Airport
Tel: 031-408 1000

Tourism KwaZulu-Natal – uShaka Marine World
Tel: 031-337 8099

Umhlanga Tourism Information Centre
Tel: 031-561 4257

K
W
A
Z
U
L
U
-
N
A
T
A
L

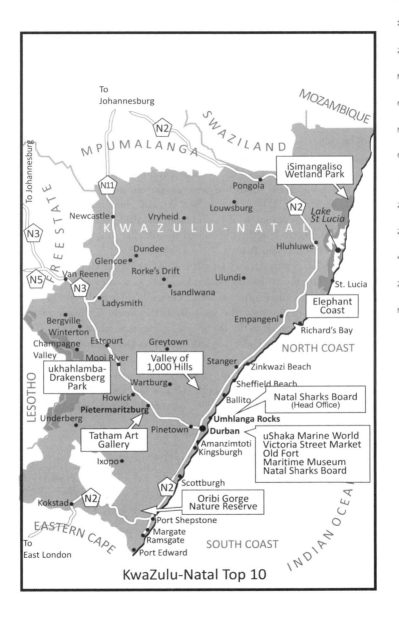

To
Johannesburg

MOZAMBIQUE

SWAZILAND

MPUMALANGA

N2

iSimangaliso
Wetland Park

To Johannesburg

N11

Pongola

Louwsburg

N2

Lake
St Lucia

Newcastle

Vryheid

KWAZULU-NATAL

N3

FREE STATE

Dundee

Hluhluwe

Glencoe

Rorke's Drift

Ulundi

St. Lucia

N5

Van Reenen

N3

Isandlwana

Ladysmith

Elephant
Coast

Bergville

Empangeni

Winterton

Richard's Bay

Champagne
Valley

Estcourt

Greytown

NORTH COAST

Mooi River

Stanger

Zinkwazi Beach

ukhahlamba-
Drakensberg
Park

Valley of
1,000 Hills

Wartburg

Sheffield Beach

LESOTHO

Howick

Ballito

Natal Sharks Board
(Head Office)

Pietermaritzburg

Umhlanga Rocks

Underberg

Tatham Art
Gallery

Pinetown

Durban

uShaka Marine World
Victoria Street Market
Old Fort
Maritime Museum
Natal Sharks Board

Amanzimtoti
Kingsburgh

Ixopo

Scottburgh

N2

Kokstad

N2

Oribi Gorge
Nature Reserve

INDIAN OCEAN

EASTERN CAPE

Port Shepstone

Margate
Ramsgate

SOUTH COAST

To
East London

Port Edward

KwaZulu-Natal Top 10

Top 10

 uKhahlamba-Drakensberg Park
Tel: 036-448 1557
Email: info@drakensberg.org.za
URL: www.drakensberg.org.za

Call it what you like, uKhahlamba-Drakensberg, the gargantuan sequence of peaks that divides sultry KwaZulu-Natal from the cloud-scraping Kingdom of Lesotho, is among the most impressive of Afro-montane landscapes. Boasting several dozen peaks that top the 3,000-metre mark, this is the highest African mountain range south of Kilimanjaro, capped by a formidable basaltic escarpment whose 200-plus-kilometre length is breached by just one solitary and remote road, the 4x4-only Sani Pass.

Inscribed as South Africa's fourth UNESCO World Heritage Site in the year 2000, the uKhahlamba-Drakensberg possesses a wide variety of attractions for discerning visitors. Scenically, it is truly spectacular, whether you opt to enjoy the view from the foothills, follow one of several overnight trails to the craggy escarpment, or snake a 4x4 vehicle to the top of Sani Pass. Culturally, uKhahlamba-Drakensberg is of great significance as it hosts the largest concentration of rock art in Africa south of the Sahara, a poignant reminder of a not-so-distant time when its slopes provided refuge to South Africa's few remaining Bushmen. (*Philip Briggs, World Heritage Sites of South Africa—uKhahlamba-Drakensberg Park, 2006*)

iSimangaliso Wetland Park
(formerly Greater St Lucia Wetland Park)
Tel: 035-590 1633
URL: www.isimangaliso.com

The word *isimangaliso* is Zulu for marvel. The park was renamed on 1 November 2007. It is situated 275 kilometres north of Durban and is South Africa's third-largest protected area, spanning 280km of coastline, from the Mozambican border in the north to Mapelane south of the St Lucia estuary, and made up of around 3,280 square kilometres of pristine natural ecosystems. The park includes the St Lucia Game Reserve, False Bay Park, St Lucia Marine Reserve, Sodwana Bay National Park, Maputaland Marine Reserve, Cape Vidal, the Ozabeni, Mfabeni and Tewate Wilderness Areas and Mkhuze Game Reserve. Like many tidal estuaries, the park has diverse wildlife reflecting the concentration of equally diverse ecosystems created by variations in the degree of salinity from season to season, year to year, and location to location within the park. The estuary is the largest in Africa and boasts, among other attractions, the world's largest forested sand dunes, which reach up to 180 metres (600 feet) in height.

 Natal Maritime Museum
Tel: 031-311 2231
URL: www.durban.gov.za/durban/discover/museums/local_
history/portnatal

The Natal Maritime Museum deals with Durban's seafaring history and is an awesome opportunity for children to get to grips with the history of naval tradition while clambering over a number of smaller craft as well as three larger vessels: the 75-year-old coal-engined *Ulundi*, the 38-year-old oil-burning-engined *JR Moore* and the 42-year-old minesweeper, the SAS *Durban*. The Britannia Exhibition Hall offers displays that encompass the entire nautical experience, from weather-prediction equipment to navigation by the stars, and communication equipment linking ships at sea to land. The museum serves as an apt reminder that Durban was, and certainly still is, Africa's busiest port.

Natal Sharks Board
Tel: 0 31-566 0400
URL: www.shark.co.za

An odd selection for a Top 10, I'll admit, but then we need to cater for everyone. Durban and its north beaches are a major national and international surfers' haven. So, daily reports on shark activity are vital and since we're for sharks and for tanned, blond surfers the Natal Sharks Board is for protecting both these curious species. They offer everything from a hotline to a safe shark-repellent device for surfers, scuba drivers, snorkellers and over-enthusiastic swimmers training for the Iron Man. Their website offers a host of information on conservation, shark species, tourism and research. You can even log on for information about the annual sardine run.

Old Fort
Tel: 031-304 4934
URL: http://travel.yahoo.com/p-travelguide-2760202-old_
fort_the_durban-i.html

This model fort is a reconstruction of the basic defences set up by the 27th Regiment, the Inniskilling Fusiliers. The original was constructed when Britain annexed Port Natal, to protect the British population from the Afrikaners who, having commenced the Great Trek, had established the Boer republic of Natalia and wanted possession of the strategic bay. Following a Boer victory at the Battle of Congella, in 1842, the Boers besieged the entrenched British garrison. Boer general Andries Pretorius kept up the attack with small-arms and artillery fire day after day. Phillip Richard 'Dick' King, an English trader, on learning of the besieged garrison, escaped the port and rode with his personal servant 960 kilometres to the Eastern Cape town of Grahamstown to convey a request from Captain Smith for immediate reinforcements, reaching Grahamstown in just ten days. King returned a month after his escape, on the *Conch*, one of the British vessels carrying the relief parties. It arrived at the bay on 24 June, and the reinforcements were in time to save Smith's garrison from imminent surrender or starvation.

Oribi Gorge Nature Reserve
Tel: 033-845 1000
Email: webmail@kznwildlife.com
URL: www.kznwildlife.com

Situated 21 kilometres inland from Port Shepstone, which is 127 kilometres south of Durban, Oribi Gorge is the eastern gorge of two gorges that cut through flat sugarcane farmlands, or the Oribi Flats. It is situated along the spectacular forest-cloaked ravine of the Mzimkulwana River. Nearly 5km wide at some points, and over 400m deep, the Oribi Gorge is perhaps better classified as a canyon than a gorge. The reserve is located at the confluence of the Mzimkulu and Mzimkulwana rivers. Aeons of erosion by these rivers have carved out nearly 30km of spectacular kloofs and crags, covered with dense subtropical vegetation. Beside the bridge there is a picnic / braai area and the starting point of a couple of trails, including the Hoopoe Falls Trail that wends its way along the riverbank, culminating in a delightful well-deserved waterfall. But be cautioned that bilharzia can be contracted from the water.

Tatham Art Gallery
Tel: 033-392 2800 / 2
Email: tatham.shop@msunduzi.gov.za
URL: www.tatham.org.za

The Tatham Art Gallery is one of South Africa's major museums, dating back to 1903. It is situated in Pietermaritzburg, oddly, the capital of the KwaZula-Natal Province. The gallery had its humble beginnings at the turn of the last century when the wife of the then president of Natal, Mrs Ada Tatham, collected money from friends also interested in the establishment of a gallery, and purchased works from overseas. The same year saw many local artists donating works to the gallery. The gallery houses the Whitwell and Bodenstein collections and regularly celebrates contemporary visual creativity by artists and crafters resident in KwaZulu-Natal.

uShaka Marine World
Tel: 031-328 8000
Email: mkt@ushakamarineworld.co.za
URL: www.ushakamarineworld.co.za
Opening Time: Summer: Monday to Sunday: 09h00; Winter:
Monday to Sunday: 09h00
Closing Time: Summer: Monday to Sunday: 17h00; Winter:
Monday to Sunday: 17h00

uShaka Marine World is a theme park with a difference as it incorporates a host of dining and shopping outlets with an underground aquarium, a dolphin and seal stadium, the water world and a variety of beach- and sea-based activities. The superstructure of a shipwreck dominates the open-plan design which incorporates land, sea and sky. It caters to all tastes, from families to young adults and the more mature. Some of its specialities include the oceanwalker experience, shark cage and snorkel lagoon. Most restaurants overlook the Indian Ocean and the retail village has everything from scuba and surfing equipment to curios.

Valley of 1,000 Hills
Tel: 031-777 1874
Email: thtouris@iafrica.com
URL: www.kzn.org.za/index.php?1000hills

Just a half hour's drive from Durban, the Valley of 1,000 Hills, in the Kingdom of the Zulu, takes its name from the thousands of hills that tumble toward the Umgeni River that starts in the distant Drakensberg Mountains and washes out in Durban. The Valley of 1,000 Hills is one of those destinations that has something for everyone: unspoilt nature and wildlife (it is home to some 15 nature reserves), magnificent scenery and warm country hospitality. For the scenery alone it's worth the drive. As you meander along the undulating roads you get a very clear scene of the place's history: of Shaka and the haunting cries of tens of thousands of his warriors. South Africa's natural beauty is best experienced on foot—if you have the time—and this region is no exception, with backpackers' and camping facilities dotted all over the landscape, and anything from day walks to three- and five-day trails can be enjoyed.

Victoria Street Market
Tel: 031-306 4021
URL: www.sa-venues.com/things-to-do/kwazulunatal/
detail.php?id=404

The Indian community in South Africa is the largest outside of Asia so it's no wonder then that a market like this is such an attraction. On the corner of Queen and Victoria streets (easy enough to remember) is a market that celebrates the merging of African and Indian cultures. First opened in the 1870s the Vic, as it's known locally, is situated in a massive building reminiscent of an authentic maharajah's glory. The ornate structure is a humming venue where you can buy anything in the way of food and spices (varying coloured varieties come by the barrel), including fish from the downstairs market—a food lover's delight.

Activities

Adventure Activities

2nd Breath Scuba Diving
Tel: 039-317 2326
Email: 2ndbreath@venturenet.co.za
URL: www.2ndbreath.co.za

Adventure Escapades
Tel: 0861-106 638
URL: www.escapades.co.za

C Freaks
Tel: 082-953 4170
Email: kartfreaks@mweb.co.za

Dive Down South
Tel: 039-682 7944
Email: admin@hibiscuscoast.org.za
URL: www.divedownsouth.co.za

Durban Skydive Centre
Tel: 072-214 6040
Email: vernon@skydivedurban.co.za
URL: www.skydivedurban.co.za

Fly Down South
Tel: 039-682 7944
Email: admin@hibiscuscoast.org.za
URL: www.flydownsouth.co.za

Karkloof Canopy Tours
Tel: 033-330 3415
Email: info@karkloofcanopytour.co.za
URL: www.karkloofcanopytour.co.za

Kart Freaks
Tel: 039-312 1514

Natal Sharks Board
Tel: 031-566 0400
URL: www.shark.co.za

South Coast Helicopter Services
Tel: 082-781 2492
Email: info@africafuntours.co.za
URL: www.infocentre.co.za/whattodo.htm

Wild Coast Waterworld
Tel: 039-305 3024
Email: flynno@worldonline.co.za
URL: www.kznsouthcoast.co.za/southcoast/
waterworld.htm

KWAZULU-NATAL

Outdoor Activities

African Skies
Tel: 032-525 4815
Email: info@flyafricanskies.co.za
URL: www.flyafricanskies.co.za

Ballito Microlight School
Tel: 082-659 5550
Email: microlight@yebo.co.za
URL: www.microlights.co.za

Boma Fun
Tel: 082-770 2099
Email: beth@bomafun.co.za
URL: www.bomafun.co.za

Clearwater Trail Centre
Tel: 039-311 1130
Email: clearwater@venturenet.co.za
URL: www.clearwater.co.za

Crocodile Creek
Tel: 032-944 3845
Email: crocodilecreek@mweb.co.za
URL: www.crocodilecreek.net

Klipspringer Xscapes
Tel: 078-221 1901
Email: info@xscapes.co.za
URL: www.xscapes.co.za

Pure Venom
Tel: 039-685 0704
Email: info@purevenom.com
URL: www.purevenom.com

Riverbend Crocodile Farm
Tel: 039-316 6204
Email: info@crocodilecrazy.co.za
URL: www.crocodilecrazy.co.za

Selsdon Park Estate Quad Biking
Tel: 083-301 2941
Email: selsdonpark@telkomsa.net

Sport

Sakabula Golf Club
Tel: 033-330 6751
Email: golfclub@sakabula.co.za
URL: www.sakabula.co.za

South Coast Bowling Greens
    Banners Rest Tel: 082-336 1998
    Margate Tel: 039-312 0351
    Munster Tel: 039-319 1541
    Port Shepstone Tel: 039-695 0141
    Scottburgh Tel: 039-314 4766
    Umkomaas Tel: 039-973 0911
    For further information please visit the Hibiscus Coast Tourism website at:
    www.zulu.org.za

Southbroom Golf Club
Tel: 039-316 6051
Email: sgc@venturenet.co.za

Zulu Kingdom Golfing Adventures
Tel: 072-373 8164
Email: info@zulukingdomgolf.co.za
URL: www.zulukingdomgolf.co.za

Stadiums

Moses Mabhida Stadium
URL: www.sa2010.gov.za/node/564
Situated in Durban

Named after a hero of the working class, the Moses Mabhida Stadium has changed the Durban skyline forever and, if you ask me, for the better, as a result of its iconic arch which is symbolic of the South African flag. The stadium will be 'broken in' so to speak during the 2010 World Cup but will host a number of sporting events thereafter; with a capacity of 70,000. It is located in central Durban next to the ABSA Stadium, better know as the Shark Tank, which is within the Kings Park Sporting Precinct.

ABSA Stadium (formerly Kings Park)
Tel: 031-308 8400
URL: www.sharksrugby.co.za
Situated in Durban

Kingsmead Cricket Ground
Tel: 031-332 9703
URL: www.dolphinscricket.co.za
Situated in Durban

Culture

Museums

Bergtheil Museum
Tel: 031-203 7107
URL: www.durban.gov.za/durban/discover/museums/local_history/bergtheil
Opening Time: 08h30 Monday to Friday; 08h00 Saturday
Closing Time: 16h45 Monday to Friday; 12h00 Saturday
Situated in Westville, Durban

Campbell Collections
Tel: 031-260 1720
Email: campbellcollections@ukzn.ac.za
URL: http://campbell.ukzn.ac.za
Situated in Durban

Comrades Museum
Tel: 033-194 3510
URL: www.sa-venues.com/things-to-do/kwazulunatal/detail.php?id=606
Opening Time: 08h30 Monday to Friday
Closing Time: 13h00 Monday to Friday
Situated in Pietermaritzburg

East Griqualand Museum
Tel: 037-727 3133
Opening Time: 09h00 and 14h00 Monday to Friday
Closing Time: 13h00 and 16h00 Monday to Friday
Situated in Kokstad

Fort Amiel
Tel: 034-328 7621 / 072-238 1983
URL: www.tourismnewcastle.co.za/fortamiel_interest.htm
Opening Time: 10h00 Monday to Saturday
Closing Time: 16h00 Monday to Friday; 13h00 Saturday
Situated In Newcastle

Fort Durnford
Tel: 036-352 6253
Email: umtshezitourism@lantic.net
URL: www.openafrica.org/participant/fort-durnford-museum
Situated in Estcourt

Greytown Museum
Tel: 033-413 2944
Email: info@greytown.biz
URL: www.greytown.biz

Himeville Museum
Tel: 033-702 1184
URL: www.drakensberg.org/sanisaunter/popup/museum htm
Opening Time: 09h00 Tuesday to Sunday
Closing Time: 12h30 Tuesday to Sunday

KwaMuhle Museum
Tel: 031-311 2237
URL: www.durban-history.co.za/index.php
Opening Time: 08h30 Monday to Saturday; 11h00 Sundays and Public Holidays
Closing Time: 16h00
Situated in Durban

Luthuli Museum
Tel: 032-559 6822
Opening Time: 08h30 Monday to Saturday; 11h00 Sundays and Public Holidays
Closing Time: 16h00 Monday to Saturday; 15h00 Sundays and Public Holidays
Situated in KwaDukuza

Mgungundlovu Museum
Tel: 035-450 2254
Email: amafahq@mweb.co.za
URL: www.places.co.za/html/dingaanskraal.html

Mission House Museum
Tel: 033-445 0405
Opening Time: 09h00 Monday to Friday
Closing Time: 12h00 Monday to Friday
Situated in Hermannsburg

Talana Museum
Tel: 034-212 2654
Email: info@talana.co.za
URL: www.talana.co.za
Situated in Dundee

The Natal Museum
Tel: 033-394 5686
Email: reception@nmsa.org.za
URL: www.nmsa.org.za
Opening Time: 08h15 Monday to Friday; 10h00 Saturday; 11h00 Sunday
Closing Time: 16h30 Monday to Friday; 16h00 Saturday; 15h00 Sunday
Tariffs: Adults: R8; Pensioners and children under 4: Free; Children: R2
Situated in Pietermaritzburg

The Siege Museum
Tel: 036-637 2992
Email: info@ladysmith.co.za
URL: www.openafrica.org/participant/ladysmith-siege-museum
Opening Time: 08h00 Monday to Friday; 09h00 Saturday
Closing Time: 16h00 Monday to Friday; 13h00 Saturday
Situated in Ladysmith

Time Warp Surf Museum
Tel: 082 452 1637
Email: surf@timewarpsurfingmuseum.com
URL: www.sa-venues.com/things-to-do/kwazulunatal/detail.php?id=608
Opening Time: 10h00 Tuesday to Sunday
Closing Time: 16h00 Tuesday to Sunday
Situated in Durban

Voortrekker Museum
Tel: 033-394 6834
Email: info@msunduzimuseum.org.za
URL: www.voortrekkermuseum.co.za
Opening Time: 09h00 Monday to Saturday
Closing Time: 16h00 Monday to Friday; 13h00 Saturday
Tariffs: Adults: R5; Students and pensions: R3; Children under 16: R2
Situated in Pietermaritzburg

Vukani Museum
Tel: 035-474 5274
Email: vukanimuseum@lantic.net
URL: www.visitzululand.co.za/museum.html
Situated in Eshowe

Winterton Museum
Tel: 036-488 1885
URL: www.antbear.co.za/information/winterton.htm
Opening Time: 09h00 Monday to Saturday
Closing Time: 15h00 Monday to Friday; 12h00 Saturday

Theatres

Catalina Theatre
Tel: 031-305 6889
Email: tsibisi@mweb.co.za
URL: www.catalinatheatre.co.za
Situated in Durban

Dockyard Theatre
Tel: 031-201 9147
Email: info@dockyardtheatre.co.za
Situated in Durban

Heritage Theatre
Tel: 031-765 4197
URL: www.heritagetheatre.co.za
Situated in Durban

Hexagon Theatre
Tel: 033-260 5537
Email: hexagon@ukzn.ac.za
URL: www.hexagon.ukzn.ac.za
Situated in Fietermaritzburg

KwaSuka Theatre
Tel: 031-305 6889
Situated in Durban

Rhumbelow Theatre
Tel: 031-205-7602
Email: roland@stansell.za.net
URL: www.rhumbelow.za.net
Situated in Durban

Galleries

African Art Centre
Tel: 031-312 3804
Email: hlengi@afri-art.co.za
URL: www.afriart.org.za
Opening Time: 08h30 Monday to Friday; 09h00 Saturday; 10h00 Sunday and Public
    Holidays
Closing Time: 17h00 Monday to Friday; 15h00 Saturday, Sunday and Public Holidays
Situated in Durban

Andrew Walford Pottery Gallery
Tel: 031-769 1363
Email: andrewwalford@telkomsa.net
URL: www.andrewwalford.co.za
Situated in Shongweni

Carnegie Art Gallery
Tel: 034-328 7622
Email: gallery@newcastle.gov.za
URL: www.carnegie-art.co.za
Opening Time: 09h00 Tuesday to Saturday
Closing Time: 17h00 Tuesday to Friday, 12h00 Saturday
Situated in Newcastle

Crouse Art Gallery
Tel: 031-312 2315
Email: michelle@crouseartkzn.co.za
URL: www.crouseartkzn.co.za
Situated in Durban

Durban Art Gallery
Tel: 031-311 2264
Email: strettonj@durban.gov.za
URL: www.durban.gov.za/durban/discover/museums/dag
Opening Time: 08h30 Monday to Saturday; 11h00 Sunday
Closing Time: 16h00 Monday to Sunday
Situated in Durban

Empangeni Art & Cultural Museum
Tel: 035-901 1617
URL: www.places.co.za/html/empartculture
Situated in Empangeni

Jack Heath Art Gallery
Tel: 033-260 5170
Situated in Pietermaritzburg

KZNSA Gallery
Tel: 031-277 1705
Email: gallery@kznsagallery.co.za
URL: www.kznsagallery.co.za
Situated in Durban

Tamasa Art Gallery
Tel: 031-207 1223
Situated in Durban

Tatham Art Gallery
Tel: 033-392 2800 / 2
URL: www.tatham.org.za
Situated in Pietermaritzburg

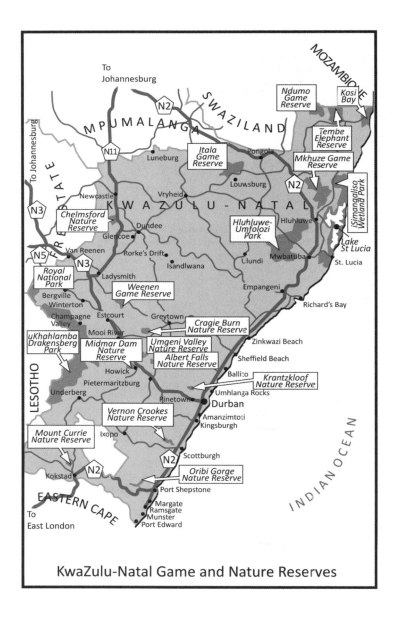

KwaZulu-Natal Game and Nature Reserves

Game and Nature Reserves (including National Parks)

Ezemvelo KZN Wildlife
Tel: 033-845 1000
Email: webmail@kznwildlife.com
URL: www.kznwildlife.com

Ezemvelo KZN Wildlife Reserves
Enseleni
Hluhluwe-Umfolozi
Itala
Mkhuze
Mount Currie
Ndumo
Opathe
Ozabeni
Phongola
Queen Elizabeth Park
Spioenkop
Tembe
Vernon Crookes
Vryheid Hill
Weenen

Albert Falls Nature Reserve
URL: www.drakensberg-tourism.com/
    albert-falls-nature-reserve

Bayete Zulu Game Lodge
Tel: 035-595 8089
Email: reservations@bayetezulu.co.za
URL: www.bayetezulu.co.za

Bonamanzi Game Park
Tel: 035-562 0181
Email: info@bonamanzi.co.za
URL: www.bonamanzi.co.za

Chelmsford Nature Reserve
URL: www.drakensberg-tourism.com/
    chelmsford-nature-reserve

Himeville Nature Reserve
Tel: 036-438 6411
Email: www.kznwildlife.com
URL: www.southafrica.net/sat/content/en

iSimangaliso Wetland Park
Tel: 035-590 1633
URL: www.isimangaliso.com

Kosi Bay
Tel: 035-590 1233
Email: info@kosibay.net
URL: www.kosibay.net

Krantzkloof Nature Reserve
URL: http://kknr.org.za

Lake Eland Game Reserve
Tel: 039-687 0395
Email: lakeelandgamereserve@saol.com
URL: www.lakeeland.co.za

Midmar Dam Nature Reserve
URL: www.drakensberg-tourist-map.com/
midmar-nature-reserve.html

Oribi Gorge Nature Reserve
Tel: 039-687 0253
Email: bookings@oribigorge.co.za
URL: www.oribigorge.co.za

Royal National Park
URL: www.drakensberg-tourism.com/royal-
natal-national-park.html

Tala Game Reserve
Tel: 031-781 8000
Email: info@tala.co.za
URL: www.tala.co.za

uKhahlamba-Drakensberg Park
Tel: 033-845 1000
Email: bookings@kznwildlife.com
URL: www.kznwildlife.com

Umgeni Valley Nature Reserve
URL: www.drakensberg-tourist-map.com/
umgeni-nature-reserve.html

Entertainment www.durbanlive.com

80's
club
Tel: 082-954 7396
Situated in Durban

Backstage
club
Tel: 039-317 1111
Situated in Margate

Burn
club
Tel: 082-325 9746
Situated in Durban

Club 54
club
Tel: 031-709 1539
Situated in Pinetown

Cool Runnings
club
Tel: 031-368 5604
Situated in Durban

Cubana
club
Tel: 031-303 2076
Situated in Durban

De la Sol
cocktail bar
Tel: 031-312 9436
Situated in Morningside, Durban

H2O
club
Tel: 031-332 9078
Situated in Durban

Joe Kool's
club
Tel: 031-332 9697
Situated on the Lower Marine Parade,
Durban

Panama Room
club
Tel: 031-312 630
Situated in Morningside, Durban

Paris Nightclub
club
Tel: 031-564 9409
Situated in Durban

Raffles
club
Tel: 031-561 7740
Situated in Umhlanga

K
W
A
Z
U
L
U
·
N
A
T
A
L

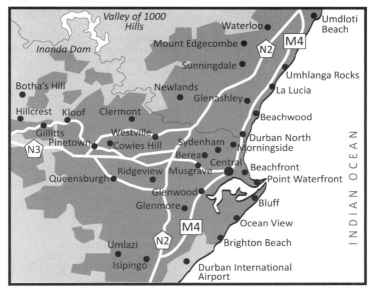

Durban: KwaZulu-Natal

Sibaya Casino & Entertainment Kingdom
casino
Tel: 031-580 5000
Email: sibaya@za.suninternational.com
URL: www.suninternational.com
Situated in Durban

The Wild Coast Sun
casino
Tel: 039-305 2777
Email: wcpro@za.suninternational.com
URL: www.suninternational.com
Situated in Durban

Skyy Bar
cocktail bar
Tel: 031-312 0947
Situated in Windermere, Durban

Tilt
club
Tel: 031-306 9356
Situated in Durban

The Lounge
club
Tel: 031-303 9030
Situated in Durban

Traxx
club
Tel: 031-303 1531
Situated in Durban

Annual Events

Africa Bike Week
URL: www.africabikeweek.co.za
Held in Marget every April

Annual South Coast Lions Show
URL: www.southcoastshow.org.za
Held on the South Coast every July

Annual Zulu Reed Dance
Tel: 031-366 7500
URL: www.trivago.co.uk
Held in Nongoma every September

Berg & Bush (cycle race)
Tel: 083 2309 091
URL: www.bergandbush.co.za
Held in the Drakensberg every October

BMW International Polo Series
Tel: 031-303 3903
Email: bridget@sapolo.co.za
URL: www.sapolo.org.za
Held in Durban every August

Comrades Marathon
Tel: 033-897 8650
Email: info@comrades.com
URL: www.comrades.com
Starts alternately from Durban /
  Pietermaritzburg every May

Durban International Astrology &
  Psychic Festival
Tel: 031-566 4781
URL: www.sa-venues.com/events
Held every September

Durban International Boat & Leisure Show
Tel: 031-266 9828
Email: creative.events@eastcoast.co.za
URL: www.durbaninternationalboatshow.
  co.za
Held every July

Durban International Film Festival
Tel: 031-260 2506.
URL: www.sa-venues.com/events
Held every July

Good Food & Wine Show
Email: reception@gourmetsa.com.
URL: www.gourmetsa.co.za
Held in Durban every July

Ladysmith Swartkop Challenge (extreme
  sports reinactment of the Siege of
  Ladysmith)
URL: www.swartkopchallenge.com
Held every April

Midmar Mile (swimming)
Tel: 0861-643 627
Email: info@midmarmile.co.za
URL: www.midmarmile.co.za
Held every February

Mr Price Pro (surfing)
URL: www.mrpricepro.com
Held in Durban every June

Nedbank Eastern Bridal Fair
Tel: 031-303 9200
Email: cu@easternbride.co.za
URL: www.easternbride.co.za
Held in Durban every July

Poetry Africa Festival
Tel: 031-260 2506
URL: www.ukzn.ac.za/cca
Held in Durban every October

Polar Bear Swim
Tel: 082-828 0401
Held in Estcourt every June

Sibaya Yearling Sale
Tel: 031-580 5555
URL: www.tba.co.za
Held in Durban every July

South Coast Christmas Market
Tel: 083-750 8447
URL: www.sa-venues.com/events
Held in Uvonga everyt December

Splashy Fen Music Festival
Tel: 033-701 1932
Emial: splashyfen@futurenet.co.za
URL: www.splashyfen.co.za
Held in Himeville / Underberg every April

The Sardine Run
Email: info@sardinerun.net
URL: www.sardinerun.net
Takes place in Durban every June

TOPS Whisky Expo
URL: www.sa-venues.com/events
Held in Durban every May

Umhlanga Summer Carnival
Tel: 031-561 4257
URL: www.blueworld.co.za/events
Held every December

Vodacom Durban July (horse race)
URL: www.vodacomdurbanjuly.co.za

White Mountain Folk Festival
Tel: 031-563 0824
Email: festival@whitemountain.co.za
URL: www.whitemountain.co.za
Held in the central Drakensberg
   every September

Kids

Chocolate Heaven Rosetta
Tel: 033-267 7299
Email: info@chocolateheaven.co.za
URL: www.chocolateheaven.co.za
Situated in Rosetta

Crocworld
Tel: 039-976 1103
Email: crocworld@cbl.co.za
URL: www.crocworld.co.za
Situated in Scottburgh

Granny Goose Animal Farm
Tel: 083-301 4676
URL: www.grannygoosefarm.co.za
Situated in San Lameer

Port Edward Space Centre
Tel: 039-311 2891
Email: spacecentresa@hotmail.com
URL: www.saao.ac.za/assa/html/natal_space_centre.html

uShaka Marine World
Tel: 031-328 8000
Email: mkt@ushakamarineworld.co.za
URL: www.ushakamarineworld.co.za
Situated in Durban

Shopping www.mallguide.co.za

Creative Beads
Tel: 031-561 4776
Email: info@creativebeads.co.za
URL: www.creativebeadsafrica.co.za
Situated in Umhlanga

Gateway
Tel: 031-514 0500
Email: gatewaypr@primelife.co.za
URL: www.gatewayworld.co.za
Situated in Umhlanga

Groundcover Leather Company
Tel: 033-330 6092
Email: info@groundcover.co.za
URL: www.groundcover.co.za
Situated in Pietermaritzburg

KwaZulu Weavers
Tel: 036-488 1657
Email: sales@kwazuluweavers.com
URL: www.kwazuluweavers.com
Situated in the central Drakensberg

Linga Lapa
Tel: 033-266 6110
Email: slimmac@telkomsa.net
URL: www.lingalapa.co.za
Situated in Durban

Shelly Centre
Tel: 039-315 1304
Email: marketing@shellycentre.com
URL: www.shellycentre.com
Situated at Shelly Beach

Spiller's Wharf
Tel: 039-684 0277
URL: www.spillerswharf.co.za

Uvongo Flea Market
Tel: 082-800 9236

Woza Woza Farmers Market & Country Fair
Tel: 033-263 2194
Situated in Pietermaritzburg

Restaurants

Ballito
Gigi's Restaurant
Cuisine: Contemporary
Tel: 032-946 3444
Address: Rey's Place

The Hops
Cuisine: Pub Meals
Tel: 032-946 2896
Address: 14 Edward Place

Berea
Café 1999
Cuisine: Contemporary
Tel: 031-202 3406
Address: Shop 2, Silvervause Centre

Mo Noodles
Cuisine: Fusion
Tel: 031-312 4193
Address: Shop 5A, Florida Centre,
   275 Florida Road

Nourish
Cuisine: Bistro
Tel: 031-202 2511
Address: 191 Musgrave Road

Palki
Cuisine: Indian
Tel: 031-201 0019
Address: 225 Musgrave Road

Durban
Almahran
Cuisine: Indian
Tel: 031-332 5127
Address: 191 Marine Parade, Beachfront

Bel Punto Restaurant
Cuisine: Italian
Tel: 031-568 2407
Address: Shop 7, Umdloti Beach Centre,
   1 South Beach Road

Engine Room Restaurant
Cuisine: Contemporary
Tel: 031-564 5458
Address: 59 Kensington Drive,
   Durban North

Famous Fish Company
Cuisine: Seafood
Tel: 031-368 1060
Address: King's Battery Point,
   Point Waterfront, Waterfront

Gaby'z Tasca
Cuisine: Portuguese
Tel: 031-563 2603
Address: Shop 1, Kensington Centre,
   Kensington Drive, Durban North

Harvey's Restaurant
Cuisine: French
Tel: 031-312 5706
Address: 465 Innes Road

Jewel of India
Cuisine: Indian
Tel: 031-337 8168
Address: 63 Snell Parade

Marco Paulo
Cuisine: Mediterranean
Tel: 031-502 2221
Address: Shop 3, 2 Golf Course Drive

Oscars
Cuisine: Bistro
Tel: 031-563 3703
Address: Woolworths Centre,
   Makeurtan Avenue

Rainbow Terrace
Cuisine: International
Tel: 031-336 8100
Address: Hilton Hotel, 12–14 Walnut Road

Riverside Café
Cuisine: International
Tel: 031-563 0600
Address: 10 Northway, Durban North

Roma Revolving Restaurant
Cuisine: Italian
Tel: 031-368 2275
Address: 32nd Floor, John Ross House,
   Esplanade, Victoria Embankment

The Brasserie
Cuisine: South African
Tel: 031-337 3681
Address: 149 Marine Parade, Beachfront

The Green Dolphin
Cuisine: Pub Meals
Tel: 031-467 4063
Address: 17 Foreshore Drive,
   Brighton Beach

The Hops
Cuisine: Pub Meals
Tel: 031-573 1657
Address: 10 Northway, Durban North

Umami
Cuisine: International
Tel: 032-525 4615
URL: www.umami.co.za
Address: Inside Dunkirk Estate

Glenashley
Andrea's Dolce Vita La Pizza Pazza
Cuisine: Italian
Tel: 031-572 4075
Address: Shop 14, Glenore Centre,
   Aubrey Drive

Splashes
Cuisine: Mediterranean
Tel: 031-572 3152
Address: Shop 1B, 36 Newport Avenue

Glenwood
Hemingway's Bistro & Café
Cuisine: Grills
Tel: 031-202 4906
Address: 131 Davenport Road

Pizzetta Restaurant
Cuisine: Italian
Tel: 031-201 1019
Address: 139 Davenport Road

Yossis Café
Cuisine: Moroccan
Tel: 031-201 0090
Address: 127 Davenport Road

Greyville
Bean Bag Bohemia
Cuisine: Fusion
Tel: 031-309 6019
Address: 18 Windermere Road

Capers
Cuisine: Grills
Tel: 031-303 9238
Address: Avonmore Centre, 9th Avenue

Vintage India
Cuisine: Indian
Tel: 031-309 1328
Address: 20 Windermere Road

Hillcrest
Aubergine & Andreotti's
Cuisine: French
Tel: 031-765 6050
Address: 20C Hillcrest Centre,
   Old Main Road

La Strada Ristorante
Cuisine: Italian
Tel: 031-765 6556
Address: Shop 11, Elangeni Shopping Centre,
   9 Inanda Road

The Pot & Kettle
Cuisine: Light Meals
Tel: 031-777 1312
Address: 168 Old Main Road, Botha's Hill

Illovo
The Oakwoods Restaurant
Cuisine: Continental
Tel: 031-916 7228
Address: Protea Hotel Karridene,
    Old South Coast Road

The Terrace
Cuisine: Light Meals
Tel: 031-916 6212
Address: Inside Illovo Nursery

The View
Cuisine: Fine Dining
Tel: 031-777 1629
please phone for directions

Margate
Eat & Meet
Cuisine: Please make sure of cuisine on flyer
Tel: 039-312 2213
Address: Marine Drive

Morningside
9th Avenue Bistro
Cuisine: Fine Dining
Tel: 031-312 9134
Address: Shop 2, Avonmore Centre,
    9th Avenue

Audacia Manor
Cuisine: Fine Dining
Tel: 031-303 9520
Address: 11 Sir Arthur Road

Billy the Bums
Cuisine: International
Tel: 031-303 1988
Address: 504 Windermere Road

Blue Zoo Restaurant
Cuisine: South African
Tel: 031-303 3568
Address: 6 Nimmo Road

Delfi
Cuisine: Greek
Tel: 031-312 7032
Address: 386 Windermere Road

Indian Connection
Cuisine: Indian
Tel: 031-312 1440
Address: 485 Windermere Road

Joops Place
Cuisine: Grills
Tel: 031-312 9135
Address: Shop 14, Avonmore Centre,
    9th Avenue

Quarters Restaurant
Cuisine: International
Tel: 031-303 5246
Address: 101 Florida Road

Snap Wine Bar & Café
Cuisine: Fusion
Tel: 031-309 4160
Address: 41 Marriot Road

Spice Restaurant & Bar Lounge
Cuisine: Fusion
Tel: 031-303 6375
Address: 362 Windermere Road

Spiga D'oro
Cuisine: Italian
Tel: 031-303 9511
Address: 200 Florida Road

Taco Zulu
Cuisine: Mexican
Tel: 031-303 9584
Address: 237 Florida Road

North Beach
Havana Grill & Wine Bar
Cuisine: Grills
Tel: 031-332 0707
Address: Sun Coast Casino

The Deck
Cuisine: Grills
Tel: 031-368 3699
Address: 139 Lower Marine Parade

KWAZULU-NATAL

Pietermaritzburg
Eaton's on Eighty
Cuisine: Fusion
Tel: 033-342 3280
Address: 80 Roberts Road

Els Amics
Cuisine: Continental
Tel: 033-345 6524
Address: 380 Longmarket Street

Little Moravia
Cuisine: Fusion
Tel: 033-390 1334
Address: F1 Chief Mhlabunzima Road

Madlula's Place
Cuisine: South African
Tel: 033-345 0013
Address: 1st Floor, Gallway House,
  2 Gallway Lane

Pesto Restaurant
Cuisine: Italian
Tel: 033-342 2778
Address: 101 Roberts Road, Wembley

Saki
Cuisine: Asian
Tel: 033-342 6999
Address: 157 Victoria Road

Strelitzia Room
Cuisine: Contemporary
Tel: 033-344 2207
Address: Botanical Gardens, Mayor's Walk

The Butchery
Cuisine: Steakhouse
Tel: 033-342 5239
Address: 101 Roberts Road, Wembley

The Café at Rosehurst
Cuisine: Contemporary
Tel: 033-394 3833
Address: 239 Boom Street

Turtle Bay
Cuisine: Contemporary
Tel: 033-347 1555
Address: Cascades Centre, McCarthy Drive

Pinetown
Black Forest Tavern
Cuisine: International
Tel: 031-702 2908
Address: 55 Glenugie Road

Butcher Block Restaurant
Cuisine: Grills
Tel: 031-702 9010
Address: 40 King's Road

Port Edward
Beaver Creek
Cuisine: Fine Dining
Tel: 039-311 2315
Address: Izingolweni Road

Port Shepstone
Waffles on the Wharf
Cuisine: Waffles
Tel: 039-682 5384
Address: Spiller's Wharf

Ramsgate
Crayfish Inn
Cuisine: Seafood
Tel: 039-314 4720
Address: Marine Drive

La Cappannina
Cuisine: Italian
Tel: 039-317 1078
Address: 206 Marine Drive, Ramsgate North

The Lobster Pot Restaurant
Cuisine: Seafood
Tel: 039-314 9809
Address: Marine Drive, Ramsgate South

The Waffle House
Cuisine: Waffles
Tel: 039-314 9424
Address: Marine Drive

Umhlanga
Blu Restaurant
Cuisine: Contemporary
Tel: 031-561 6169
Address: 88 Lagoon Drive

Figata Food Emporium
Cuisine: Gourmet
Tel: 031-566 7547
Address: 1st Floor African Palms,
  9 Palm Boulevard, Gateway

Ile Maurice
Cuisine: French
Tel: 031-561 7606
Address: 9 McCausland Crescent,
  Umhlanga Rocks

Plaka
Cuisine: Greek
Tel: 031-566 7456
Address: Palm Boulevard, Gateway

Razzmatazz
Cuisine: Seafood
Tel: 031-561 5847
Address: 10 Lagoon Drive, Umhlanga Rocks

Tare Panda
Cuisine: Japanese
Tel: 031-566 3138
Address: G12, Gateway Theatre of Shopping

Uvongo
Breakers Seafood & Grill
Cuisine: Seafoood
Tel: 039-315 6174
Address: Grado Centre, Marine Drive

Westville
Le Troquet
Cuisine: French
Tel: 031-266 5388
Address: The Village Market Centre,
  123 Jan Hofmeyer Road

Sage at Christina's
Cuisine: Fine Dining
Tel: 031-267 4700
Address: 124 Jan Hofmeyer Road

Waxy O'Connors
Cuisine: Traditional
Tel: 031-266 2565
Addres: 124 Jan Hofmeyer Road

Chains and franchises

Butcher Boys
URL: www.butcherboysgrill.co.za

Café Vacca Matta
URL: www.vaccamatta.com

Cape Town Fish Market
URL: www.ctfm.co.za

Jimmy's Killer Prawns
URL: www.jimmyskillerprawns.co.za

Mugg & Bean
URL: www.themugg.com

Piatto Mediterranean Kitchen
URL: www.piatto.co.za

Primi Restaurants
URL: www.primi-world.com

Tiago's
URL: www.southernexplorer.co.za/
  tour_9/906/tiagos.html

Accommodation

www.wheretostay.co.za/kzn
www.wheretostay.co.za/kzn/sc/holiday-resort
www.kznlive.com
www.safarinow.com/destinations/kwazulu-natal
www.staykzn.co.za
www.sa-venues.com/kzn
www.thedolphincoast.com
www.kznparks.com
www.durban-venues.co.za
www.drakensberg.org.za
www.drakensberg-tourism.com

Durban
Hotels

Albany Hotel
Tel: 031-304 4381
Email: info@albanyhotel.co.za
URL: www.albanyhotel.co.za

Fern Hill Hotel
Tel: 033-330 5071
URL: www.fernhillhotel.com

Quarters Hotel
Tel: 031-303 5246
Email: quarters@icon.co.za
URL: www.quarters.co.za

Other
Hotels

Cathedral Peak Hotel
Tel: 036-488 1888
Email: info@cathedralpeak.co.za
URL: www.cathedralpeak.co.za
Situated in the Drakensberg

Hotel Edwardian
Tel: 039-311 3618
Email: edwardian@premierhotels.co.za
URL: www.premierhotels.co.za/
    edwardian/index.html
Situated in Port Edward

Howick Falls Hotel
Tel: 033-330 2809
Email: bookings@howickfallshotel.co.za
URL: www.howickfallshotel.co.za
Situated in Howick

Kapenta Bay
Tel: 039-682 5528
Email: hotel@kapentabay.co.za
URL: www.kapentabay.co.za
Situated in Port Shepstone

Pumula Beach Hotel
Tel: 039-684 6717
Email: reservations@pumulabeachhotel.co.za
URL: www.pumulabeachhotel.co.za
Situated in Umzumbe

The Estuary Country Hotel
Tel: 039-311 2675
Email: reservations@estuaryhotel.co.za
URL: www.estuaryhotel.co.za
Situated in Port Edward

The Nest Drakensberg Mountain Hotel
Tel: 036-468 1068
Email: thenest@thenest.co.za
URL: www.thenest.co.za
Situated in the central Drakensberg

Willow Grange Country Hotel
Tel: 036-352 7102
Email: willowgrangehotel@hotmail.com
URL: www.willowgrangehotel.co.za
Situated between Mooi River and Estcourt

Lodges

Anerley Lodge
Tel: 039-681 3657
Email: anerleylodge@telkomsa.net
URL: www.anerleylodge.co.za
Situated on the South Coast

Ascot Inn
Tel: 033-386 2226
Email: info@ascot-inn.co.za
URL: www.ascot-inn.co.za
Situated in Pietermaritzburg

Avenol Country Lodge
Tel: 082-451 8848
Email: info@avenol.co.za
URL: www.avenol.co.za
Situated in Dargle Valley

Blue Haze Country Lodge
Tel: 036-352 5772
Email: info@bluehaze.co.za
URL: www.bluehaze.co.za
Situated in the Drakensberg

Bushbuck Lodge
Tel: 039-316 6399
Email: polafrosafaris@ananzi.co.za
URL: www.wakacjewafryce.pl
Situated on the South Coast

De Novo Lodge
Tel: 039-311 2711
Email: info@denovo.co.za
URL: www.denovo.co.za/contact.php
Situated in Port Edward

Dieu-Donneé River Lodge
Tel: 039-681 2733
Email: ddrlodge@venturenet.co.za
URL: www.dieudonnee.co.za
Situated in South Port

Fairway Guest Lodge
Tel: 039-315 1781
Email: j.cole@absamail.co.za
URL: www.fairwaylodge.co.za
Situated in St Michaels

Hamilton Lodge
Tel: 082-726 3289 / 033-345 0624
Email: hamiltonlodge@pietermaritzburg.co.za
URL: www.hamiltonlodge.co.za
Situated in Pitermaritzburg

Holme Lodge
Tel: 033-347 3808
URL: www.holmelodge.co.za
Situated in Pietermaritzburg

Ilanga Ntaba Guest Lodge
Tel: 039-314 9070
Email: enquiries@ilangantaba.co.za
URL: www.ilangantaba.co.za
Situated in Ramsgate

Leigthon Lodge B&B
Tel: 033-342 5676
Email: llodge@mjvn.co.za
URL: www.leightonlodge.co.za
Situated in Pietermaritzburg

Lombok Lodge
Tel: 039-695 2781
Email: jan@lomboklodge.co.za
URL: www.lomboklodge.co.za
Situated in Sea Park

Mhlangeni Lodge
Tel: 039-315 0628
Email: gregori@absamail.co.za
URL: www.mhlangenilodge.co.za
Situated in Uvongo

Mzimayi River Lodge
Tel: 039-699 3077
URL: www.mzimayi.co.za
Situated in Hibberdene

Nolangeni Lodge
Tel: 039-315 7327
Email: nolangeni@mweb.co.za
URL: www.nolangeni.co.za
Situated at Shelly Beach

Oslo Beach Lodge
Tel: 039-685 4807
Email: homeoff@venturenet.co.za
URL: www.beach-house.co.za/flat.html
Situated at Oslo Beach

Palm Dune Beach Lodge
Tel: 032-552 1588
Email: stay@palmdune.co.za
URL: www.palmdune.co.za
Situated at Blythedale Beach

Shelford Lodge
Tel: 031-202 3461
Email: cwestoby@mweb.co.za
URL: www.shelfordfarm.com
Situated in Bushy Vales

Silver Hill Lodge
Tel: 033-267 7430
Email: silverhill@icon.co.za
URL: www.silverhill.co.za
Situated in the Drakensberg

The Braes Lodge
Tel: 039-314 9854
Email: braeslodge@mweb.co.za
URL: www.braeslodge.co.za
Situated in Ramsgate

The Country Lodge
Tel: 039-316 8380
Email: countrylodge@telkomsa.net
URL: www.thecountrylodgeramsgate.co.za
Situated in Ramsgate

The View Guest Lodge
Tel: 031-903 1556
Email: info@theviewguestlodge.com
URL: www.theviewguestlodge.com
Situated in Amanzimtoti

Treetops Lodge
Tel: 039-317 2060
Email: info@treetopslodge.co.za
URL: www.treetopslodge.co.za
Situated in Margate

Wailana Beach Lodge
Tel: 039-314 4606
Email: wailana@iafrica.com
URL: www.wailana.co.za
Situated in Ramsgate

B&Bs, Guest Houses & Self-catering

40 Fraser Street B&B
Tel: 033-330 4896
Email: 40fraserbb@polka.co.za
URL: www.40fraserstreet.co.za
Situated in Howick

African Ambience
Tel: 035-590 1212
Email: lejon@digitalsky.co.za
URL: www.africanambience.com
Situated in St Lucia

Afrikhaya Guest House
Tel: 035-590 1447
Email: info@afrikhaya.co.za
URL: www.afrikhaya.co.za
Situated in St Lucia

Anna's Bed & Breakfast
Tel: 035-590 1988
Email: annas@annasbnb.com
URL: www.annasbnb.com
Situated in St Lucia

Avalone Guest House
Tel: 035-590 2112
Email: info@avalone-guesthouse.com
URL: www.avalone-guesthouse.com
Situated in St Lucia

Beachcomber Bay
Tel: 039-317 4473
Email: info@beachcomberbay.co.za
URL: www.beachcomberbay.co.za
Situated in Ramsgate

Belle Cottage
Tel: 033-347 3141
Email: belle@mjvn.co.za
URL: http://pietermaritzburg-tourism.co.za
Situated in Pietermaritzburg

Bill's Best
Tel: 0861-7267 4283 (0861 Ramsgate)
Email:bbinfo@billsbest.co.za
URL: www.billsbest.co.za
Situated in Ramsgate

Breaker View
Tel: 039-315 7160
Email: breakerview@telkomsa.net
URL: www.breakerview.co.za
Situated in Shelly Beach

Brevisbrook
Tel: 033-344 1402
Email: brevisbrook@mweb.co.za
URL: www.brevisbrook.co.za
Situated in Pietermaritzburg

Brookfield Farmhouse
Tel: 033-383 0250
Email: Brookfield@mweb.co.za
URL: www.brookfield.co.za
Situated in Hilton

Buya Futhi
Tel: 035-590 1138
Email: info@buyafuthi.co.za
URL: www.buyafuthi.co.za
Situated in St Lucia & Cape Vidal

Carissa Hill
Tel: 039-315 0752
Email: staats@saol.com
URL: www.wheretostay.co.za
Situated in Shelly Beach

Danrich Self Catering Maisonette
Tel: 031-462 6902
Email: danrich1@mweb.co.za
URL: www.wheretostay.co.za/danrich
Situated in Yellowwood Park

De Hoeve
Tel: 033-394 2527
Email: dehoeve@worldonline.co.za
Situated in Pietermaritzburg

Dick B. Morton's Holiday Flats
Tel: 083-783 1777
Email: dcmorton@mweb.co.za
URL: www.dickbmorton.co.za
Situated at Central Beach

Eagle Rock Guest House B&B
Tel: 031-563 4307
Email: shaunmc@telkomsa.net
URL: www.eaglerockguesthouse.info
Situated in Beachwood

Ebenezer Palms Bed & Breakfast
Tel: 039-317 1128
Email: hoatson@venturenet.co.za
URL: www.accommodationoncourse.co.za
Situated in Uvongo

Elephant Coast House
Tel: 035-590 1888
Email: reservations@elephantcoastbnb.co.za
URL: www.elephantcoastbnb.co.za
Situated in St Lucia

Greenlands
Tel: 033-342 6233
Email: info@greenlands.co.za
URL: www.greenlands.co.za
Situated in Pietermaritzburg

Heritage House
Tel: 033-394 4364
Email: foodwithfinesse@absamail.co.za
URL: www.pietermaritzburg.co.za
Situated in Newcastle

Hornbill House B&B
Tel: 035-590 1162
Email: info@shakabarker.co.za
URL: www.shakabarker.co.za/hornbillhouse
Situated in St Lucia

Igwalagwala Guest House
Tel: 035-590 1069
Email: igwala@mweb.co.za
URL: www.igwala.co.za
Situated in St Lucia

Janet's 'Ukuthula'
Tel: 035-550 0460
Email: goncalves@mtuba.co.za
URL: www.janetsbnb.co.za
Situated in Mtubatuba

Jean-Lee Guest Cottages
Tel: 033-346 0470
Email: info@jeanlee.co.za
URL: www.jeanlee.co.za
Situated in Pietermaritzburg

Kaiserhof
Tel: 039-314 9805
Email: kaiserh@venturenet.co.za
URL: www.kaiserhof-collection.co.za
Situated in Ramsgate

Kuta Beach
Tel: 082-824 1886
Email: broadway@zamail.co.za
Situated in Ramsgate

La La Nathi Bed & Breakfast
Tel: 039-319 1831
Email: lalanathi@lalanathikzn.co.za
URL: www.lalanathikzn.co.za
Situated at Leisure Bay

Lala Kahle B&B
Tel: 039-695 2579
Email: lalakahle@absamail.co.za
Situated in Port Shepstone

Licorna Beach
Tel: 031-561 2344
Email: licorna@intekom.co.za
URL: www.licorna.co.za
Situated in Umhlanga

Little Elba
Tel: 033-346 9025
Email: sbentley@iafrica.com
URL: www.africastay.com
Situated in Pietermaritzburg

Maputaland Guest House
Tel: 035-590 1041
Email: bookings@maputaland.com
URL: www.maputaland.com
Situated in St Lucia

Mdoni House
Tel: 039-695 1215
Email: stay@mdoni.co.za
URL: www.mdoni.co.za
Situated in Port Shepstone

Mtuba Manor
Tel: 035-550 1058
Email: info@mtubamanor.co.za
URL: www.mtubamanor.co.za
Situated in Mtubatuba

My Den Beachfront B&B
Tel: 039-682 6096
Email: myden@telkomsa.net
Situated at Oslo Beach

Nellelani Holiday Apartments
Tel: 039-312 1022
URL: www.wheretostay.co.za/nellelani
Sitaued in Margate

Ocean Grove
Tel: 039-319 1798
Email: arthur@oceangrove.co.za
URL: www.oceangrove.co.za
Situated in Munster

Pearce Place
Tel: 082-895 7089
Email: pearceplaceb.b@vodamail.co.za
URL: www.sa-venues.com
Situated in Port Shepstone

Pinnacles
Tel: 039-695 1800
Email: rickson@mweb.co.za
URL: www.bandnetwork.co.za/pinnacles
Situated in Umtentweni

Robin's Nest
Tel: 039-682 3779
Email: robin@robins-nest.co.za
URL: www.bandnetwork.co.za/robins-nest
Situated at Shelley Beach

Sandy Ridge Bed & Breakfast
Tel: 031-572 3487
Email: info@sndyridge.co.za
URL: www.sandyridge.co.za
Situated in Umhlanga

San Lameer
Tel: 039-313 0450
Email: villaren@venturenet.co.za
URL: www.sanlameer.co.za
Situated on the South Coast

Top: Table Mountain with its famed table cloth as seen from Kirstenbosch Botanical Gardens.
Above: The Victoria & Alfred Waterfront.

Top: A trendy café in Camps Bay. One of the many where you can enjoy a sundowner and certainly one of the best spots to see the sunset.
Above: Mama Africa Jazz Club in Cape Town.

Top: From Robben Island the view of Table Mountain is quite spectacular. Tours to Robben Island are weather dependant, so book in advance and don't be suprised if your trip is cancelled due to wind or rain, or both.
Above: The majority of Nelson Mandela's 27 years in prison were spent in this cell on Robben Island.

Left-hand page: The Richtersveld and the beautiful Namaqualand to its south stand in stark contrast to each other. The endless carpets of flowers give way to the drier landscape of kokkerbomme and the icy Atlantic Ocean.

Top: The Maropeng Visitor's Centre in the Cradle of Humankind.
Left: The stalactites of the Elephant Chamber in the Sterkfontein Caves.
Above right: A bust of Robert Broom and his 'find', Mrs Ples.

Left: Sunset over
the southern
Drakensberg. Trout
fishing in the many
streams is a multi-
million-rand industry.

Top centre: Bushman
paintings in the Royal
Natal National Park.

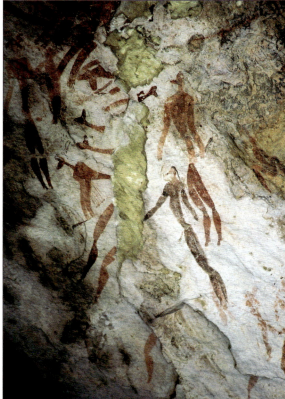

Above: Himeville in the
southern Drakensberg offers
visitors a number of quaint
places to stay.
Top right: Bushman rock
art and the natural diversity
are the reasons for the
Drakensberg's inscription as a
UNESCO World Heritage Site.
Right: The dramatic Rhino
Peak in the southern 'Berg'.

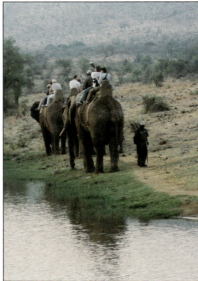

Top: Elephant-back safaris in the Pilanesberg National Park.
Left: Kiting in Sodwana, south of St Lucia in the iSimangaliso Wetland Park.
Above: A traditional fishing trap in the estuary at Kosi Bay, the northernmost part of the iSimangaliso Wetland Park.

Santa Lucia Guest House
Tel: 035-590 1151
Email: rika@santalucia.co.za
URL: www.santalucia.co.za
Situated in St Lucia

St. Lucia Wetlands Guest House
Tel: 035-590 1098
Email: wetlands@iafrica.com
URL: www.stluciawetlands.com
Situated in St Lucia

Stephward Estate
Tel: 039-315 5926
Email: info@stephward.co.za
URL: www.stephward.co.za
Situated in Uvongo

Sunbird B&B
Tel: 039-316 8202
Email: stay@sunbirds.co.za
URL: www.sunbirds.co.za
Situated in Southbroom

Tesorino Bed & Breakfast
Tel: 031-561 2719
Email: info@tesorino.co.za
URL www.tesorino.co.za
Situated in Umhlanga

The Aloe Inn
Tel: 039-311 3460
Email: aloeinn@hotmail.co.za
URL: www.wheretostay.co.za
Situate in Port Edward

The Hooting Owl
Tel: 039-313 5425
Email: hootingowl.kzn@gmail.com
URL: www.sa-venues.com
Situated at Marina Beach

The Jay's
Tel: 033-342 4510
Email: thejays@iafrica.com
URL: www.thejays.pietermaritzburg.co.za
Situated in Pietermaritzburg

The Old Orchard Bed & Breakfast
Tel: 039-727 4988
Email: theoldorchard@telkomsa.net
URL: www.theoldorchard.co.za
Situated in Kokstad

Trelawney Cottages
Tel: 039-319 2512
Email: invernes@adventurenet.co.za
URL: www.trelawney.co.za
Situated in Leisure Bay

Tropical Beach
Tel: 039-315 0573
Email: relax@tropicalbeaach.co.za
URL: www.tropicalbeach.co.za
Situated at Shelly Beach

Wendy's Country House
Tel: 035-550 0407
Email: wendybnb@iafrica.com
URL: www.wendybnb.co.za
Situated in St Lucia

Whalesong Guest House
Tel: 035-590 1561
Email: info@whalesongstlucia.co.za
URL: www.whalesongstlucia.co.za
Situated in St Lucia and Maputaland

Wild Waves
Tel: 039-315 7334
Email: wildwaves@telkomsa.net
URL: www.wildwaves.co.za
Situated at Shelly Beach

Zulani Guest House
Tel: 035-590 1427
Email: stlucia@zulani.co.za
URL: www.zulani.co.za
Situated in St Lucia

Holiday Resorts

Anguna Beachfront Holiday Apartments
Tel: 039-317 4198
Email: gusmac@xsinet.co.za
URL: www.wheretostay.co.za/anguna
Situated in Margate

Banana Beach Holiday Resort
Tel: 039-681 3229
Email: reservations@bananabeach.co.za
URL: www.bananabeach.co.za
Situated in Port Shepstone

Dumela Holiday Resort
Tel: 039-317 3301
Email: dumela@venturenet.co.za
URL: www.dumelamargate.co.za
Situated in Margate

Palm Dune
Tel: 032-552 1588
Email: stay@palmdune.co.za
URL: www.palmdune.co.za
Situated at Blythedale Beach

Paradise Holiday Resort
Tel: 039-313 0655
Email: paradise@megadial.com
URL: www.wheretostay.co.za/paradise
Situated at Palm Beach

Soeterus Holiday Resort
Tel: 083-258 3970
Email: malindad@mweb.co.za
URL: www.sa-venues.com
Situated in Port Shepstone

Port Edward Holiday Resort
Tel: 039-311 2333
Email: office@portedward.co.za
URL: www.portedward.co.za
Situated in Port Edward

Camping

Clansthal Caravan Park
Tel: 039-973 0211
Situated in Umkomaas

Corians Pennington Caravan Park
Tel: 039-975 1107
Email: corians@scottburgh.co.za
URL: www.corians.co.za
Situated in Pennington

Dragon's Rest
Tel: 082-825 7410
Email: info@bigskysafaris.co.za
URL: www.bigskysafaris.co.za
Situated in Kokstad

Ellingham Park
Tel: 039-976 0546
Email: reservations@rockybay.co.za
URL: www.rockybay.co.za
Situated in Rocky Bay

Happy Days
Tel: 039- 699 2310
URL: www.inx.co.za
Situated in Hibberdene

Hibberdene Caravamn Park
Tel: 039- 699 2308
Email: hibbpark@worldonline.co.za
URL: http://hibberdenecaravanpark.
  caravanparks.com
Situated in Hibberdene

Lalanathi Caravan Park
Tel: 039-684 5372
URL: www.lalanathi.caravanparks.co.za
Situated in Port Shepstone

Leisure View
Tel: 039-319 2367
Email: lview@vodamail.co.za
URL: www.leisureview.co.za
Situated in Port Edward

MacNicol's Caravan & Camping
Tel: 039-977 8863
Email: macnicol@scottburgh.co.za
URL: www.macnicol.co.za
Situated in Scottburgh

Margate Caravan & Camping Park
Tel: 039-312 0852
Email: mcp1@xsinet.co.za
URL: www.margatecaravanpark.co.za
Situated in Margate

Marlon Caravan and Camping Resort
Tel: 039- 681 3596
Email: marlon@saol.com
URL: www.marlonresort.co.za
Situated in Sunwich Port

Monks Cowl
Tel: 036-468 1103
Email: monkscowl@futurenet.co.za
URL: www.monkscowl.co.za
Situated in the central Drakensburg

Port O' Call
Tel: 039-313 0511
Email: portcall@telkomsa.net
URL: www.portocall.co.za
Situated in Trafalgar

Scottburgh Caravan Park
Tel: 039-976 0291
Email: caravanpark@scottburgh.co.za
URL: www.scottburghcaravanpark.co.za
Situated in Scottburgh

Shelly Caravan Park
Tel: 039-685 0764
Email: shellypark@mweb.co.za
Sitaued at Shelly Beach

Thandulula Luxury Safari
  Tent Accomodation
Tel: 039-681 3755
Email: info@thandulula.co.za
URL: www.thandulula.co.za
Situated in Southport

Xaxaza Park
Tel: 035-340 1843
Email: xaxaza@mtunzini.co.za
URL: www.xaxaza.caravanparks.com
Situated in Mtunzini

Tours

Advantage Hippo Tours
Tel: 035-590 1259
Email: advantage@zululink.co.za
URL: www.advantagetours.co.za

Any Time Africa
Tel: 083-235 4424
Email: info@anytimeafrica.co.za
URL: www.anytimeafrica.co.za

Aurora Tours
Tel: 039-311 1353
Email: auroratours@telkomsa.net
URL: www.aurora-tours.ch

Endless Summer Tours
Tel: 087-808 5091
Email: info@endlesssummertours.co.za
URL: www.endless-summer-tours.co.za

Imvuselelo Guiding Tours
Tel: 073-043 5692

Major Adventures
Tel: 033-701 1628
Email: info@majoradventures.com
URL: www.majoradventures.com

Mygration Safari Services
Tel: 031-767 3373
Email: nomadictours@mweb.co.za
URL: www.mygration.co.za

Thembela Tours
Tel: 039-687 7561 / 0253
Email: mandla@thembelatours.co.za
URL: www.thembelatours.co.za

KWAZULU-NATAL

Out to Sea

36Degrees (scuba diving)
Tel: 082-553 2834
URL: www.durban-direct.com/
   scuba-diving/36-degrees

Allure Charters
Tel: 031-466 6447
Email: fish@allurecharters.com
URL: www.allurecharters.com

Awesome Charters
Tel: 082-560 8991 / 082-370 6866
Email: info@awesomecharters.co.za
URL: www.awesomecharters.co.za

Aqua Planet Dive Centre
Tel: 039-315 7524
Email: info@aquaplanet.co.za
URL: www.aquaplanet.co.za

Casea Charters
Tel: 031-561 7381
Email: info@caseacharters.co.za
URL: www.caseacharters.co.za

Mighty Charters
Tel: 082-833 6554
Email: edred@vodamail.co.za
URL: www.mightycharters.co.za

Scuba Diving Courses
Tel: 082-856 4991
Email: scubasport@intekom.co.za

Sensational Deep Sea Charters
Tel: 083-226 5634
Email: fishmad@iafrica.com
URL: www.sensationalfishing.co.za

Spirit of Elan
Tel: 031-576 9600
Email: leighann@elan.co.za
URL: www.spiritofelan.co.za

Coaches and Buses

Margate Coach
Tel: 039-305 2778

Margate Mini Coach & Airport Services
Tel: 039-312 1406
Email: coach@margate.co.za
URL: www.margatecoach.co.za

Car Rentals

Alpha Car Rental
Tel: 0861-106 156
Email: info@alphacarhire.co.za
URL: www.alphacarhire.co.za

Avis
Tel: 0861-021 111
URL: www.avis.co.za

Bongmusa Chauffeur Services & Car Rental
Tel: 031-306 0800
Email: bongi@bongmusa.co.za
URL: www.bongmusa.com

Budget
Tel: 0861-016 622
URL: www.budget.co.za

Citi Rent Car Hire
Tel: 031-561 4600
Email: citirentcarhire@absamail.co.za
URL: www.citicarhire.co.za

Click Car Hire
Tel: 021-551 9515
URL: www.sa-venues.com/explore/
  clickcarhire/

Drive South Africa
Tel: 0860-000 060
URL: www.drivesouthafrica.co.za

Europcar
Tel: 0861-131 000
URL: www.europcar.co.za

First
Tel: 0861-011 323
URL: www.firstcarrental.co.za

Hertz
Tel: 0861-600 136
URL: www.hertz.co.za

Hlomuka Car Rentals & Tours
Tel: 031-462 1717
Email: vusin@hlomukacarrental.co.za
URL: www.hlomuka.co.za

Jared Travel & Tours
Tel: 031-404 2439

Key Car Rental
Tel: 031-462 5215
URL: www.keygroup.co.za

RIS Vehicle Hire
Tel: 035-786 1274
Email: ian@rishire.co.za
URL: www.rishire.co.za

Tempest Car Hire
Tel: 0861-836 7378
URL: www.tempestcarhire.co.za

Emergency Numbers

Ambulance Service
10177

Durban Beach Patrol
031-368 4453

Emergency Chemist
031-209 3456

Fire Department
031-361 0000

Mountain Rescue Services
082-990 5877

Police
10111

Sea Rescue Services
031-361 8567

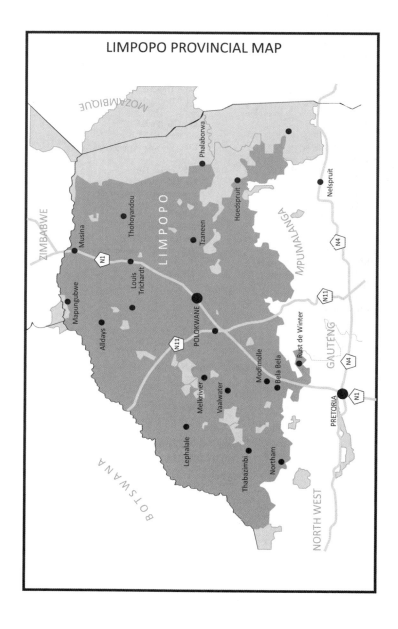

LIMPOPO PROVINCIAL MAP

Limpopo

Tourism Information Offices

Bela Bela Tourism
Tel: 014-736 3694
Email: info@belabelatourism.co.za
URL: www.belabelatourism.co.za

Limpopo Tourism & Leisure
Tel: 015-295 2121
Email: admin@emergingpublications.co.za
URL: www.leisurelimpopo.co.za

Limpopo Tourism & Parks
Tel: 0860-730 730
Email: info@golimpopo.com
URL: www.golimpopo.com

Modimolle Tourism Offices
Tel: 014-717 1818
Email: info@modimolletourism.net
URL: www.modimolletourism.net

Mookgophong Tourism
Tel: 014-743 3863
Email: info@mookgophongtourism.com.za
URL: www.mookgophongtourism.co.za

Thabazimbi Tourism
Tel: 083-770 9917
Email: info@thabazimbitourism.com
URL: www.thabazimbitourism.com

Top 10

Capricorn District
Tel: 015-294 1000
Email: communications@cdm.org.za
URL: www.cdm.org.za

Capricorn serves as a provincial tourism gateway for Limpopo. It is situated between Gauteng and the northern areas of Limpopo and between the northwest and the Kruger National Park. It is a gateway to Botswana, Zimbabwe and Mozambique. The district boasts a number of national heritage sites such as Brackenhill and Goedehoop, Makgabeng Rock Art and the ZCC pilgrimage (Moria). The city of Polokwane is the tourism Mecca of the district, endowed with a casino, museums, shopping facilities, an art gallery, cultural villages and nature reserves.

Kruger National Park
Tel: 012-428 9111
Email: reservations@sanparks.org
URL: www.sanparks.org/parks/kruger

One of the largest game reserves in Africa, the Kruger National Park takes its name from former Transvaal Republic president, Paul Kruger. The park is situated in the northeast corner of the country and has as its western border the province of Limpopo. The Kruger, as it's known locally, is almost 19,000 square kilometres and forms part of the Greater Limpopo Transfrontier Park, which includes the Gona re Zhou of Zimbabwe and the Limpopo Park of Mozambique. Truly the flagship of the South African national parks, Kruger is home to an impressive number of species: 336 trees, 49 fish, 34 amphibians, 114 reptiles, 507 birds and 147 mammals. Yet cultural treasures also abound; from bushman rock paintings to archaeological sites like Thulamela, accessed through the Pafuri Gate in the Limpopo Province. This ancient site represents the walled citadel of a community that flourished between AD 1200–1600.

L I M P O P O

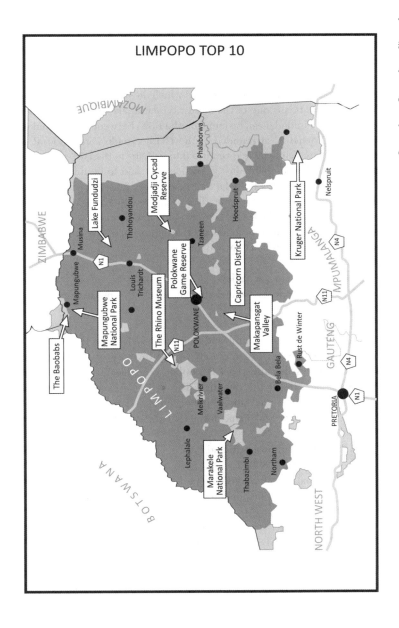

LIMPOPO TOP 10

MOZAMBIQUE

ZIMBABWE

Phalaborwa

Nelspruit

Hoedspruit

Lake Fundudzi

Modjadji Cycad Reserve

Thohoyandou

Musina

Tzaneen

Kruger National Park

MPUMALANGA

N4

Polokwane Game Reserve

Capricorn District

N1

Mapungubwe

Louis Trichardt

The Rhino Museum

POLOKWANE

N17

Mapungubwe National Park

Makapansgat Valley

Rust de Winter

The Baobabs

N11

GAUTENG

L I M P O P O

N4

Melkrivier

Bela Bela

N1

Vaalwater

PRETORIA

Lephalale

BOTSWANA

Marakele National Park

Thabazimbi

Northam

NORTH WEST

Lake Fundudzi
URL: www.mashovhela.com/culture/lake-fundudzi.html

A sacred lake of the Venda people, which lies in the heart of the Soutpansberg, this is one of the few true inland lake systems in South Africa. Lake Fundudzi can be found on the R523 between Thohoyandou and Louis Trichardt, surrounded by the Thathe Vondo Forest, so full of spirits that few Venda people venture into it. Trips to the lake are rarely granted, which is probably just as well as it is said to be infested with crocodiles. So sacred is the lake that newcomers must turn their backs on the lake and view the water from between their legs, according to the ritual after which the lake is named. Fortunately, one of the most spectacular views is found on the approach in the surrounding mountains, so visitors don't have to lose out.

Makapansgat Valley
URL: www.sa-venues.com/game-reserves/np_makapansgat

Boasting a wealth of natural and cultural biodiversity this valley is home to a network of caves, closely linked to those of the Cradle of Humankind. Fossils dating back 3.3 billion years have been lifted from the limestone sites at the diggings. The series of caves is a national monument and there is talk of it becoming a World Heritage Site. Makapansgat is near Mokopane (formerly Potgietersrus).

Mapungubwe National Park
Tel: 012-428 9111
Email: reservations@sanparks.org
URL: www.mapungubwe.com

Mapungubwe is the capital of an ancient African civilization that flourished between AD900–1300. It is the earliest known kingdom in subSaharan Africa and influenced a considerable area, covering parts of what is now South Africa, Botswana and Zimbabwe. In its later stages Mapungubwe had powerful connections with Chinese, Arab and Indian merchants on the east coast of Africa. The empire collapsed in AD1290 and its inhabitants moved on to places as legendary as the stone city of Great Zimbabwe. The Mapungubwe National Park opened its gates to the public in 2004. It is a beautiful reserve—evocative, mysterious and full of surprises. Mapungubwe is the first national park to be dedicated to a uniquely African moment; one which celebrates a history that was once denied or dismissed. The inclusivity of places like Mapungubwe is therefore something that SANParks is keen to encourage in other conservation areas. The scenery is unusual and distinctive. The rest camps are outstanding. And the park also contains the three important archaeological sites of Mapungubwe Hill, K2 and Schroda. (*David Fleminger, World Heritage Sites of South Africa—Mapungubwe Cultural Landscape, 2006*)

Marakele National Park
Tel: 014-779 0000
Email: parkmanager@marakelepark.co.za
URL: www.marakelepark.co.za

The Marakele National Park in the heart of the Waterberg Mountains, as its Tswana name suggests, has become a 'place of sanctuary' for an impressive variety of wildlife due to its location in the transitional zone between the dry western and moister eastern regions of South Africa. Contrasting majestic mountain landscapes, grass-clad hills and deep valleys characterize the park. Rare finds of yellowwood and cedar trees, five-metre-high cycads and tree ferns, are some of the plant species found here. All the large game species from elephant and rhino to the big cats as well as an amazing variety of birds, including what's probably the largest colony of endangered Cape vultures (more than 800 breeding pairs) in the world, have settled here.

Modjadji Cycad Reserve
URL: www.golimpopo.com/park-details_modjadji-nature-reserve

There are many legends about the Modjadji Rain Queens, but one of the most popular is that in the 16th century the Karanga tribe came into a time of turmoil. Fleeing south from the troubles the royal princess and her fellow travellers were enchanted by the cycad forests and decided on a new kingdom in the Duiwelskloof area north of Tzaneen. The South African Cycad Reserve has flourished to become one of the premier attractions in the region. This 560-hectare reserve forms a unique natural forest. Some of the cycads in the Modjadji Cycad Reserve reach heights of 13 metres and bear cones that weigh in at 34 kilograms, making them the giants of their species. The plants seed between December and February, which is the perfect time to view them.

Polokwane Game Reserve
URL: www.polokwane.info/polokwane-reserve

Bordering the city of Polokwane in Limpopo, the Polokwane Game Reserve is possibly one of the finest on which to cut your teeth if you're new to the pursuit of game-viewing, because of its proximity to Johannesburg—it's roughly three hours' drive—but also because its size is such that one can view quite a bit within an afternoon. One of the biggest municipal-owned game reserves in South Africa, the Polokwane Game Reserve's main attraction must be the amount of ground one can cover on foot. There are a number of walks, including a one-day 20-kilometre hiking trail with overnight accommodation. Even more exciting are the frequent sightings of White rhino and other game. One of the most important aspects of the reserve is that it conserves the Pietersburg Plateau false grassland, one of the only remaining examples of an extremely localized vegetation type that is home to important indigenous birds like the Short-clawed lark, the Ashy tit and the Kalahari scrub-robin.

The Baobabs
URL: www.sa-venues.com/attractions/limpopo/baobabs.htm

The giant baobab grows mainly in the hot, semi-arid areas north of the Soutpansberg mountains. Legend has it that in a frivolous mood, the gods planted baobabs upside down with their roots exposed to the sky. Another story is that God told the hyena to plant the first tree and having a sense of humour, he planted it upside down. The baobab tree (*Adansonia digitata*) has a long lifespan; the average age is between 300 and 500 years old. Near Sagole, a rural village in the northeast of the province, one specimen is 3,000 years old and measures 43 metres in circumference at base. Baobabs are among the most useful plants to both animals and humans with many practical, medicinal and nutritional uses. They are also a major food and moisture source for a variety of animals.

The Rhino Museum
URL: www.sa-venues.com/attractions/limpopo/rhino-
    museum.htm

As a testament to its emphasis on eco-tourism and conservation, the Waterberg boasts Africa's only rhino museum, devoted entirely to the conservation of the rhinoceros. The species, that has roamed the planet for more than 30 million years was brought to near extinction 30 years ago. War, corruption, greed and the indifference of man, led to its near demise. The Rhino Museum highlights the evolutionary history, habitats and landscapes, the rhino wars, illegal trade and use of rhino horn as well as conservation efforts to preserve the species. Considering there are only four major populations surviving in Africa today (Kenya, Zimbabwe, Namibia and South Africa) and that South Africa has the highest population of both species, Black and White, a visit to this museum is certainly worthwhile. It is situated in Lapalala Wilderness Game Reserve.

Activities

Adventure Activities

Blyde Canyon Adventure Centre
Tel: 015-795 5961
Email: bookings@blydecanyon.co.za
URL: www.blydecanyon.co.za

Camp Jabulani Elephant-back Safaris
Tel: 015-793 1265
Email: reservations@campjabulani.com
URL: www.campjabulani.com

Hot-air Ballooning SA
Tel: 083-446 9423
Email: info@hotairballooningsa.co.za
URL: www.hotairballooningsa.co.za

Magoebaskloof Canopy Tour
Tel: 083-866 1546
Email: adventures@thabametsi.com
URL: www.magoebaskloofcanopytour.co.za

Mohlatsi Adventures
Tel: 079-038 8219
URL: www.wheretostay.co.za/activities/
  mohlatsi/

Otters Den River Lodge & Hot-air
  Ballooning
Tel: 082-574 2223
Email: wynand@ottersden.co.za
URL: www.ottersden.co.za

Serendipity Eco Trails
Tel: 014-743 1665
Email: info@serendipitytrails.co.za
URL: www.serendipitytrails.co.za

Skydive Extreme
Tel: 083-759 3483
Email: info@skydivextreme.co.za
URL: www.skydivewtreme.co.za

Thaba-Metsi Adventures
Tel: 083-866 1546
Email: adventures@thabametsi.com
URL: www.thabametsi.com

Outdoor Activities

Horizon Horseback Adventures
Tel: 014-755 4003
Email: horizonranch@telkomsa.net
URL: www.ridinginafrica.com

Kolobe Bush Retreat Bird Watching
Tel: 079-711 7195
URL: www.wheretostay.co.za/activities/
  kolobebr-birdwatching/

Louis Changuion Hiking Trail
Tel: 015 276 4972
Email: mta@magoebaskloof.com
URL: www.footprint.co.za/louischanguion

Rusoord Anglers Paradise
Tel: 014-763 38001
Email: rusoord@lantic.net
URL: www.rusoordtours.com

Soutpansberg Quad Adventures
Tel: 015-516 4795
URL: www.wheretostay.co.za/activities/
  soutpansberg/

Sport

Alldays Golf Club
Tel: 015-575 1257

Amandelbult Golf Club
Tel: 014-784 1317

Drakensig Golf Club
Tel: 015-793 2105

Euphoria Golf Course
Tel: 014-743 3759
Email: info@euphoriaestate.co.za
URL: www.euphoriaestate.co.za

Giyani Golf Club
Tel: 015-812 1176

Hans Merensky Golf Course
Tel: 015-781 3931
URL: www.hansmerensky.com

KoroCreek Bushveld Golf Estate
Tel: 014-717 1181
Email: bookings@korocreek.com
URL: www.korocreek.com

Louis Trichardt Country Club
Tel: 015-516 0991

Mogol Golf Club
Tel: 014-763 4948
URL: www.mogolgolf.co.za

Polokwane Golf Course
Tel: 015-295 4118
Email: manager@ptbgolf.co.za
URL: www.ptbgolf.co.za

Zebula Country Club Golf Course
Tel: 014-734 7700
Email: reception@zebula.co.za
URL: www.zebula.co.za

Stadiums

Peter Mokaba Stadium
Tel: 015-290 2316
Email: edwardw@ellispark.co.za
URL: www.cup2010.info/stadiums/
Situated in Polokwane

The form of the largely concrete structure was inspired by the locally iconic baobab tree, with the steel structure supporting the roof plane gathered together at each corner of the stadium and supported by giant 'trunk' structures which accommodate vertical circulation ramps and service cores. In this prestigious complex, the first of its kind in the entire province of Limpopo, The Peter Mokaba Stadium will be home to local soccer teams as well as facilitate a wide range of South African sport competitions, including rugby, with a capacity of 45,000.

Culture

Museums

Arend Dieperink Museum
Tel: 015-491 9735

Masorini
Tel: 013-735 5611
URL: www.krugerpark.co.za/masorini-kruger-national-park.html

Nyani Tribal Village
Tel: 015-793 3816
URL: www.backpack.co.za/accommod/nortprov/nyani_tribal_village.html

Polokwane Art Museum
Tel: 015-290 2177

Thulamela Hill
Tel: 013-735 5611
URL: www.krugerpark.co.za/thulamela-kruger-national-park.html

Tsongakraal Open Air Museum
Tel: 015-386 8727
Opening Time: Monday to Friday: 07h30
Closing Time: Monday to Friday: 16h00

Tzaneen Museum
Tel: 015-307 2425
Opening Times: Monday to Saturday: 09h00
Closing Times: Monday to Friday: 17h00; Saturday 13h00

Galleries

DNA-Design
Tel: 079-492 4557
URL: www.dna-design.co.za

Gemco Art Gallery
Tel: 015-292 0758
Address: Plot 124, Ivydale, Polokwane

Kubasa
URL: www.kubasa.com

Polokwane Art Gallery
Tel: 015-295 3460

Sign & Art Gallery
Tel: 015-295 7981

The Place for Art
Tel: 015-295 3954
Address: 24a Biccard Street, Polokwane

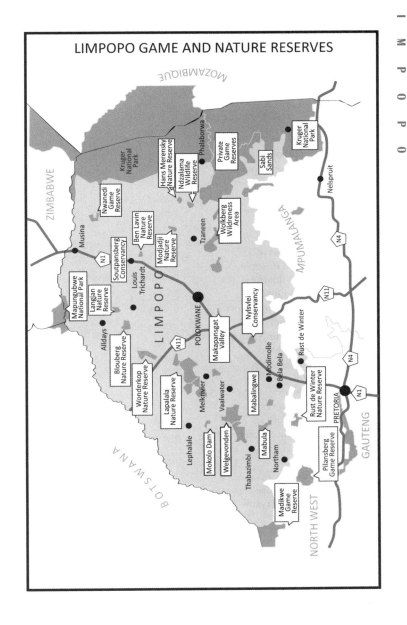

LIMPOPO GAME AND NATURE RESERVES

Game and Nature Reserves (including National Parks)

Limpopo Tourism has one of the best and most informative websites of all nine provinces. The information on their parks is extensive with links to the parks themselves.

Limpopo Parks
Tel: 015-290 7300
Email: info@golimpopo.com
URL: www.golimpopo.com

Nature Reserves
Atherstone Nature Reserve
Balule Nature Reserve
Blouberg Nature Reserve
D'Nyala Nature Reserve
Doorndraai Nature Reserve
Hans Merensky Wilderness
Mabalingwe Game Reserve
Makaladi Private Game Reserve
Makuya Nature Reserve
Manavhela Ben Lavin Nature Reserve
Masebe Nature Reserve
Modjadji Nature Reserve
Musina Nature Reserve
Nylsvlei Conservancy
Rust de Winter Reserve
Percy Fyfe Conservancy
Schuinsdraain Nature Reserve
Selati Game Reserve
Tilodi Wilderness
Timbavati Nature Reserve
Venetia Limpopo Nature Reserve
Welgevonden Private Game Reserve
Wonderkop

Provincial Parks
Lekgalameetse Reserve
Letaba Ranch Provincial Park
Mano'mbe Provincial Park
Mokolo Dam

Nwanedi Nature Reserve
Tzaneen Dam

South African National Parks
Tel: 012-426 5000
Email: reservations@sanparks.org
URL: www.sanparks.org

SANParks Reserves
Kruger National Park
Marakele National Park
Mapungubwe National Park

Entertainment

Annual Events

Aartappel Fees (Potato Festival)
Tel: 083-584 2612
Held in Vivo every May

Baobab Beat Music Festival
Tel: 072-137 3693
URL: www.baobabbeat.co.za
Held in Polokwane every September

Bridal Show
Tel: 015-290 5000
Held in Polokwane every May

Bosveld Show
Tel: 015-491 7159
Held in Mokopane every May

Burns Supper Halloween Twist
Tel: 082-575 5738
Held in Haernertsburg every January

Capricorn Endurance Horse Ride
Tel: 082-449 4009
Held in Polokwane every January,
   March and September

Christmas on the Square
Tel: 015-295 9038
Held in Polokwane every December

Dayle Hayes Super Golf
Tel: 015-781 3933
Held in Phalaborwa every March

Ebenezer Mile
Tel: 082-893 0790
URL: www.golimpopo.com/events
Held in Magoebaskloof every March

Firearms Festival
Tel: 014-763 2193
Held in Lephalale every September

Holistic Fair
Tel: 082-479 7285
Held in Haenertsburg every July

Kiwi Festival
Tel: 082-893 0790
URL: www.sa-venues.com/events/limpopo
Held in Magoebaskloof every April

Land of Legends Marathon
Tel: 074-580 2314
Held in Thohoyandou every April

Limpopo Wine Show
Tel: 015-290 8336
URL: www.sa-venues.com/events/limpopo
Held in Polokwane every April

Magoebaskloof Enduro
Tel: 082-455 7966
Held in Magoebaskloof every May

Makoppa Duathlon
Tel: 072-384 7525
Held in Tzaneen every May

Marakele National Park Marathon
Tel: 073-002 0873
URL: www.entrytime.com/index
Held every March

Marken 3&1 Marathon
Tel: 083-645 3082
Held in Marken every April

Marula Festival
Tel: 082-676 3350
URL: www.sa-venues.com/events/limpopo
Held in Phalaborwa every February

Marula Golf Tournament
Tel: 015-781 3933
Held in Phalaborwa every April

Music in the Mist
Tel: 082-893 0790
Held in Magoebaskloof every November

Musina Show
Tel: 015-534 3500
Held every July

Oppikoppi Festival
Tel: 021-327 6601
URL: www.opppikoppi.co.za
Held in Northam ever August

Polokwane Arts Festival
Tel: 015-290 2143
URL: www.polokwaneartsfestival.co.za
Held every June

Polokwane Heritage Festival
Tel: 015-290 2413
Held every September

Polokwane Show and Music Festival
Tel: 082-374 0816
URL: www.golimpopo.com/events
Held every March

Polokwane Youth Festival
Tel: 015-290 2143
Held every November

SA Birding Worldcup
Tel: 015-769 5019
Held in Phalaborwa every November

Soutpansberg Mountain Race
Tel: 074-580 2314
Held every January

Spring Festival
Tel: 082-575 5738
URL: www.sa-venues.com/events/limpopo
Held in Magoebaskloof every September

The Citrashine Bush Pilots Airshow
Tel: 015-307 1144
Held in Tzaneen every JUne

Wild & Tourism Expo
Tel: 014-777 1621
Held in Thabazimbi every May

Windpomp Fees (Windmill Festival)
Tel: 082-873 1970
Held in Mookgopong every July

Xmas in July
Tel: 082-893 0790
Held in Haenertsburg every July

Shopping www.mallguide.co.za

Limpopo Mall
Tel: 015-2971383
Situated in Polokwane

Louis Trichadt Crossing Centre
Tel: 015-516 0935
Situated in Louis Trichardt

Metropolitan Life Plaza
Tel: 015-291 4614
Situated in Polokwane

Musina Shopping Centre
Tel: 015-297 6400
Situated in Musina

Savannah Mall
Tel: 015-296 1401
Situated in Polokwane

The Farmyard Market Day
Tel: 015-263 6452
Situated in Polokwane

Restaurants

Bela Bela

Adam's Restaurant
Cuisine: South African
Tel: 014-736 2406
Address: 19 Bham Street

Black Steer
Cuisine: Steak Ranch
Tel: 014-736 5786
Address: Shop 4, Bela Bela Square

Thaba Pitsi
Cuisine: African
Tel: 014-736 5826
Address: off R101 on Nooitgedacht Road

The Pancake Inn
Cuisine: Pancake dishes
Tel: 014-736 2787
Address: 57 Voortrekker Street

The Shack
Cuisine: Pub
Tel: 014-736 4236
Address: 17km out on Alma Road

Phalaborwa

Buffalo Pub & Grill
Cuisine: Pub
Tel: 015-781 0829
Address: Olifants River Estate on R527

Cravings Restaurant & Lounge
Cuisine: South African
Tel: 078-111 7444
Address: 67 Bosvlier Avenue

Impala Inn
Cuisine: Fine Dining
Tel: 015-781 3681
Address: 52 Essenhout Street

Kaia Tani Italian Restaurant
Cuisine: Italian
Tel: 015-781 1358
Address: 29 Boekenhout Street

Lantana a la Carte Restaurant
Cuisine: Fine Dining
Tel: 015-781 5191
Address: Kiaat Street

Lateba Restaurant & Beer Garden
Cuisine: South African
Tel: 015-781 5665
Address: 7 Du Toit Street

Sefapane Restaurant
Cuisine: Fine Dining
Tel: 015-780 6700
Address: Copper Road

Polokwane

Basil's Restaurant
Cuisine: Contemporary
Tel: 015-290 5000
Address: 0699 Holandsdrift

Charamba's
Cuisine: Seafood
Tel: 015-296 2665
Address: cnr Morris & De Wet Avenue

Mawetse Fine Dining
Cuisine: South African
Tel: 015-297 4439
Address: 54 Jorissen Street

Oaks Pub & Grill
Cuisine: Pub
Tel: 015-491 4355
Address: 27 Van Riebeeck Street

Pebbles
Cuisine: Fine Dining
Tel: 015-295 6999
Address: 39 Grobler Street

The Deck
Cuisine: Mediterranean
Tel: 015-296 4956
Address: cnr Pierre & Neethling Street

The Restaurant
Cuisine: South African
Tel: 015-291 1918
Address: cnr Thabo Mbeki & Dorp Street

Tzaneen

Ashley's Continental Café
Cuisine: Bistro
Tel: 015-307 7270
Address: 30 Agatha Road

Picasso's Restaurant
Ciusine: International
Tel: 015-276 4724
Address: R71, Haenertsburg

Pot & Plow
Cuisine: Contemporary
Tel: 082-691 5790
Address: On the R71, Magoebaskloof

Zabana Steak Bar
Cuisine: Steak Ranch
Tel: 015-307 1001
Address: On the R71

Chains and Franchises

Cape Town Fish Market
URL: www.ctfm.co.za

Cappuccinc's
URL: www.cappuccinos.co.za

Dros
URL: www.dros.co.za

Mugg & Bean
URL: www.themugg.com

Ocean Basket
URL: www.oceanbasket.co.za

Panarotti's
URL: www.panarottis.com

Spur
URL: www.spur.co.za

Wimpy
URL: www.wimpy.co.za

Accommodation

www.golimpopo.co.za
www.limpopo-venues.co.za
www.wheretostay.co.za
www.sa-venues.com/limpopo_accommodation
www.sleeping-out.co.za/Limpopo-accommodation
www.kwathabeng.co.za/travel/accommodation
www.staysa.co.za/sa/10-0-0-0-1/Limpopo/accommodation
www.roomsforafrica.com/dest/south-africa/limpopo
www.safarinow.com/destinations/limpopo
http://limpopo.hotelguide.co.za

Polokwane
Hotels

Col-John Hotel
Tel: 015-295 9430
Email: reservations@col-john.co.za
URL: www.col-john.co.za

Garden Court Hotel
Tel: 015-291 2030
Email: gcpolokwane@southernsun.com
URL: www.southernsun.com

Golden Pillow
Tel: 015-295 2970
Email: adele@goldenpillow.co.za
URL: www.goldenpillow.co.za

Town Lodge Hotel
Tel: 015-292 4400
Email: tlpolok.resv@citylodge.co.za
URL: www.citylodge.co.za/poresult.htm

Lodges

Bolivia Lodge
Tel: 015-263 6205
Email: bolivia.pburg@mindsmail.co.za

Wildthingz Lodge
Tel: 083-656 5729
Email: vhbristow@mweb.co.za

B&Bs, Guest Houses & Self-catering

African Roots Guest House
Tel: 015-297 0113
Email: afrroots@mweb.co.za
URL: www.africanroots.info

Ananza Guest House
Tel: 015-491 6177
Email: ansachutte@isat.co.za
URL: www.ananza.co.za

Arli Guest House
Tel: 015-297 2504
Email: arliz@telkomsa.net

Bendor Cottage
Tel: 082-773 9274
Email: teresa@mega-pix.co.za
URL: www.bendorcottage.wordpress.com

Country Blue
Tel: 015-291 3287
Email: info@countryblue.co.za
URL: www.countryblue.co.za

Cycad Guest House
Tel: 015-291 2123
Email: mariadp@mweb.co.za
URL: www.cycadguesthouse.co.za

Eskulaap Park
Tel: 015-297 3288
Email: admin@eskulaap.co.za
URL: www.eskulaap.co.za

Kings Castle
Tel: 015-291 3915
Email: casali123@yahoo.com
URL: www.kingscastle.co.za

Marlot Guest House
Tel: 015-297 5456
Email: v.gaint@mweb.co.za
URL: www.marlot.co.za

Sleepersville Guest House
Tel: 015-291 5285
Email: sleepersvilla@mweb.co.za
URL: www.sleepersvilla.co.za

Camping

Blouberg Ivory Camp
Tel: 015-295 2829
Email: infoair@mweb.co.za
URL: www.africanivoryroute.co.za

Other
Hotels

Avuxeni Hotel Elephant Springs
Tel: 014-736 2101
Email: reservations@elephant-springs.co.za
URL: www.elephant-springs.co.za
Situated in Bela Bela

Chateau Larize
Tel: 014-736 3601
Email: info@chateaularize.co.za
URL: www.chateaularize.co.za
Situated in Bela Bela

Dongola Ranch Hotel
Tel: 015-533 1948
Email: dongola@iafrica.com
URL: www.dongola.co.za
Situated in Musina

Glenshiel Hotel
Tel: 015-276 4335
Email: info@glenshiel.co.za
URL: www.glenshiel.co.za
Situated in Magoebaskloof

Hans Merensky Hotel & Estate
Tel: 015-781 3931
Email: gitw@hansmerensky.com
URL: www.hansmerensky.com
Situated in Phalaborwa

Lonely Oak Hotel
Tel: 015-491 4560
Email: lonelyoak@telkomsa.net
Situated in Mokopane

Magoebaskloof Hotel
Tel: 015-276 5400
Situated in Magoebaskloof

Protea Hotels
Tel: 0861-119 000
Email: uwelcome@proteahotels.com
URL: www.proteahotels.com

The Coach House Hotel
Tel: 015-306 8000
Email: info@coachhouse.co.za
URL: www.coachhouse.co.za
Situated in Tzaneen

Lodges

Abba Game Lodge
Tel: 014-717 2095
Email: abbares@telkomsa.net
URL: www.abbalodge.co.za
Situated in Modimolle

Akeru Safari Lodge
Tel: 011-888 4037
Email: enquiries@adventures.co.za
URL: www.africanadrenalin.com/Akeru/
Situated in Phalaborwa

Angasii Game Lodge
Tel: 014-784 0497
Email: info@angasii.co.za
URL: www.angasii.co.za
Situated in Thabazimbi

Arbor Park Lodge
Tel: 015-307 1831
Email: arborpark@mweb.co.za
URL: www.arborparklodge.co.za
Situated in Tzaneen

Baobab Game Ranch
Tel: 082-806 9242
Email: johnny@baobabgameranch.co.za
URL: www.baobabgameranch.co.za
Situated in Mokopane

Black Forest Mountain Lodge
Tel: 082-572 9781
Situated in Tzaneen

Blyde River Canyon Lodge
Tel: 015-795 5305
Email: canyon@worldonline.co.za
URL: www.blyderivercanyon.co.za
Situated in Maruleng

Bougainvilla Lodge
Tel: 015-962 3575
Email: bvilamanager@lantic.net
URL: www.bougainvillalodge.com
Situated in Thohoyandou

Bramasole Luxury Guest Lodge
Tel: 015-276 1223
Email: reservations@bramasole.co.za
URL: www.bramasole.co.za
Situated in Tzaneen

Busisa Safari Lodge
Tel: 011-440 4075
Email: info@busisa.co.za
URL: www.busisa.co.za
Situated in Phalaborwa

Calali Bush Lodge
Tel: 082-870 4604
Email: reservations@calali.co.za
URL: www.calali.co.za
Situated in Thabazimbi

Castaro Game Lodge
Tel: 011-310 1095
Email: djfrikkie@lantic.net
URL: www.castaro.co.za
Situated in Louis Trichardt

Clifftop Lodge
Tel: 014-755 4920
Email: lodge@clifftoplodge.co.za
URL: www.clifftoplodge.com
Situated in Modimolle

Elandela Lodge
Tel: 015-793 1462
Email: yvonne@elandelalodge.co.za
URL: www.elandelalodge.com
Situated in Hoedspruit

Elephant Plains Game Lodge
Tel: 027-735 5358
Email: reservations@elephantplains.co.za
URL: www.elephantplains.co.za
Situated in Maruleng

Elephant Walk
Tel: 015-781 5860
Email: elephant.walk@nix.co.za
Situated in Phalaborwa

Fairview Country Lodge
Tel: 015-307 2679
Email: reservations@fairviewlodge.co.za
URL: www.fairviewlodge.co.za
Situated in Tzaneen

Gwalagwala Game Lodge
Tel: 015-793 3491
Email: gwala@netactive.co.za
URL: www.gwala.co.za
Situated in Phalaborwa

Hippo River Lodge
Tel: 082-927 2616
Email: kevinh@cknet.co.za
Situated in Phalaborwa

Ilala Country Lodge
Tel: 015-534 3220
Email: dorsal@lantic.net
Situated in Musina

Indabushee Game Lodge
Tel: 014-755 4113
Email: nico@indabusheesafaris.co.za
URL: www.indabusheesafaris.co.za
Situated in the Waterberg

Kambaku Safari Lodge
Tel: 015-793 2250
Email: reservations@kambakulodge.co.za
URL: www.kambakulodge.co.za
Situated in Phalaborwa

Karoi Lodge
Tel: 012-460 2704
Email: kprobert@telkomsa.net
URL: www.karoi.co.za
Situated in Modimolle

Klein Bolayi Guest Lodge
Tel: 015-534 0975
Email: lempertz@gamelodgebolayi.com
URL: www.gamelodgebolayi.com
Situated in Musina

Kokobela Lodge
Tel: 083-377 4867
Email: admin@kokobela.com
URL: www.kokobela.com
Situated in Phalaborwa

Koro Koro Safari Lodge
Tel: 082-908 4448
Email: info@koro-koro.co.za
URL: www.koro-koro.co.za
Situated in Bela Bela

Kromdraai Lodge
Tel: 014-735 0920
Email: lodgekeeper@telkomsa.net
URL: www.kromdraailodge.co.za
Situated in Thabazimbi

Leopard's View
Tel: 071-438 9562
Email: enquiries@leopardsview.co.za
URL: www.leopardsview.co.za
Situated in Maruleng

Leriba Golf Lodge
Tel: 012-660 3300
Email: leriba@netactive.co.za
URL: www.leribagolflodge.co.za
Situated in Phalaborwa

Letaba River Lodge
Tel: 015-307 7762
Email: ronel@ecopark.co.za
URL: www.ecopark.co.za
Situated in Tzaneen

Limpopo View Lodge
Tel: 015-534 2403
Email: office@limpopo-safaris.com
URL: www.limpopo-safaris.com
Situated in Louis Trichardt

Mahlahla Game Lodge
Tel: 015-793 2989
Email: info@mahlahla.co.za
URL: www.mahlahla.co.za
Situated in Maruleng

Marula Lodge
Tel: 011-869 7414
Email: marula@fcmuldergroup.co .za
URL: www.marulalodge.co.za
Situated in Lephalale

Mahutti Country Lodge
Tel: 015-307 4315
Email: mashutti@iafrica.com
Situated in Tzaneen

Matla Mamba
Tel: 014-754 4453
Email: info@matlamamba.co.za
URL: www.matlamamba.co.za
Situated in Thabazimbi

Matopi Game Lodge
Tel: 082-411 9139
Email: cstanz@netactive.co.za
URL: www.matopigamelodge.co.za
Situated in Thabazimbi

Mhondoro Lodge
Tel: 073-819 4233
Email: reservations@mhondoro.com
URL: www.mhondoro.co.za
Situated in Phalaborwa

Mopane Bush Lodge
Tel: 015-534 7906
Email: mopanebushlodge@limpopo.co.za
URL: www.mopanebushlodge.co.za
Situated in Musina

Motsomi Lodge & Tent Camp
Tel: 014-772 2082
Email: hazel@drtaxidermy.co.za
URL: www.motsomi.co.za
Situated in Thabazimbi

Nedile Lodge
Tel: 082-854 8841
Email: info@nedile.co.za
URL: www.nedile.co.za
Situated in Lephalale

Nyala Safari Lodge
Tel: 071-679 4321
Email: nyala@safarilodges.co.za
URL: www.nyalasafarilodge.co.za
Situated in Maruleng

Palala River Lodge
Tel: 014-763 4063
Email: manager@safarilands.com
URL: www.safarilands.com
Situated in Lephalale

Phumuza Bushveld Breakaway
Tel: 014-736 6453
Email: phumuza@ctec.co.za
URL: www.phumuza.co.za
Situated in Bela Bela

Pumula Lodge
Tel: 079-801 8577
Email: rautenbach5@gmail.com
Situated in Modimolle

Royal Legend Safari Lodge & Spa
Tel: 012-470 5300
Email: reservations@legendlodges.co.za
URL: www.legendlodges.co.za/royal.htm
Situated in Phalaborwa

Royal Malewane
Tel: 015-793 0150
Email: reservations@theroyalportfolio.com
URL: www.royalmalewane.com
Situated in Maruleng

Sable Lodge
Tel: 021-683 7196
Email: chrisvc@mweb.co.za
URL: www.sablelodge.co.za
Situated in Modimolle

San Village Tented Lodge
Tel: 082-447 5229
Email: nfo@bushmencamp.co.za
URL: www.bushmencamp.co.za
Situated in Lephalale

Shiduli Private Game Lodge
Tel: 011-817 5560
Email: reservations@shidulilodge.co.za
URL: www.shidulilodge.co.za
Situated in Tzaneen

Simbavati River Lodge
Tel: 012-667 3648
Email: reservations@simbavati.co.za
URL: www.simbavati.co.za
Situated in Phalaborwa

Stanford Lake Lodge
Tel: 082-322 9729
Email: gstanfor@mweb.co.za
URL: www.stanfordlake.co.za
Situated in Tzaneen

The Fig Tree Lodge
Tel: 015-964 1546
Email: Figtreelodge@lantic.net
URL: www.thefigtreelodge.com
Situated in Louis Trichardt

Tholo-Beze Game Lodge
Tel: 014-786 2903
Email: info@tholo-beze.co.za
URL: www.tholo-beze.co.za
Situated in Thabazimbi

Ubundu Lodge
Tel: 014-735 0689
Email: reservation@ubundu.co.za
URL: www.ubundu.co.za
Situated in Bela Bela

187

Umlani Bushcamp
Tel: 015-793 1483
Email: info@umlani.com
URL: www.umlani.com
Situated in Musina

Zenzele River Lodge
Tel: 012-346 7693
Email: zenzelelodge@polka.co.za
URL: www.zenzeleriverlodge.co.za
Situated in Bela Bela

Zwahili Private Game Lodge
Tel: 012-653 4340
Email: zwahili@iafrica.com
URL: www.zwahili.co.za
Situated in Modimolle

B&Bs, Guest Houses & Self-catering

Aandgloed Guest House
Tel: 015-516 4634
Email: aandgloed@absamail.co.za
Situated in Louis Trichardt

Arimagham Guest House
Tel: 082-337 7104
Email: info@arimagham.co.za
URL: www.arimagham.co.za
Situated in Tzaneen

Attic Guest House
Tel: 014-736 3026
Email: indigoskies1@gmail.com
URL: www.theatticguesthouse.co.za
Situated in Bela Bela

Azalea Glade Cottages
Tel: 015-276 2140
Email: megang@webmail.co.za
Situated in Tzaneen

Bakkers Bed & Breakfast
Tel: 015-781 1613
Email: bakkersbandb@telkomsa.net
URL: www.bakkersbandb.com
Situated in Phalaborwa

Bed in the Bush
Tel: 015-781 1139
Email: bushbed@lantic.net
URL: www.bedinthebush.co.za
Situated in Fhalaborwa

Belle Jardin
Tel: 082-672 1054
Email: leonho@mweb.co.za
URL: www.bellejardin.co.za
Situated in Bela Bela

Blue Cottages B&B
Tel: 015-795 5750
Email: info@countryhouse.co.za
URL: www.bluecottages.co.za
Situated in Maruleng

Daan & Zena's B&B
Tel: 015-781 6049
Email: daanzena@lantic.net
URL: www.daanzena.co.za
Situated in Phalaborwa

De Draai Guest House
Tel: 014-736 4755
Email: christien@dedraai.co.za
URL: www.dedraai.co.za
Situated in Bela Bela

Die Opstal Guest House
Tel: 014-736 6292
Email: monica@senco.co.za
Situated in Bela Bela

Die Stoep B&B
Tel: 015-307 5101
Situated in Tzaneen

Eagle's View Mountain Inn
Tel: 015-305 4419
Email: info@eagleview.co.za
URL: www.eagleview.co.za
Situated in Tzaneen

Ellisras Guest House
Tel: 014-763 2413
Email: ellisrasgastehuis@vodamail.co.za
Situated in Lephalale

Gorgeous Gecko Guest House
Tel: 014-717 4227
Email: ursula@nylies.co.za
Situated in Modimolle

Granny Dot's Country Spot
Tel: 015-307 5149
Email: mwbisset@mweb.co.za
URL: www.grannydots.co.za
Situated in Tzaneen

Hideaway
Tel: 014-736 4301
Email: hideawaysa@yahoo.com
URL: www.hideawaysa.com
Situated in Bela Bela

Hillbilly Haven
Tel: 083-280 4971
Email: thehillbilly@lantic.net
URL: www.hillbillyhaven.co.za
Situated in Tzaneen

Jolyne B&B
Tel: 015-795 5550
Email: jolyne@tiscali.co.za
Situated in Maruleng

Kaia Tani Exclusive Guest House
Tel: 015-781 1358
Email: info@kaiatani.com
URL: www.kaiatani.com
Situated in Phalaborwa

Khaya Guest House
Tel: 082-928 8947
Email: dplombard@absamail.co.za
URL: www.khayaguesthouse.co.za
Situated in Louis Trichardt

Klein Paradys Guest Farm
Tel: 082-490 6143
Email: kleinparadysbf@mweb.co.za
URL: www.kleinparadys.co.za
Situated in Modimolle

Komma Nader Guest House
Tel: 014-777 1376
Email: info@kommanader.co.za
URL: www.kommanader.co.za
Situated in Lephalale

Kransberg Bed & Breakfast
Tel: 014-777 1586
Email: info@kransberg-benb.co.za
URL: www.kransberg-benb.co.za
Situated in Thabazimbi

Kremetart Guest House
Tel: 015-812 4471
Email: admin@riversideguesthouse.co.za
URL: www.riversideguesthouse.co.za
Situated in Phalaborwa

Lallas Cottage Guest House
Tel: 015-491 6961
Email: lallas@cfmail.co.za
Situated in Mokopane

Lekkerbly Chalet Guest House
Tel: 014-717 3702
Email: lekkerblygh@telkomsa.net
Situated in Modimolle

MaGriet's Bed & Breakfast
Tel: 015-276 4762
Email: magrietsbnb@mweb.co.za
Situated in Tzaneen

Panzi Bushcamp
Tel: 082-751 2000
Email: panzi@mweb.co.za
URL: www.panzibushcamp.co.za
Situated in Maruleng

The Platinum Guest House
Tel: 015-491 3510
Email: theplatinum@connectit.co.za
Situated in Mokopane

Zvakanaka Farm
Tel: 015-517 7249
Email: gail@zka.co.za
URL: www.zka.co.za
Situated in Louis Trichardt

Camping

Camp Mangwele
Tel: 082-209 1827
Email: braam@lantic.net
Situated in Louis Trichardt

Doorndraai Wildlife Camp
Tel: 015-290 7355
Email: reservations@lwr.co.za
URL: www.wildliferesorts.org
Situated in Mokopane

Eden Park
Tel: 014-743 3533
Email: edenpark@pcwireless.co.za
URL: www.edenpark.co.za
Situated in Mookgophong

Eiland Spa and Eco Park
Tel: 015-386 8000
Email: fom@eiland.co.za
URL: www.eiland.co.za
Situated in Phalaborwa

El Rancho Grande
Tel: 014-736 5514
Email: elranchogrande@mweb.co.za
Situated in Bela Bela

Kaoxa Camp
Tel: 015-575 1338
Email: info@kaoxacamp.com
URL: www.kaoxa.com
Situated in Musina

Lantana Lodge and Caravan Park
Tel: 015-781 5191
Email: lantanalodge@intekom.co.za
URL: www.lantanalodge.co.za
Situated in Phalaborwa

Louis Trichardt Municipal Caravan Park
Tel: 015-519 3025
Email: magda_vanstaden@makhado.co.za
URL: www.makhado.caravanparks.co.za
Situated in Louis Trichardt

Mokolo Dam Camping Site
Tel: 015-290 7300
Email: reservations@golimpopo.com
URL: www.golimpopo.com
Situated in Lephalale

Mphephu Resort
Tel: 015-973 0282
Email: reservations@lwr.co.za
URL: www.wildliferesorts.org
Situated in Thohoyandou

Nwanedi Resort
Tel: 015-290 7300
Email: reservations@lwr.co.za
URL: www.wildliferesorts.org
Situated in Musina

Olifantspoort Bush Camp and Caravan Park
Tel: 014-717 5808
Email: melaniebosman0@gmail.com
URL: http://olifantspoort.htm1planet.com/
Situated in Modimolle

Rust de Winter Camping
Tel: 015-290 7300
Email: reservation@lwr.co.za
URL: www.wildliferesorts.org
Situated in Bela Bela

Tzaneen Wildlife Camp
Tel: 015-290 7300
Email: reservations@lwr.co.za
URL: www.wildliferesorts.org
Situated in Tzaneen

Tours

Action Travel
wildlife tours
Tel: 015-781 1188

Africa Unlimited Tours
tailor-made tours
Tel: 015-781 7825

AfriXplorer
tailor-made tours
Tel: 012-348 1708

Bushcat Safaris
tailor-made and arranged tours
Tel: 083-302 6228

Bushtec Tours & Safaris
tailor-made tours and safaris
Tel: 015-516 6617

Cruiselite Tours and Safaris
tailor-made tours
Tel: 073-223 2414

Earth Africa Tours and Safaris
wildlife tours and safaris
Tel: 013-744 0781

Firelight Tours & Safaris
South African tours and safaris
Tel: 011-793 4882

Frontline Africa Travel
tailor-made tours
Tel: 012-991 3822

Kwa'Nyathi Tours & Safaris
arranged tours
Tel: 015-307 1382

Malate Travel and Tours
tailor-made and arranged tours
Tel: 015-291 2490

Mambe Tourist Solutions
arranged tours
Tel: 015-962 4871

Panorama Tours
tailor-made tours
Tel: 021-426 1634

Serabuho Transport & Projects
arranged tours
Tel: 015-223 6787

Shoestring Eco Nature Tours
arranged tours
Tel: 078-654 9598

South Africa Vacation
tailor-made tours
Tel: 021-786 4808

Strider Expeditions
safari tours
Tel: 015-781 7529

Car Rentals

Avis
Tel: 0861-021 111
URL: www.avis.co.za

Budget
Tel: 0861-016 622
URL: www.budget.co.za

Click Car Hire
Tel: 021-551 9515
URL: www.sa-venues.com/explore/clickcarhire/

Drive South Africa
Tel: 0860-000 060
URL: www.drivesouthafrica.co.za

First
Tel: 0861-011 323
URL: www.firstcarrental.co.za

Hertz
Tel: 0861-600 136
URL: www.hertz.co.za

Europcar
Tel: 0861-131 000
URL: www.europcar.co.za

Tempest Car Hire
Tel: 0861-836 7378
URL: www.tempestcarhire.co.za

Emergency numbers

Ambulance / Fire
10177

Cell phone Emergency Number
112

National Tourism Information & Safety Line
083-113 2345

Police Emergency number
10111

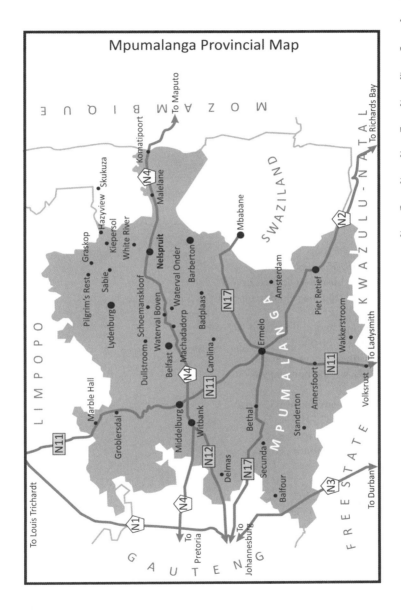

Mpumalanga

Tourism Information Offices

Barberton Community Tourism
Tel: 013-712 2880
Email: astrid@barberton.co.za
URL: www.barberton.co.za

Dullstroom Tourism
Tel: 013-254 0234
Email: info@dullstroom.co.za
URL: www.dullstroom.co.za

Lowveld Tourism
Tel: 013-755 1988
Email: business@lcbt.co.za
URL: http://lowveldtourism.com

Mpumalanga Tourism and Parks
Tel: 013-759 5300
Email: info@mtpa.co.za
URL: www.mpumalanga.com

Rendezvous Tourism Centre
Tel: 013-737 7414
Email: info@rendez.co.za
URL: www.rendez.co.za

Sabie Tourism
Tel: 013-764 1105
Email: info@sabie.co.za
URL: www.sabie.co.za

Top 10

Blyde River Canyon Reserve
URL: www.nature-reserve.co.za/blyde-river-canyon-natural-preserve.html

Blyde River Canyon is the third largest in the world and one of South Africa's scenic wonders. The scenery of the 25,000-hectare reserve in South Africa's lowveld is unsurpassed and is set against the Greater Drakensberg escarpment, stretching from the high mistlands down to the hotter and drier lowveld at the Blyde River Dam. Its vegetation is both varied and lush and the selection of birdlife includes a breeding colony of the rare Bald ibis. The Blyde River Canyon can be reached from Graskop via the R532. The canyon starts at Bourke's Luck Potholes and ends at the Three Rondavels. It is situated on the R532 north of Graskop. The unique geological features at Bourke's Luck Potholes, the Three Rondavels and God's Window are all easily accessible on tarred roads from the picturesque village of Graskop. There is ample accommodation throughout the area. Several hiking trails meander through the reserve and cater for all ages and levels of fitness.

Bourke's Luck Potholes
URL: www.sabie.co.za/gallery/Bourkes%20Luck%20Potholes.html

Situated 35km north of Graskop on the R532 this natural water feature marks the beginning of the Blyde River Canyon. Through countless eons the swirling whirlpools which occur as the Treur River plunging into the Blyde River caused waterborne sand and rock to grind huge, cylindrical potholes into the bedrock of the river. The potholes were named after a gold digger, Tom Burke, who staked a claim nearby. Although his claim did not produce a single ounce of gold, he correctly predicted that large gold deposits would be found in the area.

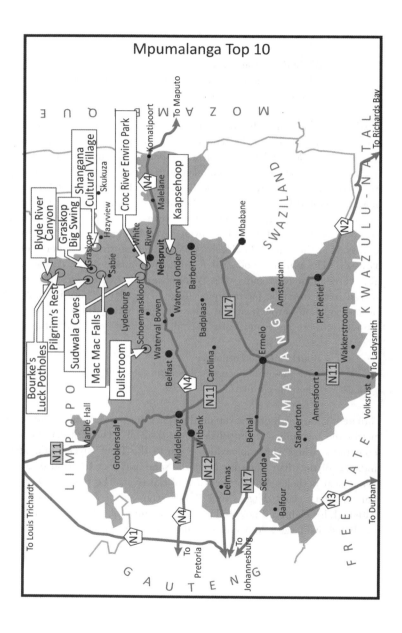

Mpumalanga Top 10

Blyde River Canyon

Graskop Big Swing

Shangana Cultural Village

Croc River Enviro Park

Kaapsehoop

Bourke's Luck Potholes

Pilgrim's Rest

Sudwala Caves

Mac Mac Falls

Dullstroom

M P U M A L A N G A

Croc River Enviro Park
Tel: 013-752 5511
URL: www.booknowsa.com/listings/SouthAfrica/
Mpumalanga/CrocRiverEnviroPark .asp

The largest reptile park in Africa! Reptiles are housed in a terraquarium with 88 glass enclosures in which indigenous and exotic species are housed. The tropical house is offset from the terraquarium and features a nine-metre-high indoor waterfall. Live presentations are given in the demonstration pit. Guests can visit the tea garden situated on the banks of the Crocodile River.

Dullstroom
Tel: 013-254 0234
Email: info@dullstroom.co.za
URL: www.dullstroom.co.za

The Dullstroom website says it best: flyfishing, fireplaces, fine dining, fresh air and fauna and flora. Dullstroom is only a two-hour drive from Gauteng on the way to the Kruger National Park. It's perfect for quick breakaways. It is steeped in history and idyllic scenery with quaint buildings and a plethora of antique stores, second-hand bookshops, places to eat and above all places to fish. There are fancy hotels, comfy guesthouses and plenty of self-catering accommodation. Mpumalanga is dotted with gorgeous towns: Pilgrim's Rest, Graskop and of course Dullstroom, although Dullstroom pips the rest to the post.

Graskop Big Swing
Tel: 013-767 1886
Email: info@graskop.co.za
URL: www.graskop.co.za

Also known as the Gorge Swing, this 68-metre bungee jump is into an 80-metre gorge in the Blyde River Canyon—that's an 18-storey freefall with acceleration from 0–160km/h in 2.3 seconds. The swing is R300 per person, which is comparatively cheap. To complement this activity, 'The Edge Bar', the multi-tiered deck on the opposite side of the gorge, allows you to sit back and enjoy a drink while watching the jumpers.

Kaapsehoop
URL: www.kaapsehoop.com /
www.countryroads.co.za/content/Kaapsehoop.html

Situated 25km southwest of Nelspruit, Kaapsehoop is a fairytale town, rich in historical history. So named because the valley is often covered in mist when the plateau resembles a cape in a sea of clouds. A land of legends, of gold and horses, dating back to 1721 to the Delagoa Bay (now Maputo) of yesteryear where gold was traded. In 1882 Bernard Chomse claimed to have found gold in the bed of a stream on a high, narrow plateau that projects like a finger between the valleys of the Elands and the Little Crocodile rivers. Situated in the hills above Ngodwana 32 kilometres from Nelspruit, this picturesque village has a charming country atmosphere. A herd of wild horses has roamed the hills around Kaapsehoop for many years, reported to have originated from escaped pit ponies over a hundred years ago.

Mac Mac Falls
URL: www.sabie.co.za/gallery/mac-mac-falls.html /
www.countryroads.co.za/content/mac-mac-falls.html

The Mac Mac Falls are 13km from Sabie on the R532 toward Graskop. The turnoff and parking area is at the curio stalls and a nominal entrance fee is charged. A steep walk along a cement pathway (with many steps) takes you to the viewing platform above the falls. The 65-metre-high Mac Mac Falls on the Mac Mac River have been declared a National Monument. This waterfall was originally a single stream, but gold miners blasted it with dynamite to divert the river in an attempt to work the rich gold-bearing reef over which it plunges.

Pilgrim's Rest
Tel: 013-768 1060
URL: www.pilgrimsrest.org.za

A living museum—the entire town has been declared a National Monument—taking visitors back to the days of the old Transvaal Gold Rush. Pilgrim's Rest was proclaimed a goldfield in 1873, soon after digger Alec 'Wheelbarrow' Patterson had found gold deposits in Pilgrim's Creek. The valley proved to be rich in gold and by the end of the year there where about 1,500 diggers working in the area. As a result, Pilgrim's Rest became the social centre of the diggings. A mere 40-minute drive north from Nelspruit, Pilgrim's Rest is situated on the magnificent Panorama Route on the eastern escarpment region of the Mpumalanga Province.

Shangana Cultural Village
Tel: 013-737 5804/5
Email: reservations@shangana.co.za
URL: www.shangana.co.za

Midway between the Blyde River Canyon and the southern Kruger National Park, the residents of the traditional villages of Shangana invite guests to share in the way of life of the Shangaan people. The picturesque villages are set in the shade of ancient trees in a reserve of forest and grassland and are open to visitors every day. Bustling African markets form the core of Shangana, where local craftspeople make and trade their goods. From here, trained guides lead guests down to the various villages on daytime tours, midday tours with lunch and the famed Evening Festival in the Chief's Kraal. Shangana was created and built by local Shangaan people and is a source of great pride as a means of preserving their rich heritage.

Sudwala Caves
Tel: 013-733 4152
Email: info@sudwalacaves.co.za
URL: www.sudwalacaves.co.za
Opening Time: 08h30
Closing Time: 16h30
Tariffs: Adults R50; Pensioners R40; Children R25

Looming above the wooded valley of a bustling mountain torrent there is a majestic massif; a rock upon a rock or a crag upon a crag. In this great dolomite massif rock lies one of the most astonishing caves in southern Africa; a complex of passages and giant chambers extending into the heart of the mountain. The Sudwala Caves are the oldest known caves in the world and, as such, are a must-see on any visitor's itinerary. These incredible caverns lie in the Drakensberg escarpment which divides the highveld from the lowlands of Mpumalanga. The caves are situated in Pre-cumbrian dolomite rocks of the Malmani Group, formed over a period of some 3,000 million years, capturing in stone a time when the area was covered by warm, shallow inland seas. These are among the second-oldest-known sedimentary rocks on earth. Represented in the cave are fossils of the first oxygen-producing plants on earth, Collenia. One can clearly see in the different layers and textures of the rock the result of the different weather patterns that took place in the building of an ancient seabed. Besides the awesome rock displays the caverns also boast an array of calcium formations, aged but active, anciently and patiently still growing.

Activities

Adventure Activities

Balloons Over Africa
Tel: 013-737 6950
Email: db@balloonsoverafrica.co.za
URL: www.balloonsoverafrica.co.za

Ecotraining
Tel: 013-745 7777
Email: admin@ecotraining.co.za
URL: www.ecotraining.co.za

Hardy Ventures
Tel: 013-751 1693
URL: www.hardyventure.com

Induna Adventures
Tel: 013-737 8308 / 1
Email: info@indunaadventures.com
URL: www.indunaadventures.com

Leading Edge Flight School
Tel: 083-400 1405
Email: dkraidy@gmail.com
URL: www.lefssa.co.za

Letubi Quad Biking
Tel: 082-851 7762
Email: info@letubiquadbiking.co.za
URL: www.letubiquadbiking.co.za

Mountain Biking
Tel: 013-764 2123
Email: ghoeks@iafrica.com

Mpumalanga Helicopter Co.
Tel: 084-505 2052
Email: info@mhelicopter.co.za
URL: www.mhelicopter.co.za

Rhino Walking Safaris
Tel: 011-467 1886
Email: info@rws.co.za
URL: www.rws.co.za

Roc 'n Rope Adventures
Tel: 013-257 0363
Email: climb@rocrope.com
URL: www.rocrope.com

Sabie Backpackers & Xtreme Adventures
Tel: 013-764 2118
Email: visitsabie@iafrica.com
URL: www.sabiextreme.co.za

Sabie River Adventures
Tel: 013-737 8266
Email: info@sabieriveradventures.co.za
URL: www.sabieriveradventures.co.za

Skyway Trails
Tel: 082-825 0209
Email: info@skywaytrails.com
URL: www.skywaystrails.com

Transfrontiers Wildlife Walking Safaris
Tel: 015-793 3816
Email: info@transfrontiers.com
URL: www.krugerwalkingsafaris.com/
www.transfrontiers.com

Outdoor Activities

Big Sky Fishing & Outdoor
Tel: 013-764 2682
Email: bigskyout@mweb.co.za

Horse Riding – Ponieskrantz
Tel: 013-768 1465
URL: www.pilgrimsreststables.co.za

Horse Trails – Pelipa Ranch
Tel: 013-745 7140
Email: enquiry@pelipa-ranch.org
URL: www.pelipa-ranch.org

Mavungana Flyfishing
Tel: 013-254 0270
Email: info@flyfishing.co.za
URL: www.flyfishing.co.za

Paintball – Pelipa Ranch
Tel: 013-745 7140
Email: enquiry@pelipa-ranch.org
URL: www.pelipa-ranch.org

River Horse Out-rides
Tel: 083-382 5098
Email: riverhorse@afvac.co.za

Sport

Graceland Golf Course
Tel: 017-620 1000
URL: www.graceland.co.za
Situated in Secunda

Greenways Woods Golf Course
Tel: 013-751 1094
URL: www.greenway.co.za
Situated in White River

Leopard Creek
Tel: 013-791 2000
URL: www.leopardcreek.co.za
Situated near Malelane

Nelspruit Golf Course
Tel: 013-744 0952
Email: nelspgc@mweb.co.za
URL: www.nelspruitgolfclub.co.za

White River Golf Course
Tel: 013-751 3781
Email: info@whiterivercountryclub.co.za
URL: www.whiterivercountryclub.co.za

Stadiums

Mbombela Stadium
URL: www.fifa.com/worldcup/destination/
stadiums/stadium

The new Mbombela Stadium is built on open land just seven kilometres outside Nelspruit. It was designed to ensure it enjoys a prosperous life beyond the 2010 World Cup as an adaptable, relevant multi-sport entertainment and exhibition venue. With a capacity of 40,000, the stadium will be used for the first and second rounds of the 2010 World Cup.

Jan van Riebeeck Stadium
Tel: 013-656 2647/8
Email: pum@mweb.co.za
Situated in Nelspruit

Culture

Museums

Barberton Museum
Tel: 013-712 4208
URL: www.southafrica.com/mpumalanga/barberton/museum
Opening Time: 09h00
Closing Time: 16h00

Belhaven House Museum
Tel: 013-712 4208
Email: knzolo@nel.mpu.gove.za
URL: www.barberton.info/museum.html
Situated in Barberton

Bethal Museum
Tel: 017-624 3021
URL: www.govanmbeki.gov.za/activitiesp2.htm

Botshabelo Museum
Tel: 0132-43 5020 / 015-516-2082
Situated in Middleburg

Kgodwana Ndebele Village & Museum
Tel: 013-932 0894
URL: www.sahistory.org.za/pages/artsmediaculture
Situated in Kwa Mhlanga

Komatiland Forestry Museum
Tel: 013-764-1058 / 013-764-2071
Situated in Sabie

Krugerhof Museum
Tel: 013-712-4208 / 013-712-4208
Situated in Waterval Onder

Theatres

The Basement Theatre
Tel: 017-634 7577
Email: theatre@lakeumuzi.co.za
URL: www.basementtheatre.co.za
Situated in Secunda

Galleries

Artique Gallerie
Tel: 013-751 1120
Situated in White River

Bank Gallery
Tel: 017-847 0164
Situated in Chrissiesmeer

Cachet Art
Tel: 013-744 9968
Situated in Nelspruit

Curio D'Afrique
Tel: 013-767 1685
Situated in Graskop

Dullstroom Art Gallery
Tel: 013-254 0994
Situated in Dullstroom

Graskop Hotel Gallery of Contemporary Art
Tel: 013-767 1244
Situated in Graskop

Le Gallerie
Tel: 013-767 1093
Situated in Graskop

Mojari Studios
Tel: 013-755 4134
Situated in Nelspruit

Sunlight Art Gallery
Tel: 083-334 2496
Situated in Graskop

The Collectibles Gallery
Tel: 013-767 1673
Situated in Graskop

The White Lily Gallery
Tel: 083-469 4750
Situated in Graskop

The Window Gallery
Tel: 013-767 1364
Situated in Graskop

Van Reenen Art Studio
Tel: 083-267 9757
Situated in Dullstroom

Game and Nature Reserves (including National Parks)

Mpumalanga Parks Board
Tel: 013-759 5300
URL: www.mpumalangaparksboard.com

Mpumalanga Reserves
Barberton Nature Reserve
Blyde River Canyon Nature Reserve
Loskop Dam Nature Reserve
Lydenburg Fisheries and Sterkspruit Nature Reserve
Mabusa Nature Reserve
Mahushe Shongwe Reserve
Mdala Game Reserve

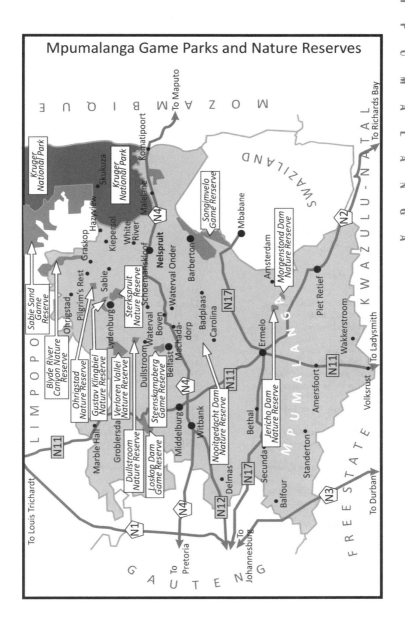

Mpumalanga Game Parks and Nature Reserves

Mkhombo Nature Reserve
Mthethomusha Game Reserve
Nooitgedacht Dam Nature Reserve
Ohrigstad Dam Nature Reserve
Songimvelo Game Reserve
SS Skosana Nature Reserve
Verloren Valei Nature Reserve

South African National Parks
Tel: 012-426 5000
Email: reservations@sanparks.org
URL: www.sanparks.org

SANParks Reserves
Kruger National Park

Other Parks

Exeter Private Game Reserve
Tel: 031-583 2840
URL: http://exeter.krugerpark.co.za/

Gazebo Game Lodge
Tel: 082-492 0696
Email: gazebo@icon.co.za
URL: www.gazebo.co.za

Idube Private Game Reserve
Tel: 011-431 1120
Email: res@lukimbi.com
URL: http://idube.com

Inyati Private Game Reserve
Tel: 011-880 5907
Email: inyatigl@iafrica.com
URL: www.inyati.co.za

Kwa Madwala Private Game Reserve
Tel: 013-792 6700
Email: res@kwamadala.co.za
URL: www.kwamadwala.net

Leopard Hills Private Game Reserve
Tel: 013-735 5142
Email: Duncan@leopardhills.com
URL: www.leopardhills.com

Lion Sands Private Game Reserve
Tel: 011-484 9911
Email: res@lionsands.com
URL: www.lionsands.com

Londolozi Private Game Reserve
Tel: 011-280 6655
URL: www.londlozi.com

Mala Mala Private Game Reserve
Tel: 011-442 267
Email: reservations@malamala.com
URL: www.malamala.com

Sabi Sabi Private Game Reserve
Tel: 011-447 7172
Email: res@sabisabi.com
URL: www.sabisabi.com

Sabi Sands Private Game Reserve
Tel: 021-424 1037
URL: www.sabisands.co.za

Savanna Private Game Reserve
Tel: 013-751 2474
URL: www.sa-venues.com/visit/savanna/

Ulusaba Safari Camp
Tel: 011-325 4405
Email: enquiries@ulusaba.virgin.com
URL: www.ulusaba.virgin.com

Entertainment

Emnotweni Casino
casino
Tel: 013-757 4300
URL: http://emnotweni.tsogosun.co.za
Situated in Nelspruit

Graceland Hotel Casino & Country Club
casino
Tel: 017-620 1000
URL: www.graceland.co.za
Situated in Secunda

Stables
nightclub
Tel: 013-755 4697
Situated in Nelspruit

The Mayfly
cocktail lounge
Tel: 013-254 0999
Situated in Dullstroom

The Ridge Casino
casino
Tel: 013-655 9399
URL: http://theridge.tsogosun.co.za
Situated in Witbank

Annual Events

Alfred Dunhill Championship
Tel: 011-347 1338
URL: www.alfdun.co.za
Held in Nelspruit every December

Dullstroom Arts Festival
Tel: 013-254 0020
URL: www.sa-venues.com
Held every December

InniBos Kunstefees
Tel: 013-741 5294
URL: www.innibos.co.za
Held in Nelspruit every September

Jock Cycle Classic
Tel: 011-707 2800
URL: www.cycletour.co.za
Held in Nelspruit every July

Lowveld Show
URL: www.lowshow.co.za
Held in Nelspruit every March

Lydenburg Kwena Festival MTB
Tel: 083-441 7782
URL: www.mpumalangahighlands.travel/
    event/496912001

Sabie Experience
Tel: 011-462 0016
URL: www.sabiexperience.co.za
Held every December

Sundwala Mankele MTB Challenge
Tel: 082-774 5821
URL: www.adventurezone.co.za
Held in Nelspruit every August

The Big Induna Mountain Bike Race
Tel: 013-737 8308
URL: www.indunaadventures.com
Held in Hazyview every May

Tonteldoos Country Festival
Tel: 082-565 3402
URL: www.adventurezone.co.za
Held in Dullstroom every April

Uplands Festival
Tel: 013-759 7707
URL: www.uplands-festival.co.za
Held in White River every May

WESSA Living Green Expo
Tel: 082-900 1453
URL: www.wessa.org.za/living_green_expo
Held in Nelspruit every August

Shopping www.mallguide.co.za

Acornhoek Shopping Centre
Tel: 013-753 2624
Situated in Hazyview

Besterbrown Shopping Centre
Tel: 013-753 2624
Situated in Nelspruit

Ermelo Mall
Tel: 012-401 4830
Situated in Ermelo

Highveld Mall
Tel: 013-692 6010
Situated in Witbank

Mall@Emba
Tel: 017-685 2437
Situated in Secunda

Riverside Mall
Tel: 013-757 0080
Situated in Nelspruit

Secunda Mall
Tel: 017-634 1156
Situated in Secunda

Restaurants

Dullstroom

2 Chefs Bistro
Cuisine: Continental
Tel: 013-254 0920
Address: Willowbrook Centre, Main Street

Canimambo Restaurant
Cuisine: Portuguese
Tel: 013-254 0977
Address: 84 Naledi Street

Fibs
Cuisine: Cosmopolitan
Tel: 013-254 0059
Address: 567 Voortrekker Street

Harrie's Pancakes
Cuisine: Pancakes
Tel: 013-254 0801
Address: Main Road

Mrs Simpson's Restaurant
Cuisine: South African
Tel: 013-254 0088
Address: 197 Teding Street, cnr
  Van Berkhould Street

Peebles Country Retreat
Cuisine: South African
Tel: 013-254 8000
Address: cnr Bosman & Lyon Cachet Street

Pickles & Things
Cuisine: Bistro
Tel: 013-254 0115
Address: Naledi Drive

Plat du Jour
Cuisine: French
Tel: 072-320 5370
Address: Naledi Drive

The Duck & Trout
Cuisine: Fine Dining
Tel: 013-254 0421
Address: Main Road

The Dullstroom Inn
Cuisine: Pub
Tel: 013-254 0071
Address: cnr Chunky Masango &
  Oranje Nassau Street

The Flying Dutchman
Cuisine: Steakhouse
Tel: 013-254 0939
Address: The Gables Shopping Centre,
  Naledi Street

Nelspruit
10 On Russel
Cuisine: Contemporary
Tel: 013-755 2376
Address: 10 Russel Street

Chez Vincent
Cuisine: French
Tel: 013-744 1146
Address: 56 Ferreira Street

Costa do Sol
Cuisine: Contemporary
Tel: 013-752 6382
Address: Paul Kruger Street

Makulu Manzi
Cuisine: South African
Tel: 013-757 0396
Address: Botanical Gardens Lowveld

Old Joe's Kaia
Cuisine: South African
Tel: 013-733 3045
Address: N4, Schoemanskloof

Orange
Cuisine: Fusion
Tel: 013-744 9507
Address: 4 Du Preez Street

Parillo's
Cuisine: International
Tel: 013-752 7680
Address: General Dan Pienaar Street

Rabbit & Rooster
Cuisine: Portuguese
Tel: 082-697 0711
Address: R37 Sabie-Lydenburg Road

Summerfields Kitchen
Cuisine: Fine Dining
Tel: 013-737 6500
Address: R536 Hazyview-Sabie Road

Trattoria Stefano
Cuisine: Italian
Tel: 013-744 9310
Address: Steiltes Shopping Centre,
  Aurora Drive

Chains and Franchises

Cape Town Fish Market
URL: www.ctfm.co.za

Cappuccino's
URL: www.cappuccinos.co.za

Dros
URL: www.dros.co.za

Mugg & Bean
URL: www.themugg.com

Ocean Basket
URL: www.oceanbasket.co.za

Panarotti's
URL: www.panarottis.com

Spur
URL: www.spur.co.za

Wimpy
URL: www.wimpy.co.za

Accommodation

www.mpumalanga-venues.co.za
www.safarinow.com/destinations/mpumalanga
www.mpumalanga-africaninvitation.co.za
www.sa-venues.com/mpumalanga_accommodation
www.kwathabeng.co.za/.../accommodation
www.wheretostay.co.za
http://mpumalanga.hotelguide.co.za
www.countryroads.co.za/mpumalanga-accommodation
www.mpumalangainfo.co.za
www.mpumalanga-accommodation.co.za

Nelspruit

Hotels

Emnotweni Sun Hotel
Tel: 013-757 3000
Email: contactus@southernsun.com
URL: www.southernsun.com

Express by Holiday Inn Nelspruit
Tel: 013-757 0000
URL: www.hiexpress.com

Graskop Hotel
Tel: 013-767 1244
Email: graskophotel@mweb.co.za
URL: www.graskophotel.co.za

Hotel Formula 1
Tel: 013-741 4490
URL: www.hotelformula1.co.za

Mercure Hotel
Tel: 013-741 4222
Email: H2918@accor.com
URL: www.mercure.com

Orion Hotel Promenade
Tel: 013-753 3000
Email: promenade@promendaehotel.co.za
URL: www.oriongroup.co.za

Lodges

Ngongoni Private Game Lodge
Tel: 084-081 8928
Email: info@unlimitedescapes.co.za
URL: www.ngongoni.co.za

B&Bs, Guest Houses, Self-catering

Alkmaar Farmstay
Tel: 013-733 3029
Email: info@alkmaarfarmstay.co.za
URL: www.alkmaarfarmstay.co.za

Alpenland Guest House
Tel: 013-744 9819
Email: cobus@gpmm.co.za
URL: www.alpenland.co.za

Brush Cherry House
Tel: 013-752 2018
Email: brushcherry@webmail.co.za

Galla Manor Guest House
Tel: 013-744 1882
Email: info@gallamanor.co.za
URL: www.gallamanor.co.za

Jorn's Gastehaus
Tel: 013-744 1894
Email: mwjorn@mweb.co.za
URL: www.jorns.co.za

Kavinga
Tel: 013-755 3193
Email: kavinga@mpu.co.za
URL: www.kavinga.co.za

Loeries Call
Tel: 013-744 1251
Email: info@loeriescall.co.za
URL: www.loeriescall.co.za

Matopos Guest House
Tel: 013-753 3549
Email: matopos@mweb.co.za
URL: www.matopos.co.za

Nomanini Guest House
Tel: 013-741 3633

Phumeleni Guest House
Tel: 013-744 9301
Email: phumelani@mweb.co.za

Rose & Crown
Tel: 013-744 1877
Email: suzy@soft.co.za
URL: www.rose-and-crown.co.za

Sunset Manor
Tel: 013-745 7972
Email: sunsetmanor@lantic.net
URL: www.sunsetmanor.co.za

The Arches
Tel: 013-741 4937
URL: http://thearches.co.za

Camping

Safubi River Lodge & Caravan Park
Tel: 013-741 3253
Email: info@safubi.co.za
URL: www.safubi.co.za

Other
Hotels

Graceland Hotel
Tel: 0860 777 900
Email: reservations@graceland.co.za
URL: www.gracelands.co.za
Situated in Secunda

Hotel Formula 1
Tel: 013-692 4387
URL: www.hotelformula1.co.za
Situated in Witbank

Protea Hotel
Tel: 0861-119 000
Email: info@proteahotals.com
URL: www.proteahotels.com

Royal Hotel Pilgrim's Rest
Tel: 013-768 1100
URL: www.royal-hotel.co.za
Situated in Pilgrim's Rest

Sanbonani Resort Hotel
Tel: 013-737 5600
Email: info@sanbonani.com
URL: www.sanbonani.com
Situated in Hazyview

Lodges

Buhala Game Lodge
Tel: 013-792 4372
Email: buhala@telkomsa.net
URL: www.buhala.co.za
Situated in Malelane

Djuma Game Reserve
Tel: 013-735 5118
Email: djuma@djuma.co.za
URL: www.djuma.co.za
Situated in Hluvukani

Elephant Walk Retreat
Tel: 013-793 7543
Email: enquiries@elephantwalk.co.za
URL: www.elephantwalk.co.za
Situated near the Crocodile Bridge Gate to
    the Kruger National Park

Hannah Game Lodge
Tel: 013-238 8100
Email: info@hannahlodge.co.za
URL: www.hannahlodge.co.za
Situated in Ohrigstad

Hoyo Hoyo Tsonga Lodge
Tel: 013-735 8915
Email: bookings@imbali.com
URL: www.hoyohoyo.co.za
Situated in Skukuza

Iketla Lodge
Tel: 013-238 8900
Email: relax@iketla.com
URL: www.iketla.com
Situated near Ohrigstad

Jock Safari Lodge
Tel: 041-407 1000
Email: reservations@mantiscollection.com
URL: www.jocksafarilodge.co.za
Situated in the Kruger National Park

Komati Gorge Lodge
Tel: 017-843 3920
Email: komatigorge@telkomsa.net
URL: www.komatigorge.co.za
Situated in Carolina

Lukimbi Safari Lodge
Tel: 011-431 112
Email: res@lukimbi.co.za
URL: www.lukimbi.co.za
Situated in the Kruger National Park

Malapo Country Lodge
Tel: 013-235 1056
Email: info@malapo.co.za
URL: www.malapo.co.za
Situated in Lydenburg

Olifants River Lodge
Tel: 013-243 9401
Email: olirivlo@mweb.co.za
URL: www.olifants-river-lodge.co.za
Situated in the Olifants River Valley

Shishangeni Game Lodge
Tel: 013-735 3300
Email: shishangeni@mweb.co.za
URL: www.shishangeni.com
Situated inside the Kruger National Park

Stonecutters Lodge
Tel: 013-235 4225
Email: cobbles@mweb.co.za
URL: www.stonecutters.co.za
Situated in Lydenburg

B&Bs, Guest Houses & Self-catering

Ambience Inn
Tel: 013-751 1951
Email: ambience@lantic.net
URL: www.ambienceinn.co.za
Situated in White River

Charilo Guest House
Tel: 013-254 0250
Email: charilo@lantic.net
URL: www.charilo.co.za
Situated in Dullstroom

Hippo Hollow Country Estate
Tel: 013-737 7752
Email: reservations@hippohollow.co.za
URL: www.hippohollow.co.za
Situated in Hazyview

KU DE TA
Tel: 013-751 1773
Email: live@kudeta.co.za
URL: www.kudeta.co.za
Situated in White River

Log Cabin & Settlers Village
Tel: 013-767 1974
Email: llprod@global.co.za
URL: www.logcabin.co.za
Situated in Graskop

Tours

Balloon Over Africa
hot-air balloon tours
Tel: 013-737 6950

Black Pot Safaris
self-drive safaris
Tel: 013-733 3124

Bush Unlimited
tailor-made tours
Tel: 082-965 3102

Bushveld Safaris, Tours & Transfers
safaris and tailor-made tours
Tel: 013-750 1155

Clivima Tours
tailor-made tours
Tel: 072-406 3959

Earth Africa Tours & Safaris
South Africa & wildlife tours
Tel: 013-744 0781

Emoyeni Tours & Lodge
South Africa tours
Tel: 013-744 9551

Goldenoldies Tours
Tel: 082-697 6058

Hlakaniphani XPS Tours
South Africa tours
Tel: 076-482 1118

Katambori Safaris
tailor-made tours
Tel: 013-751 3339

Khanya Tours
South Africa tours
Tel: 013-796 1618

L & J Tours
tailor-made tours
Tel: 013-744 7169

Regent Exclusive Safaris
tailor-made tours
Tel: 082-490 8202

Vula Tours
tailor-made tours
Tel: 013-741 2238

Car Rentals

Avis
Tel: 0861-021 111
URL: www.avis.co.za

Budget
Tel: 0861-016 622
URL: www.budget.co.za

Click Car Hire
Tel: 021-551 9515
URL: www.sa-venues.com/explore/
  clickcarhire/

Drive South Africa
Tel: 0860-000 060
URL: www.drivesouthafrica.co.za

Europcar
Tel: 0861-131 000
URL: www.europcar.co.za

First
Tel: 0861-011 323
URL: www.firstcarrental.co.za

Hertz
Tel: 0861-600 136
URL: www.hertz.co.za

Tempest Car Hire
Tel: 0861-836 7378
URL: www.tempestcarhire.co.za

Emergency Numbers

Ambulance / Fire
10177

Cell phone Emergency Number
112

National Tourism Information & Safety Line
083-113 2345

Police Emergency number
10111

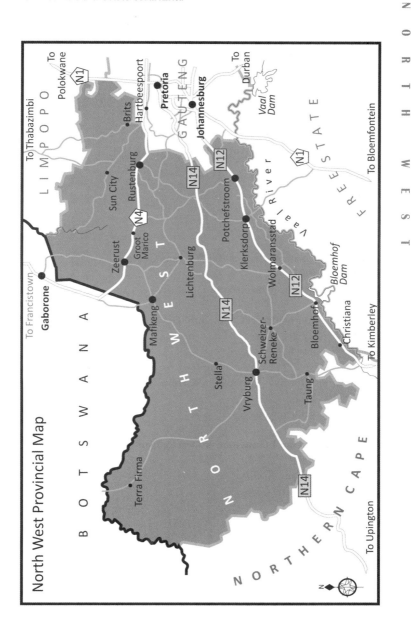

North West Provincial Map

North West

Tourism Information Offices

Hartbeespoort Tourism Bureau
Tel: 012-253 0266
Email: webmaster@hartbeespoortdam.com
URL: www.hartbeespoortdam.com

North West Tourism
Tel: 018-386 1225
Email: info@tourismnorthwest.co.za
URL: www.tourismnorthwest.co.za

Sun City Information Office at the Welcome Centre
Tel: 014-557 1907
Email: infodesksunc@mweb.co.za

Pilanesberg Information & Community Development Centre
Tel: 014-555 5362
Email: tidcpberg@mweb.co.za

Potchefstroom Tourism Information & Development Centre
Tel: 018-293 1611
Email: tidcpotch@mweb.co.za

Rustenberg Tourism Information & Development Centre
Tel: 014-597 0904
Email: tidcrust@mweb.co.za

Top 10

Ann van Dyk Cheetah Centre
(De Wildt Cheetah & Wildlife Trust)
Tel: 012-504 9906/7/8
Email: cheetah@dewildt.co.za
URL: www.dewildt.co.za

De Wildt has recently been renamed the Ann van Dyk Cheetah Centre after the woman who has devoted her life to the preservation of the species. This centre is located 15 minutes northeast of Hartbeespoort Dam on the northern side of the Magaliesberg Mountains. The centre offers guided tours where visitors will not only learn about cheetah but also caracal, the African wild dog … and cat! The Shingwedzi Ranch, situated 58km from Bela Bela (Warmbaths) and only 160km (about 2 hours) north of Pretoria, boasts a panoramic view of the Hoekberge, the foothills of the majestic Waterberg range. Vegetation is broad-leaf bushveld at its best, game is varied and plentiful and the area is malaria-free. Accommodation consists of three unique, completely private, thatched chalets, each with its own lapa, braai and pool. Tastefully furnished (including electric fans) the chalets are fully equipped for self-catering.

Aardklop Festival
Tel: 018-294 7509
Email: admin@aardklop.co.za
URL: www.aardklop.co.za
Held in Potchefstroom

120 kilometres southwest of Jo'burg, Potchefstroom is a small, educational town, much like Grahamstown (which also hosts an annual arts festival). Potch is predominantly an Afrikaans-speaking town; and the people are hospitable and friendly and will go out of their way to speak English to those who don't *praat die taal* (speak the language). This arts festival is held for a week in the latter half of the year (28 September–2 October 2010) and showcases a multitude of theatre genres and music (everything from one man in a pub to full orchestral stuff and rock concerts). Being an Afrikaans town the food stalls are to

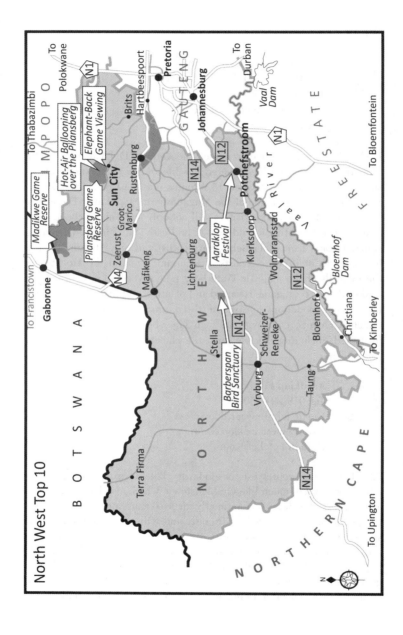

North West Top 10

die for; the *volk* love to eat and cook in equal measures so the culinary delights one can grab between shows are endless. Even the boarding schools open their doors to offer additional accommodation so if you're lucky and get a bed at Potch Girls High you may even be sleeping in my old dorm. The festival is lively, friendly and showcases the local arts scene like few other festivals in South Africa.

Barberspan Bird Sanctuary
Tel: 053-948 1854
Email: barbersp@lantic.net
URL: www.tourismnorthwest.co.za/barberspan
Opening Time: Daily: 06h00
Closing Time: Daily: 18h00
Tariffs: Adults: R25; Children and pensioners: R10

The Barberspan Bird Sanctuary is a huge 2,000-hectare body of water located between Delareyville and Sannieshof. The reserve is a pioneer in ornithological research. Bird Life South Africa has declared it an important national birding site. Given then that it is also a RAMSAR Convention-accredited Wetland of International Importance for migratory birds and waterfowl, it is well worth a visit—365 bird species have been recorded. The pans, which are fed intermittently by the Harts River, are an important refuge for waterfowl which arrive in numbers from the surrounding pans to wait out the dry season. Barberspan and the adjacent Leeupan, connected by a shallow channel, are over 4,000 hectares in extent, comprising shallow alkaline waters ideally suited to the many species which favour such conditions. The area around Barberspan is undulating grassland and agricultural land, leaving the pans largely undisturbed. Certain areas are designated for anglers to enjoy excellent fishing opportunities for carp, barbel and yellowfish. Boating is offered and a number of photographer's hides are available. To reach Barberspan take any number of routes to Delareyville. The pans are located 17km northwest of Delareyville on the N14 to Sannieshof, 307km from Johannesburg—an easy 3-hour drive.

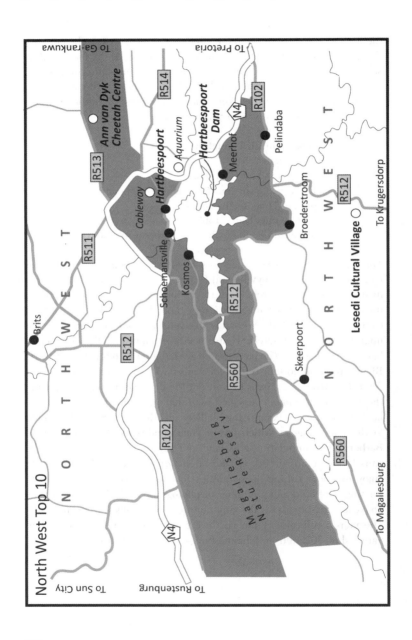

North West Top 10

North West

Hartbeespoort

Hartbeespoort Dam

Ann van Dyk Cheetah Centre

Aquarium

Cableway

Meerhof

Pelindaba

Broederstroom

Schoemansville

Kosmos

Skeerpoort

Lesedi Cultural Village

Brits

Magaliesberge Nature Reserve

R514
R513
R102
R512
R511
R512
R560
R560

N4

To Ga-rankuwa

To Pretoria

To Krugersdorp

To Magaliesburg

To Rustenburg

To Sun City

Elephant-Back Game Viewing
Tel: 014-552 5020
Email: adventures@gametrac.co.za
URL: www.pilanesbergelephantback.co.za

In terms of wildlife, game viewing and adventure you'd go far to beat this experience. These elephants are mostly orphans or young adults from broken homes—herds that have been poached to near extinction. They come into this peaceful environment and into the care of selfless people where they are trained, not as elephants in the Far East, to allow us to ride them. Sitting atop a full-grown elephant is a humbling experience and yet it is not in the least bit frightening. Before mounting the ellies, you are introduced to them. They come up close, smelling you out gently and tugging at your clothing. You can stroke their massive heads and their inquisitive trucks. Their skin is foreign to the touch but not unpleasant. Each one is distinct from the next, with its own personality entirely. Riding them is a truly meditative experience; the movement is gentle yet expansive. Afterwards one gets to feed them and thank them, another completely mind-blowing feeling when you place your hand inside the biggest mouth you've ever seen—close up that is. This experience is about the elephants.

Hartbeespoort Dam
Tel: 012-253 1567
Email: webmaster@hartbeespoortdam.com
URL: www.hartbeespoortdam.com

Surrounded by the Magaliesberg Mountains, Hartbeespoort Dam is very popular for weekend getaways or day trips. All water sports are enjoyed, including para-sailing, windsurfing, water and jet skiing. For the more adventurous there is paragliding, hang-gliding or hot-air ballooning. There is an aquarium, a private zoo with a snake park, an elephant sanctuary (different from the Pilanesberg sanctuary), a monkey sanctuary and a predator park. Explore and discover the scenic beauty, entertaining attractions, fun activities and places of interest in this area. Situated only an hour from Johannesburg it is an easy getaway with craft markets and a host of eating spots along the way.

Hot-Air Ballooning over the Pilanesberg
Tel: 014-552 5020
Email: balloon@gametrac.co.za
URL: www.airtrackers.co.za

Airtrackers operates from one of the most scenic and breathtakingly beautiful hot-air balloon locations in the world, the Pilanesberg National Park. Airtrackers is presently the only hot-air balloon company in southern Africa that permanently operates from within a National Park. This gives them exclusivity to fly in this unique location, viewing the Big Five, namely lion, leopard, rhino, elephant and buffalo, from a completely new perspective. Trips are offered daily (weather permitting of course, no fun being drizzled on at that height).

Lesedi Cultural Village
Tel: 087-940 9933
URL: www.lesedi.com

Established in 1993 to provide an authentic showcase for the cultures of some of the better-known South African tribes, representatives of these tribes facilitated the design of the villages to ensure a historically accurate portrayal of their cultures, highlighting their traditional way of life. Members of these communities live at Lesedi and continue to breathe life into their fascinating way of life. Situated within the Cradle of Humankind, a visit to the North West is incomplete without a visit to Lesedi—the cradle of living Africa. In an informative and entertaining way, Lesedi provides the visitor with a better understanding of the rich background of the traditional peoples of South Africa, offering guests accommodation, conference facilities and fine dining, all to enhance the overall experience.

Madikwe Game Reserve
Tel: 018-350 9931
Email: madikweadmin@telkomsa.net
URL: www.madikwe-game-reserve.co.za

The Madikwe Game Reserve, situated against the Botswanan border, 90 kilometres north of Zeerust, just three hours' drive from both Johannesburg and Pretoria, is now one of South Africa's premier safari destinations. Madikwe is a Big Five game reserve covering some 75,000 hectares and it is one of the largest game reserves in South Africa. The rich diversity of vegetation ensures a wide range of game and the topography offers ideal game-viewing opportunities.

Pilanesberg National Park
Tel: 014-555 1600
Email: pilanesberg@nwptb.co.za
URL: www.pilanesberg-game-reserve.co.za

Visitors are offered many opportunities to experience the wonders of Pilanesberg. There are nearly 200 kilometres of excellent-quality roads for either self-drives or guided drives with professional guides. Numerous hides and scenic picnic sites enable the tourist to experience 'out-of-the-car' unspoiled bushveld. The area is fringed by three concentric ridges or rings of hills—this formation rises from the surrounding plains like a bubble: ancient, even by geological standards, this extinct volcano is the most perfect example of an alkaline ring complex. A number of rare (but not necessarily canonically important) minerals occur in the park. Pilanesberg rates high among the world's outstanding geological phenomena, surviving eons of erosion and standing high above the surrounding bushveld plains. The early presence of man can be seen in the numerous Stone and Iron Age sites that are scattered throughout the park.

Sun City Resort
Tel: 014-557 1000
URL: www.suninternational.com

Sun City, unique in the context of world resorts, with a combination of features unmatched anywhere, draws thousands of visitors each year to its four top-quality hotels, a Vacation Club plus magnificent sporting and recreational facilities including two world-class golf courses, the magical Lost City water-park and The Valley of the Waves. Only 187 kilometres from Johannesburg, the resort, situated in the Bushveld, is surrounded by the imposing mountains of the Pilanesberg. The Sun City Resort has been awarded Gold Classification by the Heritage Programme for being an environmentally friendly destination that is committed to the principles of sustainable and responsible environmental practice. Not bad considering this is essentially a casino resort.

Activities

Adventure Activities

Airtrack Adventures (Sun City)
Tel: 014-552 1552
URL: www.tourismnorthwest.co.za

Dome Adventures
Tel: 018-291 1569
Email: info@domeadventures.co.za
URL: www.domeadventures.co.za

Go Vertical
Tel: 082-731 4696
Email: info@govertical.co.za
URL: www.gotrekking.co.za

Magaliesberg Canopy Tours
Tel: 014-535 0150
Email: info@magaliescanopytour.co.za
URL: www.magaliescanopytour.co.za

Miracle Waters Scuba Resort
Tel: 082-062 1717 / 071-699 7291
Email: miraclewaters@vodamail.co.za
URL: www.miraclewaters.co.za

Outdoor Adventure Centre—Gametrackers
Tel: 014-552 5020
URL: www.gametrac.co.za

Zip 2000—Extreme Adventure Slide
Tel: 014-557 1544
Email: time@zip2000.com
URL: www.zip2000.co.za

Outdoor Activities

Bokamoso Bicycle Project
Tel: 083-474 6801
Email: info@voluntours.co.za
URL: www.voluntours.co.za

Segway South Africa Tours
Tel: 014-557 4052
Email: jonathan@segway.co.za
URL: www.segway.co.za

Sun City Waterworld
Tel: 014-552 1553
Email: info@suncitywaterworld.com
URL: www.suncitywaterworld.com

Sport

Brits Golf Club
Tel: 012-250 2522
Email: britsgolf@lantic.co.za
URL: www.golfoncourse.co.za
Situated in Brits

Gary Player Country Club
Tel: 014-557 1245
URL: http://garyplayer.com
Situated in Sun City

Hunters Rest Golf Club
Tel: 014-537 8300
Email: hunters@mweb.co.za
URL: www.huntersrest.co.za
Situated just outside Rustenburg

Leopard Park Golf Course
Tel: 018-386 3086
Email: admin@leopardpark.co.za
URL: www.leopardpark.co.za
Situated in Mafikeng

Lost City Golf Course
Tel: 014-557 1246
URL: www.aboutsuncity.com/golf.htm
Situated in Sun City

Pecanwood Golf & Country Club
Tel: 012-244 8000
URL: www.pecanwoodgolf.co.za
Situated at Hartbeespoort Dam

Potchefstroom Country Club
Tel: 018-293 0210
Situated in Potchefstroom

Rustenburg Golf Club
Tel: 014-597 1814
Email: rustgolf@mweb.co.za
URL: http://golf.ifm2.com/rustenburg
Situated in Rustenburg

Stadiums

Royal Bafokeng Stadium
URL: www.sa2010.gov.za/node/568
Situated in Rustenburg

Reflecting natural features with its saddle shape, the Royal Bafokeng is set to play an important role, and is used more for soccer matches than for rugby. The stadium is one of the ten stadiums to host the 2010 World Cup soccer tournament. Its capacity has been increased from 38,000 to 42,000.

Olen Park
Tel: 018-297-5304/5
Email: nwr-unie@iafrica.com
Situated in Potchefstroom

Mmabatho Stadium
Tel: 018-392-4295
Situated in Mmabatho

Culture

Museums

Ampie Bosman Cultural History Museum
Tel: 018-462 3546
Email: museum@lichtenburg.co.za
Opening Time: Tuesday to Saturday: 10h00
Closing Time: Tuesday to Thursday: 17h00; Friday: 16h00; Saturday: 12h00
Situated in Lichtenburg

Diggers Museum
Tel: 018-632 5051
Email: museum@lichtenburg.co.za
Opening Time: Monday to Friday: 10h00 and again at 14h00
Closing Time: Monday to Friday: 13h00 and again at 16h00
Situated in Lichtenburg

Goetz Fleischack Museum
Tel: 018-299 5031
Opening Time: Monday to Friday: 09h00 and again at 14h00
Closing Time: Monday to Friday: 13h00 and again at 16h30
Situated in Potchefstroom

Klerksdorp Museum
Tel: 018-462 3546
URL: www.koshinfo.co.za/culture/museum/index.html
Opening Time: Monday to Friday: 10h00 and again at 14h00; Saturday: 09h30;
   Sunday and Public Holidays: 14h00
Closing Time: Monday to Friday: 13h00 and again at 16h30; Saturday: 12h00;
   Sunday and Public Holidays: 17h00

Lesedi Cultural Village
Tel: 087-940 9933
Email: marketing@lesedi.com
URL: www.lesedi.com
Situated in the Cradle of Humankind area (R512 to Lanseria)

Mafikeng Museum
Tel: 018-381 6102
Opening Time: Monday to Friday: 08h00; Saturday 10h00
Closing Time: Monday to Friday: 16h00; Saturday: 12h30

Mapoch Ndebele Village
Tel: 083-474 6801 / 082-441 2749
Email: info@ndebelevillage.co.za
URL: www.ndebelevillage.co.za
Opening Time: Daily: 10h00
Closing Time: Daily: 16h00
Situated in Klipgat

North West Agricultural Museum
Tel: 081-632 5051
Email: museum@lichtenburg.co.za
Opening Time: Monday to Friday: 10h00 and again at 14h00
Closing Time: Monday to Friday: 13h00 and again at 16h00
Situated in Lichtenburg

Paul Kruger Country House Museum
Tel: 014-573 3218
Situated in Potchefstroom

Potchefstroom Museum
Tel: 018-299 5022
Opening Time: Monday to Friday: 09h00 and again at 14h00; Saturday: 09h00;
   Sunday 14h30
Closing Time: Monday to Thursday: 13h00 and again at 19h00; Friday: 13h00
   and again at 16h30; Saturday: 13h00; Sunday: 17h00

President Pretorius Museum
Tel: 018-299 5036
Opening Time: Monday to Friday: 09h00 and again at 14h00
Closing Time: Monday to Friday: 13h00 and again at 16h30
Situated in Potchefstroom

Rainbow Cultural Village
Tel: 012-258 0333
Email: lesedi@pixie.co.za
Situated at Hartbeespoort Dam

Taung Skull Heritage Site
URL: www.tourismnorthwest.co.za/taung_heritage/index.html
Situated at Buxton Quarry

Totius House Museum
Tel: 018-299 5046
Opening Time: Monday to Friday: 09h00 and again at 14h00
Closing Time: Monday to Friday: 13h00 and again at 16h30
Situated in Potchefstroom

Galleries

Adlou Art Gallery
Tel: 012-253 0520
Email: info@adlou.co.za
URL: www.adlou.co.za
Situated at Hartbeespoort Dam

Christiaan Nice Art Gallery
Tel: 012-259 1287
Situated at Hartbeespoort Dam

Dietmar Wiening Gallery
Tel: 012-205 1193
Email: lesley@dietmarwiening.com
URL: www.dietmarwiening.com
Situated at Hartbeespoort Dam

Hartbeespoort Art Gallery
Tel: 012-253 2915
Situated at Hartbeespoort Dam

Jo Roos Studio Gallery
Tel: 082-292 8581
Email: joroosgallery@gmail.com
URL: www.icon.co.za/~joroos/
Situated in the Brits District

Kosmos Art Gallery
Tel: 012-253 1727
Situated in Kosmos

Waterfall Gallery
Tel: 014-537 3320
Situated in Rustenburg

Willem Annandale Art Gallery
Tel: 018-632 5051
Situated in Lichtenburg

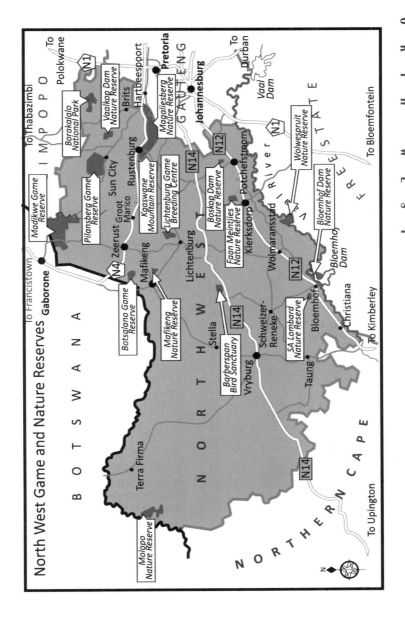

North West Game and Nature Reserves

Game and Nature Reserves (including National Parks)

North West Parks
URL: www.tourismnorthwest.co.za

North West Parks Reserves
Barberspan
Bloemhof Dam
Borakalalo
Boskop Dam
Botsalano
Madikwe
Mafikeng
Molopo
Kgaswane
SA Lombard
Vaalkop Dam
Wolwespruit

South African National Parks
Tel: 012-426 5000
Email: reservations@sanparks.org
URL: www.sanparks.org

SANParks Reserves
Marakele National Park

Other Parks

Bloemhof Dam Nature Reserve
Tel: 053-433 1706
Email: bloemhofdam@cybertrade.co.za
URL: www.tourismnorthwest.co.za

Botsalano Game Reserve
Tel: 018-381 8900
Email: mafgr@mweb.co.za
URL: www.tourismnorthwest.co.za

Kgaswane Mountain Reserve
Tel: 014-533 2050
Email: marcusl@mweb.co.za
URL: www.tourismnorthwest.co.za

Mafikeng Game Reserve
Tel: 018-381 5611
Email: Mafgr@mweb.co.za
URL: www.tourismnorthwest.co.za

Molopo Game Reserve
Tel: 072-596 0945
Email: molopo@nwptb.co.za
URL: www.tourismnorthwest.co.za

SA Lombard Nature Reserve
Tel: 053-433 1953
URL: www.tourismnorthwest.co.za

Entertainment

Sun City Resort Casinos
casino
Tel: 014-557 1000
URL: www.suninternational.com/
    Destinations/Resorts/SunCity

The Carousel
casino
Tel: 012-718 7777
Email: malefyane.monareng@
    za.suninternational.com
URL: www.suninternational.com/
    Destinations/Casinos/Carousel

Tusk Mmabatho
casino
Tel: 018-389 1111
Email: info@mmabathopalms.co.za
URL: www.mmabathopalms.co.za

Tusk Rio Casino Resort
casino
Tel: 018-469 9100
URL: www.riocasino.co.za

Zanzibar Sports Café
nightclub & bar
Tel: 014-597 3210

Annual Events

Aardklop National Arts Festival
Tel: 018-294 7509
Held in Potchefstroom every September

Adventure Tourism Exhibition
Tel: 014-537 3113
Held in Rustenburg every June

Brightly Coloured Sight
URL: www.sa-venues.com
Held in Potchefstroom every June

Lichtenburg Zebra Zemba Race
Tel: 082-371 1703
URL: www.sa-venues.com
Held in Lichtenburg every November

Magaliesberg Classic Country Festival
Tel: 011-783 4148
URL: www.magfest.co.za
Held in Magaliesberg every September

Nedbank Golf Challenge
URL: www.nedbankgolfchallenge.com
Held in Sun City every December

'Om die dam' Ultra Marathon
URL: www.omdiedam.co.za
Held at Hartbeespoort Dam every March

Oppiewerf Arts & Antiques Fair
Tel: 018-299 8036
URL: www.sa-venues.com
Held in Potchefstroom every May

Posi+ive Festival
URL: www.positivecollection.co.za
Held in Sun City every September

Quilt Festival
URL: www.sa-venues.com
Held in Klerksdorp every August

Rustenburg Show (Agricultural)
Tel: 014-592 1318
Held every May

Shopping www.mallguide.co.za

Flamwood Walk Shopping Centre
Tel: 018-462 6810
Situated in Klerksdorp

Mid Town Mall
Tel: 014-597 2808
Situated in Rustenburg

Mooi Rivier Mall
Tel: 018-293 2004
Email: www.mrmall.co.za
Situated in Potchefstroom

River Walk Shopping Centre
Tel: 018-293 0594
Situated in Potchefstroom

Rustenburg Plaza
Tel: 014-592 6897
Situated in Rustenburg

Sun Village Shoppping Centre
Tel: 014-552 1691
Situated in Sun City

The Crossing
Tel: 018-381 3881
Situated in Mafikeng

Restaurants

Hartbeespoort Dam
AfricanSwiss
Cuisine: South African
Tel: 083-476 0507
Address: Plot 119, Broederstroom

Arendskrantz Restaurant
Cuisine: Fusion
Tel: 012-253 1227
Address: Cable Way, Main Road

Klem
Cuisine: South African
Tel: 012-205 1412
Address: Plot 144, Broederstroom

La Dolce Vita
Cuisine: Italian
Tel: 012-253 5949
Address: 105 Joslyn Street

Leopard Lodge Restaurant
Cuisine: South African
Tel: 012-207 1130
Address: R560 Skeerpoort

The Silver Orange Bistro
Cuisine: South African
Tel: 012-253 2136
Address: Altyd Mooi Farm, off the R512

The Windmill
Cuisine: International
Tel: 012-259 0955
Address: Plaas Jasmyn, Jan Smuts Drive

Mafikeng
Toto's Pizza, Pasta and Burgers
Cuisine: Italian
Tel: 018-381 5891
Address: cnr Nelson Mandela &
    Molopo Road

Welkom Kafee & Restaurant
Cuisine: South African
Tel: 018-381 6138
Address: 46 Stasieweg / Station Road

Potchefstroom
Neptune's Fishmonger
Cuisine: Seafood
Tel: 018-294 3949
Address: Shop 16-18, Cachet Park,
    cnr Steve Biko & Meyer Street

Ribs for Africa
Cuisine: South African
Tel: 018-297 4493
Address: 104 Church Street

Theo's Gourmet Restaurant
Cuisine: International
Tel: 018-293 2412
Address: 76 James Moroka Street

Rustenburg
Majababothle Restaurant
Cuisine: South African
Tel: 014-592 0106
Address: 7 Plein Street

Seafood Tavern
Cuisine: Seafood
Tel: 014-591 6493
Address: 51 Arend Road

Tico Tico Restaurant
Cuisine: Contemporary
Tel: 014-592 4631
Address: 115 Smit Street

Rosita Eating House
Cuisine: South African
Tel: 014-599 1014
Address: Bleskop

The Pulse Bar
Cuisine: Contemporary
Tel: 014-592 5010
Address: 1 Church Street, Midtown Mall

Chains and Franchises

Cape Town Fish Market
URL: www.ctfm.co.za

Cappuccino's
URL: www.cappuccinos.co.za

Cattle Baron
URL: www.cattlebaron.co.za

Dros
URL: www.dros.co.za

Mike's Kitchen
URL: www.mikeskitchen.co.za

Mugg & Bean
URL: www.themugg.com

Ocean Basket
URL: www.oceanbasket.co.za

Panarotti's
URL: www.panarottis.com

Spur
URL: www.spur.co.za

The Brazen Head
URL: www.brazenhead.co.za

The Famous Butcher's Grill
URL: www.butchersgrill.com

Wimpy
URL: www.wimpy.co.za

Accommodation

www.sa-venues.com/nw_province_hotels
www.wheretostay.co.za/nw
www.northwest-venues.co.za
www.safarinow.com/destinations/north-west
www.sleeping-out.co.za/South-Africa-accommodation
www.tourismnorthwest.co.za/accommodation/index
www.stayinsa.co.za/themaps/NorthWest1
http://staynorthwest.co.za
www.south-african-hotels.com/north-west-province-hotels
www.countryroads.co.za/north-west-accommodation

Hotels

Cabanas
Tel: 014-557 1580
URL: www.suninternational.com

Kedar Country Hotel
Tel: 011-950 6000
Email: sales@rali.co.za
URL: www.kedar.co.za

Protea Hotels
Tel: 0861-119 000
URL: www.proteahotels.com

Rustenburg Boutique Hotel
Tel: 014-592 4645
Email: info@rustenburgbh.co.za
URL: www.rustenburgbh.co.za

The Cascades
Tel: 014-557 4850
URL: www.suninternational.com

The Palace of the Lost City at Sun City
Tel: 014-557 4301
URL: www.suninternational.com

The Sun City Hotel
Tel: 014-557 5110
URL: www.suninternational.com

Lodges

Akwaaba Lodge
Tel: 014-592 5321
Email: reservations@akwaabalodge.co.za
URL: www.akwaabalodge.co.za

Bona Bona Game Lodge
Tel: 018-451 1188
Email: info@bonabona.co.za
URL: www.bonabona.co.za

Impodimo Game Lodge
Tel: 018-350 9400
Email: info@impodimo.com
URL: www.impodimo.com

Ivory Tree Game Lodge
Tel: 014-556 8100
Email: francois@anthology.co.za
URL: www.ivorytreegamelodge.com

Kwamahla Lodge
Tel: 012-277 2123
Email: enquiries@kwamahlalodge.co.za
URL: www.kwahmahlalodge.co.za

Kwa Maritane Bush Lodge
Tel: 014-552 5100
Email: kwamaritane@legacyhotels.co.za
URL: www.kwamaritane.co.za

Rothbury Country Lodge
Tel: 012-205 1110
Email: info@rothbury.co.za
URL: www.rothbury.co.za

Thaba Phuti Safari Lodge
Tel: 082-800 3292
Email: info@thabaphuti.com
URL: www.thabaphuti.com

Tshukudu Bush Lodge
Tel: 014-552 6255
Email: tshukudu@legacyhotels.co.za
URL: www.tshukudu.co.za

Willinga Lodge
Tel: 012-253 0032
Email: willinga@mweb.co.za
URL: www.willingalodge.co.za

B&Bs, Guest Houses & Self-catering

Adato Guest House
Tel: 018-294 5244
Email: adato@lantic.net
URL: www.potchefstroom.co.za/adato/

Afri-Chic Guest House
Tel: 014-592 2763
Email: bookings@afri-chic.co.za
URL: www.afri-chic.co.za

African Moon
Tel: 082-921 0482
URL: www.wheretostay.co.za/africanmoon

Birdsong B&B
Tel: 014-592 6800
URL: www.wheretostay.co.za/birdsongbandb

Blue Hills Guest House
Tel: 082-854 3940
Email: info@bluehillslodge.co.za
URL: www.bluehillslodge.co.za

Blue Roan Guest Farm
Tel: 014-577 0237
Email: blueroan@ugo.co.za
URL: www.ugo.co.za/blueroan

Boubou B&B
Tel: 083-457 9954
URL: ww.northwest-venues.co.za/bou-bou

Clindee Chalets
Tel: 014-536 3063
Email: info@clindee.co.za
URL: www.clindee.co.za

Cosy Cottage B&B
Tel: 018-290 5710
Email: cosy@absamail.co.za
URL: www.cosy-cottage.co.za

La Chaumière Guest House
Tel: 012-205 1007
Email: mekruger@absamail.co.za
URL: www.lachaumiere.co.za

Mary's View B&B
Tel: 014-533 3092
Email: anita@marysview.co.za
URL: www.marysview.co.za

North Hills Country House
Tel: 018-468 6416
Email: info@northhills.co.za
URL: www.northhills.co.za

Olive Tree Farm
Tel: 014-577 2601
Email: info@olivetreefarm.co.za
URL: www.olivetreefarm.co.za

Scott's Manor Guest House
Tel: 018-632 0255
URL: www.scottsmanor.co.za

Camping

The Cynthiana Hotel & Caravan Park
Tel: 014-537 2361
Email: cynthiana@telkomsa.net
Situated in Rustenburg

Eastco Resort
Tel: 011-660 9824
Email: liezel@wdbs.co.za
URL: www.eastcomagalies.co.za

Lovers Rock Family Resort
Tel: 014-577 1327
Email: info@loversrock.co.za
URL: www.loversrock.co.za

Magalies River Lodge
Tel: 014-577 1300
Email: ljgrobler@mweb.co.za

Magalies Sleepy River Park
Tel: 014-577 1524
URL: www.magaliessleepyriver.co.za

Makalani
Tel: 012-253 0436
URL: www.hartbeespoortdam.com

Mogobe Camp
Tel: 018-381 5392
Email: kghalagadi@lantic.net
URL: www.tourismnorthwest.co.za

Mountain Sanctuary Park
Tel: 014-534 0114
Email: owen@mountain-sanctuary.co.za
URL: www.mountain-sanctuary.co.za

Rustenburg Kloof
Tel: 014-594 1038
Email: rtbkloof@mweb.co.za
URL: www.rustenburgkloof.co.za

Tours

African Hopper Tours
Tel: 018-469 2016
Email: sales@hoppertours.com
URL: ww.hoppertours.com

Firelight Tours & Safaris
Tel: 082-809 0038
Email: peterm@firelighttours.co.za
URL: www.firelighttours.co.za

Gametrackers Outdoor Adventures
Tel: 014-594 2459
Email: gametrackers@gametrac.co.za
URL: www.gametrac.co.za

Langau Touring
Tel: 014-555 6355
Email: info@lengautours.com
URL: www.lengautours.com

Lathita Expeditions
Tel: 072-221 4106
Email: info@lathita.co.za
URL: www.lathita.co.za

Lethakhu Tours
Tel: 012-541 1482
Email: info@lethakhu.com
URL: www.lethakyu.com

Livingstone Trails
Tel: 082-654 9478
Email: tours@livingstonetrails.co.za
URL: www.livingstonetrails.co.za

Mankwe Heritage Tours & Safaris
Tel: 014-555 7056
Email: mankwesafari@mweb.co.za
URL: www.mankwesafaris.co.za

Nare Travel & Tours
Tel: 014-567 1342
Email: info@naretours.co.za
URL: www.naretours.co.za

Planet Thuso Travel
Tel: 014-555 7883
Email: info@planetthusotravel.co.za
URL: www.planetthusotravel.co.za

Porcupine Tours & Transfers
Tel: 018-299 1812
Email: info@porcupinetours.co.za
URL: www.porcupinetours.co.za

Tautona Safaris
Tel: 014-552 1272
Email: tautonasafaris@telkomsa.net
URL: www.tautonasafaris.co.za

Car Rentals

Avis
Tel: 0861-021 111
URL: www.avis.co.za

Budget
Tel: 0861-016 622
URL: www.budget.co.za

Click Car Hire
Tel: 021-551 9515
URL: www.sa-venues.com/explore/clickcarhire/

Drive South Africa
Tel: 0860-000 060
URL: www.drivesouthafrica.co.za

First
Tel: 0861-011 323
URL: www.firstcarrental.co.za

Hertz
Tel: 0861-600 136
URL: www.hertz.co.za

Europcar
Tel: 0861-131 000
URL: www.europcar.co.za

Tempest Car Hire
Tel: 0861-836 7378
URL: www.tempestcarhire.co.za

Emergency Numbers

Ambulance / Fire
10177

Cell phone Emergency Number
112

National Tourism Information & Safety Line
083-113 2345

Police Emergency number
10111

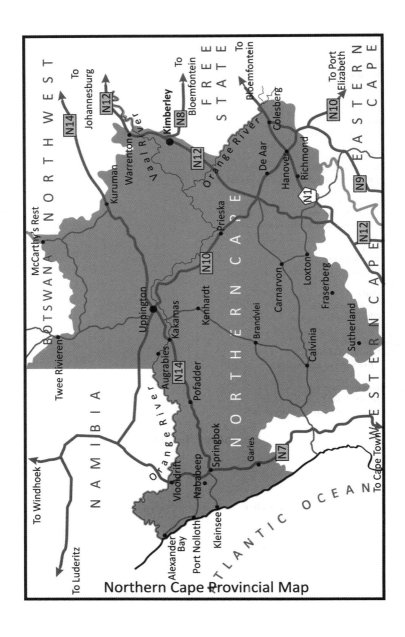

Northern Cape Provincial Map

Northern Cape

Tourism Information Offices

Northern Cape Tourism Authority
Tel: 053-832 2657
Email: northerncapetourism@telkomsa.net
URL: www.northerncape.org.za

Diamond Fields Tourism
Tel: 053-182 7298
Email: northerncapetourism@telkomsa.net
URL: www.northerncape.org.za

Explore Kalahari
Tel: 053-712 0117 / 076-844 9492
Email: info@explorekalahari.com
URL: www.explorekalahari.com/index.html

Karoo Tourism
Tel: 053-631 4176

Karoo Hoogland Tourism Offices
Tel: 023-571 1265
URL: www.karoohoogland.co.za
Email: hooglandtourism@telkomsa.net

Namakwa Tourism
Tel: 027-213 5552
Email: info@namakwa.com
URL: www.namakwa.com

Springbok Regional Tourism
Tel: 027-712 8035 / 6
URL: www.northerncape.org.za/getting_around/towns/Springbok

Top 10

Augrabies Falls National Park
Tel: 054-452 9200
URL: www.sanparks.org/parks/augrabies/

The Nama people, who have lived in the area for centuries and adapted well to its harsh conditions call the falls on the Orange River, *Aukoerebis*, meaning Place of Great Noise, as it plunges 60 metres, downstream of Upington. Picturesque names such as Moon Rock, Ararat and Echo Corner are descriptive of this rocky region. The 55,383 hectares on both the northern and southern sides of the Orange River provide sanctuary to a diversity of species, from the very smallest succulents, birds and reptiles to springbok, gemsbok and the endangered Black rhino. Klipspringer and Kokerboom (quiver trees) stand in stark silhouette against the African sky, silent sentinels in a strangely unique environment where only those that are able to adapt ultimately survive.

Barkly West
Tel: 053-531 0673
URL: www.northerncape.org.za/getting_around/towns/
    Barkly%20West/

This quaint town is situated 32 kilometres northwest of Kimberley on the R21, almost equidistant between Kimberley and Warrenton and just east of the Vaalbos National Park. The discovery of diamonds at Klipdrift on the Vaal River in 1869 drew thousands of prospectors to the area. The area was renamed Barkly West in 1873 after becoming part of the Crown Colony of Griqualand West. Renowned writer Sarah Gertrude Millin grew up here, where her father operated a shop. One of the first towns to be affected by the diamond rush, the district's economy is now driven by stock and irrigation farming and mining.

Northern Cape Top 10

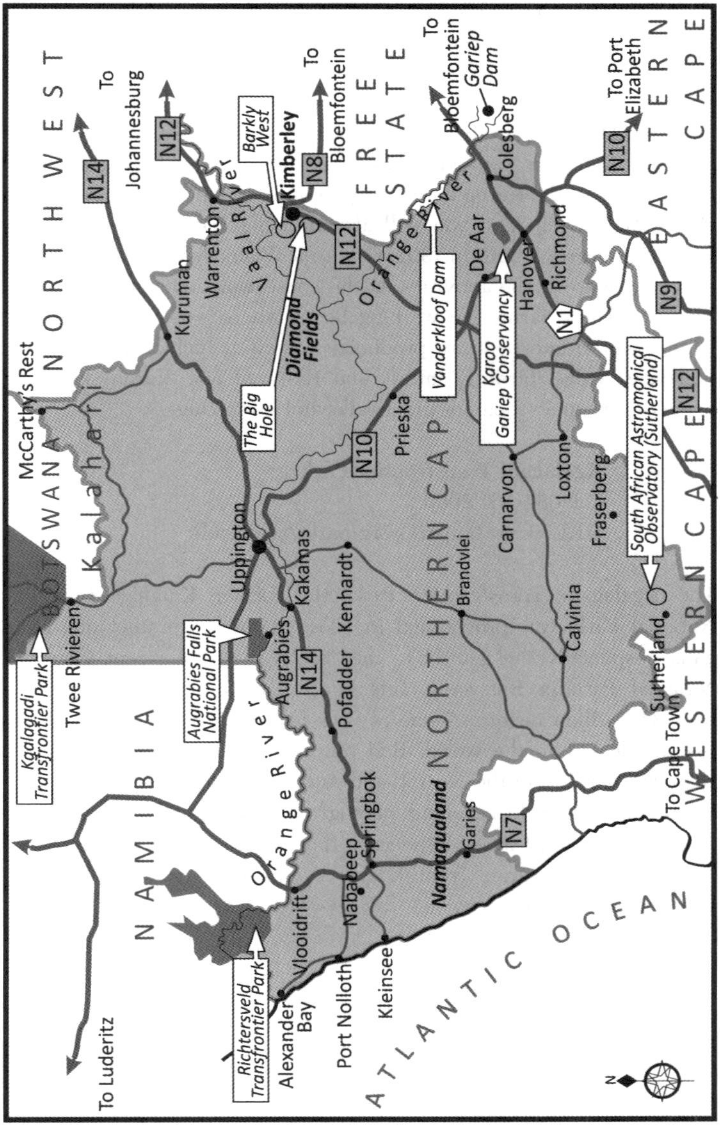

Karoo Gariep Conservancy
Tel: 053-643 0193
Email: karoogariep@mjvn.co.za
URL: www.karoogariep.co.za

On this 12,000-hectare block of land situated in the district of Hanover, you will find two four-star guesthouses—New Holme Karoo Guest Farm, home of the Karoo Hippo Project and Mieliefontein Karoo Guest Farm. At Mieliefontein you will also find the Karoo Gariep abattoir which Ian Ferreira built in 1992. Guests at Wolmade self-catering lodge have access to all the activities on the conservancy, managed by Elma Ferreira. These farms are working farms where wool, ostrich, Karoo lamb, venison and beef are produced. Activities include horse riding, donkycart rides, birding, safaris and fly-ins. Clear Karoo skies also make these venues ideal for nightwalks and stargazing.

Kgalagadi Transfrontier Park
Tel: 054-561 2000
URL: www.sanparks.org/parks/kgalagadi/

The Kgalagadi Transfrontier Park, the former Kalahari Gemsbok National Park, was proclaimed in 1931, mainly to protect migratory game, especially the gemsbok. Together with the adjacent Gemsbok National Park in Botswana, this Peace Park comprises an area of over 3.6 million hectares—one of very few conservation areas of this magnitude left in the world. Red sand dunes, sparse vegetation and the dry riverbeds of the Nossob and Auob boast antelope and predator species and provide excellent photographic opportunities. Kgalagadi is a haven for bird lovers especially those interested in birds of prey. Accommodation varies from luxury camps to the slightly rougher wilderness and rest camps.

Kimberley Diamond Fields
URL: www.sa-venues.com/attractionsnc/diamondfields-attractions.htm

During the world's greatest diamond rush, hordes of prospectors converged on the region, scouring the river banks and sifting soil in their frenetic quest for wealth, with as many as 30,000 diggers labouring all day and far into the night. Although the name Kimberley evokes images of glamour and romance, the diamond heyday was an era of blood, sweat and tears, high stakes and ruthless power struggles. Kimberley developed around the huge hole in the ground, formerly a small hill known as Colesberg Koppie, where diamonds were discovered early in 1871. An observation platform provides a good view of the Big Hole, about 365 metres deep and covering an area close on 15.5 hectares. Between 1871 and 1914, men toiled to remove some 25 million tons of earth from the site, which yielded about 14.5 million carats of diamonds.

Namaqualand
Tel: 027-744 1770
URL: www.namaqualand.com

South of the Richtersveld Conservancy is the world-renowned Namaqualand which stretches from Springbok in the north to just north of the Cederberg, although there are some beautiful flower-spotting areas all the way south to Darling, just outside Cape Town. Since this region is famous for its spring flowers, flower-spotting is the main activity of the region, when the season and the rains and the heavens deem it so. The N7 is the major transport corridor through the area and the main access road for the annual spring flower spectacle. The Namaqualand is home to not only the famed carpets of flowers but also a host of pretty towns, festivals and, farther south, wine farms.

Richtersveld National Park
Tel: 027-831 1506
URL: www.sanparks.org/parks/richtersveld/

The Richtersveld National Park (RNP) is, quite simply, breathtaking. It is a place out of time, out of the ordinary and out of this world. Here, in the most mountainous part of the Richtersveld, the rocks are laid bare. The mountain slopes are starved of soil and the dry desert plains are barren and beautiful in equal measure. You need a 4x4 to drive in this rugged park, and it's really only geared for camping, but recent improvements to the park's infrastructure make it relatively easy to explore. This, South Africa's eighth UNESCO World Heritage Site, includes the National Park and the Richtersveld Conservancy, the latter situated directly south of the National Park.

South African Astronomical Observatory
Bookings are essential
Tel: 023-571 14113
Email: suthbookings@saao.co.za
URL: www.saao.ac.za

The South African Astronomical Observatory (SAAO), situated in Sutherland, is the national centre for optical and infrared astronomy in South Africa. Its prime function is to conduct fundamental research in astronomy and astrophysics by providing a world-class facility and by promoting astronomy and astrophysics in southern Africa. The main telescopes used for research are located at the SAAO observing station near Sutherland, a four-hour drive from Cape Town. The observatory provides a host of astronomical delights for visitors including day and night tours.

The Big Hole
Tel: 053-830 423
URL: www.thebighole.co.za

We are welcomed to the brand-new Diamonds & Destiny Visitor Centre! Kimberley is the capital of the Northern Cape and as such is fast reclaiming its prominence of the late 1800s. A tour of the Big Hole is already interesting, but the new exhibition centre will turn this experience into an unforgettable foray into the diamond fields of yesteryear. At the Visitors' Centre guests will have the opportunity to join a tour with an information officer, every hour on the hour, starting from 08h00. The last tour is at 16h00. The old town gives you a unique opportunity to see how Kimberley would have looked in its heyday.

Vanderkloof Dam
URL: www.vanderkloofdam.co.za

The Vanderkloof Dam is situated approximately 130km downstream from Gariep Dam, and is fed by the Orange River, South Africa's largest river. The Vanderkloof Dam plays an important role in providing water for irrigation to more than 100,000 hectares of productive agricultural land. The dam is also ideal for angling and water-related sports, including sailing, skiing and windsurfing. Building the dam gave birth to the beautiful town Vanderkloof, popular with holidaymakers and travellers alike.

Activities

Adventure Activities

Aquatrails
Tel: 021-782 7982
Email: info@aquatrails.co.za
URL: www.aquatrails.co.za

Bakkie Skiing
Tel: 053-781 0492
Email: info@thotalodge.co.za
URL: www.thotalodge.co.za/activities.html

Broadwater River Escapes
Tel: 082-332 2266
Email: broadwater@vodamail.co.za
URL: www.broadwater.co.za

Felix Unite River Adventures
Tel: 021-670 1300
Email: dboots@felix.co.za
URL: www.felixunite.com

Fly De Aar School of Paragliding
Tel: 053-631 1555
Email: flydeaar@telkomsa.net
URL: www.flydeaar.co.za

Gravity Adventures
Tel: 021-683 3698
Email: adventure@gravity.co.za
URL: www.gravity.co.za

Kriek Helicopters
Tel: 083-321 8707
Email: johann@kriekheli.com
URL: www.kriekheli.com

Rotary Airforce SA
Tel: 054-331 3534
Email: eben@rafgyro.co.za
URL: www.rafsa.co.za

Upington Microlight Training Centre
Tel: 054-331 1328
Email: eben@microlightkalahari.co.za
URL: www.microlightkalahari.co.za

Wildthing Adventures
Tel: 021-556 1917
Email: info@wildthing.co.za
URL: www.wildthing.co.za

Outdoor Activities

Camel Rides
Tel: 083-564 4613 / 082-336 9110
Email: koppieskraal@gmail.com
URL: www.koppieskraal.co.za

Hot-air Ballooning SA
Tel: 083-446 9423 / 011-802 4318
Email: info@hotairballooningsa.co.za
URL: www.hotairballooning.co.za

Inkwazi Flyfishing Safaris
Tel: 083-626 0467
Email: rolston@iafrica.com
URL: www.inkwaziflyfishing.co.za

Wildebeest Kuil Rock Art Centre
Tel: 053-833 7069
Email: dmorris@inext.co.za
URL: www.wildebeestkuil.itgo.com

Sport

Calvinia Golf Club
Tel: 027-341 1267

Hartswater Golf Club
Tel: 053-342 2232

Kimberley Golf Club
Tel: 053-841 0179 / 0127
URL: www.kimberleygolfclub.co.za

Loeriesfontein Golf Club
Tel: 027-662 1496

Sutherland Golf Club
Tel: 023-571 1033

Upington Golf Club
Tel: 054-338 0239

Stadiums

ABSA Park Stadium
Tel: 053-832 8773
Email: andre@megapro.co.za
URL: www.griquas.co.za
Situated in Kimberley

Culture

Museums

Colesberg-Kemper Museum
Tel: 051-753 0678
Email: belinda@mjvn.co.za
URL: www.northerncape.org.za/getting_around/towns/colesberg/
Situated in Colesberg

Kalahari-Oranje Museum
Tel: 054-332 6064
URL: www.roaringkalahari.co.za
Opening Time: Monday to Friday: 09h00 and 14h00; Saturdays 09h00
Closing Time: Monday to Friday: 12h30 and 17h00: Saturdays 12h00
Situated in Upington

Kimberley Mine Museum
Tel: 053-833 1557
Email: broodt@debeers.co.za
URL: http://kimberley-bighole.museum.com
Opening Time: Daily 08h00
Closing Time: Daily 18h00
Tariffs: R15.00 per adult, R10.00 per child

Loeriesfontein Windmill Museum
Tel: 027-662 1023
URL: www.loeriesfontein.co.zal

Magersfontein Battlefield Museum
Tel: 053-833 7115
URL: www.museumsnc.co.za/aboutus/SateliteContactInfo.pdf
Opening Time: Monday to Sunday: 08h00
Closing Time: Monday to Sunday: 17h00
Situated near Kimberley

Mary Moffat Museum
Tel: 053-343 0180
URL: www.southafricaholiday.org.uk/history/le_robert_moffat.htm
Opening Time: Monday to Friday: 08h00 and again at 14h00
Closing Time: Monday to Friday: 12h00 and again at 17h00
Situated in Kimberley

McGregor Museum
Tel: 053-839 2700
Email: cfortune@museumsnc.co.za
URL: www.museumsnc.co.za
Opening Time: Monday to Saturday: 09h00; Sunday 14h00; Public Holidays 10h00
Closing Time: 17h00
Tariffs: R12.00 per adult; R6.00 per child
Situated in Kimberley

Pellissier House Museum
Tel: 051-76269
URL: www.fs.gov.za/Departments/SAC/MUSEUM/bethulie.html
Opening Time: Tuesday and Thursday: 10h00; Saturday: 14h00
Closing Time: Tuesday and Thursday 12h30; Saturday: 17h00
Situated in Bethulie

Pioneers of Aviation Museum
Tel: 053-839 2722
URL: www.museumsnc.co.za/other/SateliteMuseumInfoPDF.pdf
Opening Time: Monday to Friday: 09h00
Closing Time: Monday to Friday: 17h00
Situated in Kimberley

Wildebeest Kuil
Tel: 053-833 7069
Email: dmorris@museumsnc.co.za
URL: www.museumsnc.co.za/other/SateliteMuseumInfoPDF.pdf
Opening Time: Monday to Friday: 09h00, Weekends and Public Holidays: 10h00
Closing Time: Monday to Friday, Weekends and Public Holidays: 16h00
Situated in Kimberley

Wonderwerk Caves
Tel: 053-712 1036
Email: cj-joubert@telkomsa.net
URL: www.museumsnc.co.za/aboutus/depts/archaeology/wonderwerk.html
Situated in Kuruman

Galleries

Duggan-Cronin Gallery
Tel: 053-839 2743
Email: photos@museumsnc.co.za
URL: www.openafrica.org/participant
/duggan-cronin-gallery
Situated in Kimberley

William Humphreys Art Gallery
Tel: 053-831 1724 / 5
Email: info@whag.co.za
URL: www.whag.co.za
Situated in Kimberley

Game and Nature Reserves (including National Parks)

South African National Parks
Tel: 012-426 5000
Email: reservations@sanparks.org
URL: www.sanparks.org

SANParks Reserves
|Ai-|Ais|Richtersveld Transfrontier Park
Augrabies Falls National Park
Kgalagadi Transfrontier Park
Mokala National Park
Namaqua National Park
Tankwa Karoo National Park
Vaalbos National Park

Other Parks

Doornkloof Nature Reserve
Tel: 051-753 1315
URL: www.sa-venues.com/things-to-
do/northerncape/detail.php?id=353

Goegap Nature Reserve
Tel: 027-718 9906
URL: www.linx.co.za/tripreports/
goegap-nature-reserve/index.php

Mattanu Private Game Reserve
Tel: 083-235 1993
URL: http://mattanu.com

Mokala National Park
Tel: 053-204 0158 / 164
URL: www.sanparks.org/parks/mokala/

Oorlogskloof Nature Reserve
Tel: 027-218 1010
Email: wpretorius@sp.ncape.gov.za
URL: www.footprint.co.za/oorlogskloof

Rolfontein Nature Reserve
Tel: 053-664 0170
URL: www.sa-vanues.com/game-reserves/
nc-rolfontein.htm

Rooipoort Game Farm
Tel: 049-843 1707
URL: www.rooipoort.co.za

Skilpad Wild Flower Reserve
Tel: 027-672 1948
URL: www.namaquainfo.co.za/1ni0402.htm

Tswalu Kalahari Reserve
Tel: 011-679 2994
Email: res@tswalu.com
URL: www.tswalu.com

Witsand Nature Reserve
Tel: 053-313 1061 / 2
Email: witsandkalahari@telkomsa.net
URL: www.witsandkalahari.co.za **249**

Northern Cape Game and Nature Reserves

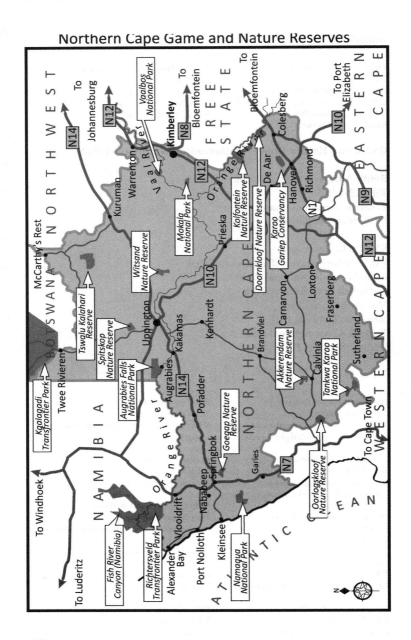

Entertainment

Desert Palace
casino
Tel: 054-338 4100
Situated in Upington

Flamingo Casino
casino
Tel: 053-830 2600
Situated in Kimberley

Nations Nightclub and Bar
club
Tel: 054-331 1007
Situated in Upington

Annual Events

AfrikaBurn
Email: info@afrikaburns.com
URL: www.afrikaburns.com
Held in Tankwa Karoo every September

Apollo Film Festival
Tel: 082-858 2015
URL: www.apollofilmfestival.co.za
Held in Victoria West every September

Cultural Festival
Tel: 084-597 7889
URL: www.sa-venues.com/events/
Held in Okiep every September

Fraserburg Logan Drama Festival
Tel: 023-741 1252
URL: www.sa-venues.com/events/
Held every August

Gariep Kunstefees
Tel: 053-832 5014
URL: http://gariepfees.co.za
Held in Kimberley every September

Hantam Vleisfees
Tel: 083-355 8155
URL: www.hantamvleisfees.co.za
Held in Calvinia every August

Kakamas Sultana Kultuurfees
Tel: 073-012 2480
URL: www.sa-venues.com/events/
Held every March

Kalahari Augrabies Extreme Marathon
Tel: 083-309 7755
URL: www.extrememarathons.com
7-day trail run every October

Kalahari Kuierfees
Tel: 054-332 1100
URL: www.kalahari-kuierfees.co.za
Held in Upington every September

Namakwa Festival
Tel: 084-956 1865
URL: www.sa-venues.com/events/
Held in Springbok every December

NWCA NDFT Daisy Marathon
Tel: 083-491 0227
URL: www.sa-venues.com/events/
Held in Springbok every September

Orange River Canoe Race
URL: www.sa-venues.com/events/
Held every April

Upington Landbou Skou
Tel: 054-331 2105
URL: http://upington.co.za/expo
Held every May

251

Shopping www.mallguide.co.za

Diamond Pavillion Shopping Mall
Tel: 053-832 9200
Situated in Kimberley

Kathu Centre
Tel: 053-723 4652
Situated in Kathu

Kimberley Kim Park
Tel: 051-430 2341
Situated in Kimberley

Newpark Centre
Tel: 053-831 4152
Situated in Kimberley

Riveiro Shopping Centre
Tel: 053-861 3860
Situated in Kimberley

Sanlam Centre
Tel: 051-430 2341 / 083-832 7298
Situated in Kimberley

Restaurants

Calvinia
Blou Nartjie Restaurant
Cuisine: South African
Tel: 027-341 1263
Address: 35 Water Street

Kimberley
Barnato's
Cuisine: Cosmopolitan
Tel: 053-833 4110
Address: 6 Dalham Road

China Restaurant
Cuisine: Chinese
Tel: 053-831 4444
Address: Currey Street

Dieda's Corner
Cuisine: Fine Dining
Tel: 053-831 3075
Address: cnr York & Jones Streets

Edgerton House
Cuisine: Cosmopolitan
Tel: 053-831 1150
Address: 5 Edgerton Road

George and Dragon
Cuisine: South African
Tel: 053-833 2075
Address: 187 Du Toitspan Road, Belgravia

Gossip Lounge
Cuisine: Cosmopolitan
Tel: 053-833 5110
Address: 14 Long Street

Halfway House
Cuisine: Pub
Tel: 053-831 6324
Address: Halfway House, 229 Du Toitspan
    Road, Belgravia

Mario's
Cuisine: Cosmopolitan
Tel: 053-831 1738
Address: 159 Du Toitspan Road, Belgravia

Old Diggers Inn
Cuisine: Steakhouse
Tel: 053-832 8577
Address: Old Bloemfontein Road

Star of the West
Cuisine: Cosmopolitan
Tel: 053-832 6463
Address: cnr North Circular &
    Barkley Roads

Teemane Pub & Grill
Cuisine: Cosmopolitan
Tel: 053-832 6211
Address: 231 De Beers Road

The Half
Cuisine: Cosmopolitan
Tel: 053-831 6324
Address: 229 Du Toitspan Road, Belgravia

The Lemon Tree
Cuisine: South African
Tel: 053-831 7730
Address: 33 Angel Street

Tiffany's Restaurant
Cuisine: South African
Tel: 053-832 6211
Address: 19 De Beers Road

Umberto's Restaurant & Pizzeria
Cuisine: Italian
Tel: 053-832 5741
Address: Halfway House, 229 Du Toitspan Road, Belgravia

Kuruman
22nd on Main Restaurant & Grill
Cuisine: Grill
Tel: 053-712 3391
Address: Palmgate Shopping Centre, 22 Main Street

Nieuwoudtville
Van Zijl Guesthouses & Restaurant
Cuisine: South African
Tel: 027-218 1535
Address: 1 Neethling Street

Springbok
El Dago
Cuisine: South African
Tel: 027-718 1475
Address: 39 Voortrekker Street

Grasdak Steak Ranch
Cuisine: Pub
Tel: 027-718 3488
Address: Tolweg 19

Upington
Bi Lo Bistro
Cuisine: Grills
Tel: 054-338 0616
Address: 9 Groen Punt Road, Keidevees

Collector's Restaurant
Cuisine: Cosmopolitan
Tel: 054-331 2290
Address: 4 Schroder Street

De Werf
Cuisine: South African
Tel: 054-461 1635
Address: Main Road

Friends
Cuisine: South African
Tel: 054-332 3331
Address: 51 Scott Street

Le Must Restaurant
Cuisine: South African
Tel: 054-332 6700
Address: 11A Schroder Street

Le Raisin
Cuisine: Cosmopolitan
Tel: 054-332 2351
Address: 67 Mark Street

Chains and Franchises

Cappuccino's
URL: www.cappuccinos.co.za

Cattle Baron
URL: www.cattlebaron.co.za

Dros
URL: www.dros.co.za

Mugg & Bean
URL: www.themugg.com

Ocean Basket
URL: www.oceanbasket.co.za

Panarotti's
URL: www.panarottis.com

Spur
URL: www.spur.co.za

Accommodation

www.northcape-venues.co.za
www.safarinow.com/destinations/northern-cape/hub.aspx
www.wheretostay.co.za/nc
www.sa-venues.com/northern_cape_accommodation
www.countryroads.co.za/northern-cape-accommodation.html
www.roomsforafrica.com/dest/south-africa/northern-cape
www.northerncape-direct.com
www.places.co.za/accommodation/northern_cape_accommodation
www.northern-cape-accommodation.co.za

Kimberley
Hotels

Hotel Formula 1
Tel: 053-831 2552
URL: www.hotelformula1.co.za

The Kimberley Club
Tel: 053-832 4224
Email: info@kimberleyclub.co.za
URL: www.kimberleyclub.co.za

Jungnickel Guest House
Tel: 053-832 5630 / 073-588 7600
Email: jungnickel@mweb.co.za
URL: www.jungnickel.co.za

Welgewandel Guest House
Tel: 053-832 0468
URL: www.welgewandel.co.za

Lodges

Mattanu
Tel: 083-235 1993
Email: info@ecotourismafrica.com
URL: http://mattanu.com

Camping

Riverside Country Club & Caravan Park
Tel: 053-581 7120
URL: www.riversideresort.co.za

Other
Hotels

B&Bs, guesthouses & self-catering

Aletheim Guest House
Tel: 082-553 1366
Email: aletheim@exact-net.com
URL: www.aletheimguesthouse.co.za

Heerengracht Guest House
Tel: 053-831 1531
Email: info@kelesedi.co.za
URL: www.kelesedi.co.za

Garden Court Hotels
Tel: 0861-447 744 / 053-883 1751
Email: gckimberley@southernsun.com
URL: www.southernsun.com

Kamieskroon Hotel
Tel: 027-672 1614
Email: kamieshotel@kingsley.co.za
URL: www.kamieskroonhotel.com/?m=1
Situated in Kamieskroon

Le Must Premier Collection
Tel: 054-332 3971
Email: manor@lemustupington.com
URL: www.lemustupington.com
Situated in Upington

Masonic Hotel
Tel: 027-712 1505
URL: www.jcbotha.co.za
Situated in Springbok

Okiep Country Hotel
Tel: 027-744 1000
Email: okiep@intekom.co.za
URL: www.okiep.co.za
Situated in Okiep

Protea Hotels
Tel: 0861-119 000
Email: info@proteahotels.com
URL: www.proteahotels.com

River City Inn
Tel: 054-337 8500
Email: rivercity@upthotels.co.za
URL: www.upingtonhotels.co.za
Situated in Upington

Scotia Inn
Tel: 027-851 8353
Email: scotiainn@telkomsa.net
URL: www.richtersveld.net/index.php
Situated in Port Nolloth

Sutherland Hotel
Tel: 023-571 1096
Email: info@sutherlandhotel.co.za
URL: www.sutherlandhotel.co.za
Situated in Sutherland

Lodges

Bedrock Lodge
Tel: 027-851 8865
Email: bedrocklodge@telkomsa.net
URL: www.bedrocklodge.co.za
Situated in Port Nolloth

Blue Diamond Lodge
Tel: 027-718 2624
Email: bluediamond@worldonline.co.za
Situated in Springbok

Dundi Lodge
Tel: 054-451 9200
Email: info@dundilodge.co.za
URL: www.dundilodge.co.za
Situated near Augrabies Falls

Harmony Estate Guest Lodge
Tel: 027-718 1779
Email: HarmonyEstateGL@gmail.com
Situated in Springbok

Libby's Lodge
Tel: 054-332 2661
Email: lgerber@mweb.co.za
URL: www.wheretostay.co.za/libbyslodge
Situated in Upngton

Namakwari Lodge
Tel: 053-723 2987
Email: info@namakwari.co.za
URL: www.namakwari.co.za
Situated in Kathu

Springbok Lodge
Tel: 036-637 9604
URL: www.thespringboklodge.co.za
Situated in Springbok

Xaus Lodge
Tel: 021-701 7860
Email: info@tfpd.co.za
URL: www.xauslodge.co.za
Situated in Kgalagadi Transfrontier Park

B&Bs, Guest Houses & Self-catering

@Belurana
Tel: 054-332 4323
Email: belurana@mweb.co.za
URL: www.beluranaupington.com
Situated in Upington

A La Fugue Guest House
Tel: 054-338 0424
Email: a-la-fugue@mweb.co.za
URL: www.lafugue-guesthouse.com
Situated in Upington

Annie's Cottage B&B
Tel: 027-712 1451
Email: annie@springbokinfo.com
URL: www.springbokinfo.com
Situated in Springbok

Country Club Accommodation
Tel: 027-851 7433
Email:accommodation@countryclubpn.net
URL: www.countryclubpn.co.za
Situated in Port Nolloth

Desert Rose Guest House
Tel: 027-712 2330
Email: desertrose@telkomsa.net
URL: www.desertrose.co.za
Situated in Springbok

Die Blou Nartjie Guest House
Tel: 027-341 1263
Email: hermanf@hantam.co.za
URL: www.placesforafrica.com/blounartjie
Situated in Calvinia

Elkoweru Guest House
Tel: 027-718 1202
Email: elkoweru.spk@intekom.co.za
URL: www.elkoweru.co.za
Situated in Springbok

Gousblom B&B
Tel: 027-672 1004
Email: ed@isat.co.za
URL: www.placesforafrica.com
Situated in Kamieskroon

Greenfield Gardens
Tel: 054-332 4242
Email: info@greenfieldgardens.co.za
URL: www.greenfieldgardens.co.za
Situated in Upington

Habitat Guest Village
Tel: 054-332 4311
Email: mail@habitatvillage.co.za
URL: www.habitatvillage.co.za
Situated in Upington

Kleinplasie Guest House
Tel: 027-712 1141
Email: info@kleinplasie.com
URL: www.kleinplasie.com
Situated in Springbok

Mountain View Guest House
Tel: 027-712 1438
Email: mountview@worldonline.co.za
URL: www.mountview.co.za
Situated in Springbok

Port Indigo Guest House & Self Catering
Tel: 027-851 8012
Email: portindigo@telkomsa.net
URL: www.portindigo.co.za
Situated in Port Nolloth

Soebatsfontein Road Farm Accomodation
Tel: 027-672 1637 / 027-672 1726
Email: grootvalletjie@telkomsa.net
Situatedin Kamieskroon

Strelitzia Guest House
Tel: 054-331 1519
Email: isaac@medicnet.co.za
Situated in Upington

The Olive Tree Guest House
Tel: 027-718 1808
Email: info@tot.co.za
URL: www.tot.co.za
Situates in Springbok

Three Gables Guest House
Tel: 083-264 2982
Email: lana.schmidt@mweb.co.za
URL: www.threegables.co.za
Situated in Upington

Voetbaai Self-catering
Tel: 027-712 1141
Email: info@kleinplasie.com
URL: www.kleinplasie.com
Situated in McDougalls Bay

Camping

Agama Tented Camp
Tel: 072-040 0614
Email: bookings@agamacamp.co.za
URL: www.agamacamp.co.za
Situated in Garies

Aquacade Camp
Tel: 027-761 8777
Email: aquacade@telkomsa.net
URL: www.aquacade.co.za
Situated in Viooldsrift

Doornkloof Nature Reserve
Tel: 051-753 1315
URL: www.aatravel.co.za
Situated in Colesberg

Kalahari Monate Lodge & Caravan Park
Tel: 054-332 1336
Email: teuns@intekom.co.za
URL: www.spitskopmonate.co.za
Situated in Upington

Kalahari Water Holiday Adventure Farm
Tel: 054-461 2404 / 1521
Email: info@kalahariwater.co.za
URL: www.kalahariwater.co.za
Situated in Keimoes

Oorlogskloof Nature Reserve
Tel: 027-218 1010
Email: wpretorius@sp.ncape.gov.za
URL: www.footprint.co.za/oorlogskop.htm
Situated in Nieuwoudtville

Orange River Tented Camp
Tel: 051-755 5055
Email: ivansinclair@intekom.co.za
URL: www.orangerivertentscamp.com
Situated in Colesberg

Winton Guest Farm
Tel: 053-791 0516
Email: info@guestfarm.co.za
URL: www.guestfarm.co.za
Situated in Kathu

Tours

A Grade Tours & Event Management
cultural tours
Tel: 027-341 2987
Email: agrade@telkomsa.net
URL: www.northerncape.org.za/
  getting_around/tour_operators/

Augrabies Canoe Trails
river adventures
Tel: 082-476 8213
Email: info@kalahari.co.za
URL: www.kalahari.co.za

Aukwatowa Tours
cross-country 4x4
Tel: 027-851 8026
Email: aukwatowa@yahoo.com

Bushwhacked Outdoor Adventures
Orange River adventures
Tel: 027-761 8953
Email: info@bushwhacked.co.za
URL: www.bushwhacked.co.za

Cape Fox Tours & Photography
photographic and 4x4 safaris
Tel: 082-572 0065
Email: info@capefox.co.za
URL: www.capefox.co.za

Club Travel Upington
travel agency
Tel: 054-338 6420
Email: infou@clubtravel.co.za
URL: www.clubtravel.co.za

Diamond Coast
tours throughout the Diamond Coast
Tel: 027-877 0028
Email: coast.of.diamonds@gmail.com
URL: www.coastofdiamonds.co.za

Diamond Tours
guided tours and safaris
Tel: 011-965 0575
Email: info@diamondtours.co.za
URL: www.diamondtours.co.za

Kalahari Outventures
Kalahari safaris
Tel: 082-476 8213
Email: info@kalahari.co.za
URL: www.kalahari.co.za

Kalahari Safaris
guided tours
Tel: 054-332 5653
Email: pieter@kalaharisafaris.co.za
URL: www.kalaharisafaris.co.za

Karoo Biking
motorcycle tours in the Karoo
Tel: 082-533 6655
Email: jurgen@karoo-biking.de
URL: www.karoo-biking.de/en

Khamkiri
tailor-made tours
Tel: 082-821 6649
Email: info@khamkirri.co.za
URL: www.khamkirri.co.za

Kimberley Helicopter Services
game-viewing and charter services
Tel: 084-552 2063
Email: khsadmin@inext.co.za
URL: www.northerncape.org.za/
   getting_around/tours_operators

Koperberg Tours and Safaris
Namaqualand tours
Tel: 027-713 8755
Email: koperberg@mweb.co.za
URL: www.namaqualand.net/tours.html

Kriek Helicopters
heli fly-fishing
Tel: 083-321 8707
Email: johann@kriekheli.com
URL: www.kriekheli.com

Noah's River Adventures
paddling through Richtersveld
Tel: 076-863 7658
Email: info@noahsriveradventures.co.za
URL: www.noahsriveradventures.co.za

Richtersveld Tours
custom 4x4 camping tours
Tel: 082-335 1399
Email: mail@richtersveldtours.co.za
URL: www.richtersveldtours.co.za

Southern Cross Adventures
guided and self-catering tours
Tel: 027-712 2624
Email: scadventures@kingsley.co.za
URL: www.scadventures.co.za

Spitskop Safaris
game safaris
Tel: 083-257 3746
Email: adam@spitskop.co.za
URL: www.spitskop.co.za

T'Ky Gariep Flyfishing Trail
Yellowfish flyfishing tours
Tel: 053-861 4983
Email: dtours@kimnet.co.za
URL: www.diamondtours.co.za

Tata Ma Tata Tours
guided tours
Tel: 082-535 8830
Email: edsmith2@webmail.co.za
URL: www.tatamatata.co.za

Umkulu Safaris
safari and canoe trail operator
Tel: 021-853 7952
Email: info@umkulu.co.za
URL: www.umkulu.co.za

Uniglobe Thembelihle Travel
Northern Cape tours
Tel: 079-013 0167 / 084-588 9182
Email: winnie.kondowe@gmail.com
URL: www.uniglobetravel.co.za

NORTHERN CAPE

Virosatours
tailor-made tours
Tel: 073-229 5014
Email: piet@virosatours.com
URL: www.virosatours.com

Wildthing Adventures & River Camp
outdoor adventures
Tel: 021-556 1917
Email: safaris@wildthing.co.za
URL: www.orangeriver.co.za

Car Rentals

Avis
Tel: 0861-021 111
URL: www.avis.co.za

Europcar
Tel: 0861-131 000
URL: www.europcar.co.za

Budget
Tel: 0861-016 622
URL: www.budget.co.za

Kalahari 4x4
Tel: 054-337 7133
URL: www.kalahari4x4hire.co.za

Click Car Hire
Tel: 021-551 9515
URL: www.sa-venues.com/explore/
   clickcarhire/

Kgalagadi 4x4
Tel: 054-337 7100
URL: www.kgalagadi4x4.com

Leisure Mobile Rent a Car
Tel: 011-475 8135
URL: www.sa-venues.com/explore/
   leisuremobiles/

Drive South Africa
Tel: 0860-000 060
URL: www.drivesouthafrica.co.za

First
Tel: 0861-011 323
URL: www.firstcarrental.co.za

Tempest Car Hire
Tel: 0861-836 7378
URL: www.tempestcarhire.co.za

Hertz
Tel: 0861-600 136
URL: www.hertz.co.za

Emergency Numbers

Ambulance / Fire
10177

Cell phone Emergency Number
112

National Tourism Information & Safety Line
083-113 2345

Police Emergency number
10111

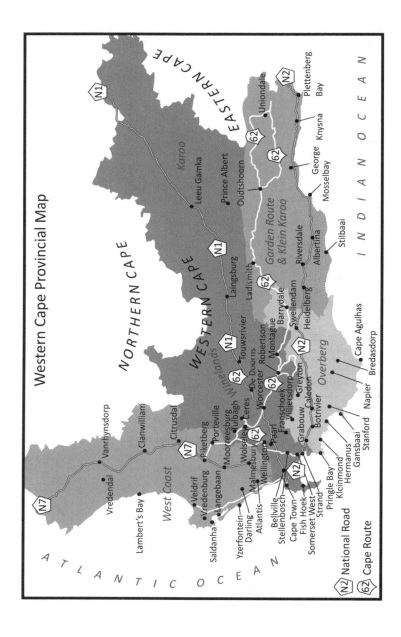

Western Cape Provincial Map

Western Cape

Tourism Information Offices

Cape Info Africa
Tel: 021-425 6463
Email: info@capeinfoafrica.co.za
URL: www.capeinfoafrica.co.za

Cape Town International Airport Visitor Information Centre
Tel: 021-935 3160
URL: airport@capetown.travel

Cape Town Routes Unlimited
Tel: 021-426 5639
URL: www.tourismcapetown.co.za

South Africa Tourism
URL: www.southafrica.net/sat/content/en/za/home

South Africa Tourism Services Association
Tel: 011-886 9996
URL: www.satsa.com

V&A Waterfront Gateway Information Centre
Tel: 021-405 4500
Email: info@tourismcapetown.co.za

Western Cape Tourism
Tel: 0861-843 639 72
Email: info@thewesterncape.co.za
URL: www.thewesterncape.co.za

Top 10

Boulders Beach
Tel: 0861-843 639 72
Email: info@thewesterncape.co.za
URL: www.aboutcapetown/penguins
Tariff: R15 for adults and R5 for children.

An inlet of granite boulders, this sheltered beach, in the Table Mountain National Park, is home to a large colony of African penguins that first settled there in 1982 and have showed no signs of relocating. If you have no appetite for the crowded little beaches, the overhead boardwalk provides an excellent view of the penguins. Situated just south of historical Simon's Town, in False Bay, Boulders Beach is a perfect excursion for animal lovers and visitors with children.

Calitzdorp
Tel: 044-213 3775
Email: calitzdorpinfo@kannaland.co.za
URL: www.calitzdorp.co.za

Known as the wine capital of South Africa, this quaint little town can be found on Route 62 in the heart of the Klein Karoo. It is home to three wine cellars—Boplass, Calitzdorp and De Krans—and was host to the 2009 Port Festival. Exploring this town will reveal a dozen places to kick back and relax or overnight while enjoying the beauty of the Garden Route. Accommodation varies from B&Bs to private resorts and caters for visitors with both rustic and luxury tastes. There are restaurants and coffee spots, delis and bakeries, offering everything from traditional home-cooking to pub grub. However, the charm of Calitzdorp is its setting, surrounded by majestic sandstone mountains cut by deep ravines. It is the heart of wild flower and birding country and is the ideal getaway for hikers, fishermen, birders and the more relaxed tourist who enjoys reading a good book, surrounded by spectacular views.

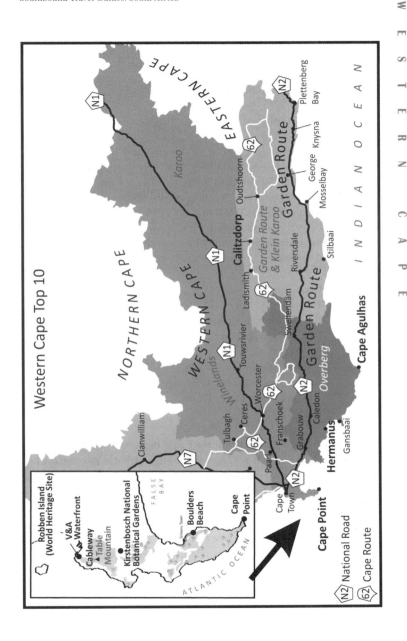

Western Cape Top 10

Cape Agulhas
Tel: 028-424 2584
Email: suidpunt@brd.dorea.co.za
URL: www.sanparks.org/parks/agulhas/

The southernmost tip of Africa is home to a host of seaside towns, most notably, Cape Agulhas, with endless beaches and craggy mountains sweeping into the Indian Ocean to the east and the Atlantic to the west. Although an angler's paradise, these rocks are notorious for the myriad shipwrecks that litter this stretch of coastline. Nestled in the Bredasdorp Mountains, Cape Agulhas and its neighbouring towns, offer tourists an insight into the Western Cape's rich history, with an old gold mine, and a plethora of monuments and museums. The more energetic visitor can enjoy hiking and birding in one of the several nature reserves in the area. Sea charters offer an exciting alternative for fishermen.

Cape Point
Tel: 021-780 9010
Email: info@capepoint.co.za
URL: www.capepoint.co.za
Opening time: October to March: 06h00;
   April to September: 07h00
Closing time: October to March: 18h00;
   April to September: 17h00
Tariffs: R60

Cape Point is the culmination of the Cape Peninsula and the southern tip of Table Mountain. It is the western edge of False Bay, its eastern counterpart being Hangklip. Cape Point falls within the Good Hope section of the Table Mountain National Park that occupies the entire southern tip of the peninsula and is one of the eight parks which comprise the Cape Floral Region Protected Areas World Heritage Site, proclaimed for its vast floral biodiversity. A walk up to the lighthouse and then all the way to the viewing deck at the point itself will leave you breathless, but on a clear day the view is well worth it. If it's overcast and rainy, don't bother.

Garden Route
Tel: 044-873 6314
Email: info@gardenroute.org.za
URL: www.gardenroute.co.za

This picturesque route along the southern coast of the Western Cape stretches from Mossel Bay in the west to the Tsitsikamma Mountains in the east. The N2 highway connects the Garden Route to Cape Town in the west and Port Elizabeth in the east. It is possible to fly to George and hire a car to explore this renowned route. Ten nature reserves embrace the varied ecosystems of the area as well as unique marine reserves, home to soft coral reefs, dolphins, seals and a host of other marine life. Various bays along the Garden Route are nurseries to the endangered Southern right whale which come to calve in the winter and spring (June to December). The annual Knysna Oyster Festival is a highlight and takes place for ten days every July.

Hermanus
Tel: 0861-234 777
Email: admin@maxitec.co.za
URL: www.hermanus.co.za and www.whalefestival.co.za

The best land-based whale-watching destination in the world, Hermanus is home to the world's only whale crier who blows his kelp horn when whales are spotted along the central sea route. Hermanus is a beautiful town situated to the north of Walker Bay and southwest of Caledon on the N2. Southern right whales visit Walker Bay from June to December each year. The annual September Whale Festival has become a feature on the town's calendar.

Kirstenbosch National Botanical Gardens
Tel: 021-799 8899
URL: www.sanbi.org/frames/kirstfram.htm
Opening time: 08h00
Closing time: September to March: 19h00;
    April to August: 18h00
Tariffs: Adults: R32; SA Students: R20;
    Children: R10; Children under 6: Free

Founded in 1913 and set against the eastern slope of Table Mountain, the Kirstenbosch National Botanical Gardens are world-renowned for their floral biodiversity. They exhibit only indigenous South African plants within 528 hectares and support diverse fynbos flora and natural forest. Its cultivated garden displays collections of plants predominantly from South African's winter-rainfall regions. During the summer months (December to March), sunset music concerts are held on the lawns every Sunday and craft markets are held in the stone cottages (opposite Kirstenbosch) on the last Sunday of every month, except during mid-winter (June to August).

Robben Island
Tel: 021-409 5100
URL: www.robben-island.org.za
Opening time: 09h00
Closing time: Last ferry departs at 15h00
Tariffs: Adults over 18: R180; Children: R90

The Robben Island Ferry leaves from the Nelson Mandela Gateway at the V&A Waterfront every two hours. For four centuries Robben Island was a place of banishment, isolation and imprisonment. The Robben Island Museum at the Nelson Mandela Gateway is a stark reminder of this history. Although the prison and Nelson Mandela's cell are the obvious highlights of the tour the island has a history that started long before that. The military gun emplacements, the female asylum and the Baths of Bethesda (a tidal pool constructed for lepers to bathe in) are all testimony to its long and torturous history. Booking for this trip is essential, especially over the December holiday season. Bookings can be made on the website but don't be surprised when the booking is cancelled due to bad weather. The channel between Cape Town and Robben Island has treacherous currents, so these weather restrictions are in place for the tourists' safety.

Table Mountain Cableway
Tel: 021-424 8181
URL: www.tablemountain.net

Opening time: 16 January to 30 April and 16 September to 15 January 08h00; 1 May to 15 September 08h30
Closing time: 16 January to 31 January: Last Car Up 20h30, Last Car Down 21h30;
1 February to 28 February: Last Car Up 19h30, Last Car Down 20h30;
1 March to 31 March: Last Car Up 18h30, Last Car Down 19h30;
1 April to 30 April: Last Car Up 17h30, Last Car Down 18h30;
1 May to 15 September: Last Car Up 17h00, Last Car Down 18h00;
16 September to 31 October: Last Car Up 18h00, Last Car Down 19h00;
1 November to 30 November: Last Car Up 19h00, Last Car Down 20h00;
1 December to 15 December: Last Car Up 20h30, Last Car Down 21h30;
16 December to 15 January: Last Car Up 21h00, Last Car Down 22h00
Tariffs: Adults: R145; Children over 4: R76

There are few things you can actually do in Cape Town if the wind is blowing, which it regularly does. The cableway isn't one of them, nor is the trip to Robben Island. Later in this chapter you will find a directory to the Cape wine farms; it is strongly recommended that on windy days you sample wine. However, on a clear, windless day the cableway to the top of Table Mountain is a must. The cableway opened almost 80 years ago and has since transported over 18 million visitors to the summit. A recent upgrade to the cable cars means 65 people can now make the journey up the mountain in a car whose floor rotates 360 degrees so that passengers can see what everyone else is seeing without having to jab wet dummies in unsuspecting childless couples' necks for a better look. Once at the top you can look southward to the Table Mountain National Park, then scan the western coastline. Looking north you will see Lion's Head, Robben Island, Table Bay and the entire city bowl. Gazing east will reveal the Cape Flats and the southern coastline extending east past Somerset West. It really is quite a view! The more energetic tourist will appreciate the view all the more for making the hike. There are various paths up the mountain and it is recommended that if you are not a local you make use of the experience of a guide. Don't be one of the silly tourists who ends up on the evening news.

Victoria & Alfred (V&A) Waterfront
Tel: 021-408 7600
URL: www.waterfront.co.za

This vast complex surrounding the harbour accommodates more malls, boutiques, restaurants, bars and trinket shops then one could ever hope to count let alone visit in three life times. It is also home to some of the most luxurious hotels Cape Town has to offer. Aside from being a consumer's paradise it is from here that the Robben Island tours are launched. It also houses the aquarium, a must-see.

Activities

Adventure Activities

Action Africa
Tel: 021-438 8181
Email: jenny@actionafrica.co.za
URL: www.actionafrica.co.za

Adrenaline Sailing
Tel: 083-701 8473
Email: brent@drumafrica.co.za
URL: www.drumafrica.co.za

Adventure Sports & Tours 4U
Tel: 021-696 3631
URL: www.adventure4u.co.za

Aquila Microlight safaris & Training
Tel: 021-712 1913
Email: tskorge@mweb.co.za
URL: www.aquilamicrolight.com

Blue Rock Cable Waterski
Tel: 021-858 1330
Email: waterski@bluerock.co.za
URL: www.bluerock.co.za

Cape Town Tandem Paragliding
URL: www.paraglide.co.za

Downhill Adventures
Tel: 021-422 0388
Email: info@downhilladventures.com
URL: www.downhilladventures.com

Frixion Adventures
Tel: 021-447 4985
Email: scott@frixion.co.za
URL: www.frixion.co.za

Gourits Bungy
Tel: 044-697 7001
Email: gourits@faceadrenalin.com
URL: www.faceadrenalin.com

Para-Pax
Tel: 082-881 4724
Email: stefsa@gmail.com
URL: www.parapax.com

Shark Watch
Tel: 028-384 1005
Email: dive@sharkwatchsa.com
URL: www.sharkwatchsa.com

Shark Zone
Tel: 082-894 4979
Email: info@sharkzone.co.za
URL: www.sharkzone.co.za

Skydive Cape Town
Tel: 082-800 6290
Email: info@skydivecapetown.za.net
URL: www.skydivecapetown.za.net

Unreal Dive
Tel: 083-273 4920
URL: www.unrealdive.com

Quad & Motorcycle Adventures
Tel: 021-859 1989
Email: motorcycles@iafrica.com
URL: www.naturediscovery.co.za

Outdoor Activities

African Horse Company
Tel: 082-667 9232
Email: contact@africanhorseco.com
URL: www.africanhorseco.com

Agama Mountain Adventures
Tel: 072-024 6537
Email: robinkayser7@yahoo.com

Arumdale Outdoor Experiences
Tel: 021-848 9683

Cape Town Ostrich Ranch
Tel: 021-972 1669
Email: info@ostrichranch.co.za
URL: www.ostrichranch.co.za

Horse Trail Safaris
Tel: 021-703 4396
URL: www.horsetrailsafaris.co.za

Inkwazi Flyfishing
Tel: 083-626 0467
URL: www.inkwaziflyfishing.co.za

Kenilworth Racecourse
Tel: 021-700 1621

Klapmuts Conservatory
Tel: 021-884 4752
Email: theteam@dirtopia.co.za

Mineral World
Tel: 021-419 9429
URL: www.scratchpatch.co.za

Monkeyland
Tel: 044-534 8906
Email: info@monkeyland.co.za
URL: www.monkeyland.co.za

Table Mountain Cableway
Tel: 021-424 8181
URL: www.tablemountain.net

Table Mountain Bikes
Tel: 021-438 6073
Email: cauaburi@yahoo.com

The Elephant Sanctuary
Tel: 044-534 8145
Email: crags@elephantsanctuary.co.za
URL: www.elephantsanctuary.co.za

Two Oceans Aquarium
Tel: 021-418 3823
Email: aquarium@aquarium.co.za
URL: www.aquarium.co.za

Tygerberg Zoo
Tel: 021-884 4494

Sport

Cape Sports Centre	Red Sands Golf
Tel: 021-772 1114	Tel: 082-872 8838
Email: info@capesport.co.za	Email: info@redsandsgolf.co.za
URL: www.capesport.co.za	URL: www.redsandsgolf.co.za
Situated in Langebaan, Cape Town	Situated in Cavendish, Cape Town
Golfmac	Rondebosch Golf Club
Tel: 021-785 5659	Tel: 021-689 4179
Email: mark@golfmac.co.za	Email: rgc@mweb.co.za
URL: www.golfmac.co.za	URL: www.rondeboschgolfclub.com
Situated in Cape Town	

Stadiums

Greenpoint Stadium
Tel: 021-430 0410/8
Email: info@greenpointstadiumvc.co.za
URL: www.greenpointstadiumvc.co.za

This latest addition to Cape Town's sport venues will be the city's premier 2010 World Cup destination. It is located in Green Point, between Signal Hill and the Atlantic, close to the city centre. A state-of-the-art, modern construction, the revamped stadium has a capacity of 68,000.

Newlands Rugby Stadium	Newlands Cricket Ground
Tel: 021-686-4955	Tel: 021-657 2050
Email: wpprwag@iafrica.com	URL: www.wpcc.co.za
URL: www.wprugby.com	Situated in Cape Town
Situated in Cape Town	

Culture

Museums

Gold of Africa Museum
Tel: 021-405 1540
Email: info@goldofafrica.com
URL: www.goldofafrica.com
Situated in Cape Town

Irma Stern Museum
Tel: 021-685 5686
URL: www.irmastern.co.za
Situated at the University of Cape Town

Iziko Museums
Tel: 021-481 3800
Email: info@iziko.org.za
URL: www.iziko.org.za
Various Cape Town-based locations

Robben Island Museum
Tel: 021-413 4220
Email: infow@robben-island.org.za
URL: www.robben-island.org.za
Situated at the V&A Waterfront, Cape Town

South African Jewish Museum
Tel: 021-465 1546
Email: info@sajewishmuseum.co.za
URL: www.sajewishmuseum.co.za
Situated in central Cape Town

The Afrikaans Language Museum
Tel: 021-872 3441
Email: hgm@taalmuseum.co.za
URL: www.taalmuseum.co.za
Situated in Faarl

Worcester Open-air Museum
Tel: 023-342 2225
Email: manager@kleinplasie.org.za
URL: www.kleinplasie.co.za

Theatres

Artscape Theatre Centre
Tel: 021-410 9800
Email: artscape@artscape.co.za
URL: www.artscape.co.za
Situated in central Cape Town

Baxter Theatre Centre
Tel: 021-685 7880
Web address: www.baxter.co.za
Situated in Rondebosch, Cape Town

Cape Philharmonic Orchestra
Tel: 021-410 9809
Email: capephil@artscape.co.za
Based at the Artscape Theatre Complex

Paul Cluver Forest Amphitheatre
Tel: 021-884 0605
Situated in Grabouw

Woza Cape Town
Tel: 079-770 4686
Email: bookings@theatreinthedistrict.co.za
URL: www.theatreinthedistrict.co.za
Situated in District Six, Cape Town

WEST ERN CAPE

Galleries

Rembrandt van Rijn Art Gallery
Tel: 021-886 4340
Situated in Stellenbosch

Silver Art Gallery
Tel: 021-424 2691
Email: info@silvergallery.co.za
Situated in Gardens, Cape Town

The Albie Bailey Art Gallery
Tel: 021-419 2679
Email: clement@netactive.co.za
URL: www.clementina.co.za
Situated in Woodstock, Cape Town

The Cape Gallery
Tel: 021-423 5309
Email: cgallery@mweb.co.za
URL: www.capegallery.co.za
Situated in central Cape Town

The Edge Glass Gallery
Tel: 021-423 3370
Situated in Cape Town

The Fenix
Tel: 021-854 8618
Email: info@thefenix.co.za
URL: www.thefenix.co.za
Situated in the Strand

Winelands

Ashanti
Tel: 021-862 0789
URL: www.ashantiwines.com
Opening time: 10h00 Monday to Friday
Closing time: 16h00
Situated in Paarl

Backsberg Estate
Tel: 021 8755141
Email: info@backsberg.co.za
URL: www.backsberg.co.za
Situated in Paarl

Bergkelder
Tel: 021-8098025
Email: sschoeman@distell.co.za
URL: www.bergkelder.co.za
Opening time: 08h00 Monday to Friday;
    09h00 Saturday
Closing time: 09h00 Monday to Friday;
    14h00 Saturday
Situated in Stellenbosch

Bellingham
Tel: 021-874 1019
Email: info@bellingham.co.za
URL: www.bellingham.co.za
Opening time: 08h00 Monday to Saturday
Closing time: 17h00
Situated in Franschhoek

Blaawklippen
Tel: 021-880 0133
Email: hospitality@blaauwklippen.co.za
URL: www.blaawklippen.co.za
Opening time: 09h00 Monday to Sunday;
Closing time: 17h00 Monday to Friday;
    13h00 Saturday and Sunday
Situated in Stellenbosch

Boland Kelder
Tel: 021-862 6190
Email: info@bolandkelder.co.za
URL: www.bolandwines.co.za
Opening time: 08h00 Monday to Saturday
Closing time: 17h00 Monday to Friday;
    14h00 Saturday
Situated in Paarl

Boschendal Wines
Tel: 021-870 4272/3/4/5
URL: www.boschendal.com
Opening time: 08h30 Monday to Sunday
Closing time: 16h30
Situated in Franschhoek

Bosman Family Vineyards
Tel: 021-873 3170
Email: carla@bosmanwines.com
URL: www.bosmanwines.com
By appointment only
Situated in Wellington

Bovlei Winery
Tel: 021-873 1567
Email: wines@bovlei.co.za
URL: www.bovlei.co.za
Opening time: 08h00 Monday to Friday;
    09h00 Saturday and Public holidays
Closing time: 17h00 Monday to Friday; 13h00
    Saturdays; 16h30 Public Holidays
Situated in Wellington

Buitenverwachting
Tel: 021-794 5190
Email: info@buitenverwachting.com
URL: www.buitenverwachting.co.za
Opening time: Novermber to April: 12h00
    Mondays to Saturday
Closing time: 16h00; closed Christmas and
    New Year's days
Situated in Cape Town

Cabriere Estate
Tel: 021-876 8500
Email: marketing@cabriere.co.za
URL: www.cabriere.co.za
Opening time: 09h00 Monday to Friday;
    10h30 Saturdays
Closing time: 16h30 Monday to Friday;
    15h30 Saturdays
Situated in Franschhoek

Chamonix
Tel: 021-876 8400
URL: www.chamonix.co.za
Opening time: 09h30 Monday to Sunday
Closing time: 17h00
Situated in Franschhoek

WESTERN CAPE

WINE | WINE | WINE | WINE | WINE | WINE | WINE | WINE | WINE | WINE | WINE

Colmant Cap Classique & Champagne
Tel: 021-876 4348
Email: info@colmant.co.za
URL: www.colmat.co.za
Opening time: 10h00 Monday to Saturday
Closing time: 18h00 Monday to Friday;
    13h00 Saturdays
Situated in Franschhoek

De Compagnie Wine Estate
Tel: 021-864 1241
Email: mail@decompagnie.co.za
By appointment only
Situated in Wellington

De Zoete Inval Wine Estate
Tel: 021-863 1535
Email: info@dezoeteinval.co.za
URL: www.dezoeteinval.co.za
Opening time: 09h00 Monday to Saturday;
    10h00 Public holidays
Closing time: 17h00 Monday to Saturday;
    15h00 Public holidays
Situated in Paarl

Diemersfontein Wine and Country Estate
Tel: 021-864 5050
URL: www.diemersfontein.co.za
Opening time: 10h00 Monday to Sunday
Closing time: 17h00
Situated in Wellington

Delheim
Tel: 021-888 4600
Email: delheim@delheim.com
URL: www.delheim.com
Opening time: 09h00
Closing time: 17h00
Situated in Stellenbosch

Dieu Donné
Tel: 021-876 2493
Email: info@dieudonnevineyards.com
URL: www.dieudonnevineyards.com
Opening times: 09h00 Monday to Friday;
    10h30 Saturday and Sunday
Closing times: 16h00
Situated in Franschhoek

Doolhof Wine Estate
Tel: 021-873 6911
URL: www.doolhof.com
Opening time: 08h00 Monday to Friday;
    09h00 Saturdays
Closing time: 17h00 Monday to Friday;
    13h00 Saturdays
Situated in Wellington

Eikendal
Tel: 021-855 1422
Email: info@eikendal.co.za
URL: www.eikendal.com
Opening time: 09h30 Monday to Saturday;
    10h00 Sundays and public holidays
Closing time: 16h30 Monday to Saturday;
    16h00 Sundays and public holidays
Situated in Stellenbosch

Eshkol Winery
Tel: 021-856 1113
Email: info@capvin.co.za
By appointment only
Situated in Wellington

Fairview
Tel: 021-863 2450
Email: info@fairview.co.za
URL: www.fairview.co.za
Opening time: 08h30 Monday to Saturday;
    09h30 Sundays
Closing time: 17h00 Monday to Friday;
    16h00 Saturday and Sunday
Situated in Paarl

Franschhoek Vineyards
Tel: 021-876 2086
URL: www.franschhoek.co.za
Opening time: 09h30 Monday to Friday;
    10h00 Saturdays and public holidays; 11h00
    Sundays
Closing time: 17h00 Monday to Friday;
    16h00 Saturdays and public holidays; 15h00
    Sundays
Situated in Franschhoek

Glen Carlou
Tel: 021-875 5528
Email: welcome@glencarlou.co.za
URL: www.glencarlou.co.za
Opening time: November to March: 08h30
  Monday to Friday; 10h00 Saturday and
  Sunday; April to October: 09h00 Saturdays
Closing time: November to March: 16h45
  Monday to Friday; 15h00 Saturday and
  Sunday; April to October: 12h45 Saturdays
Situated in Paarl

Groot Constantia
Tel: 021-794 5128
Email: enquiries@grootconstantia.co.za
URL: www.grootconstantia.co.za
Opening time: 09h00 Monday to Sunday;
  Closed on Good Friday, Christmas Day
  and New Year's Day
Closing time: 18h00
Situated in Cape Town

Hartenberg
Tel: 021-865 2541
Email: info@hartenbergestate.com
URL: www.hartenbergestate.com
Opening time: 09h00 Monday to Saturday
  and public holidays; 10h00 Sundays
Closing time: 17h15 Monday to Friday,
  15h00 Saturdays and public holidays;
  15h30 Sundays
Situated in Stellenbosch

Hoopenburg
Tel: 021-8844 221
Email: info@hoopenburg.com
URL: www.hoopenburg.com
Opening time: 09h30 Monday to Saturday
  and public holidays
Closing time: 16h30 Monday to Friday; 14h00
  Saturdays and public holidays
  Closed May to September
Situated in Stellenbosch

Jacaranda Wine Estate
Tel: 02-8641235
Opening time: 10h00 Monday to Saturday
Closing time: 17h00 Monday to Friday;
  13h00 Saturdays
Situated in Wellington

Jordan
URL: www.jordanwinery.co.za
Opening time: 10h00 Monday to Friday and
  Sundays; 09h30 Saturdays
Closing time: 16h30 Monday to Friday; 14h30
  Saturdays and Sundays
Situated in Stellenbosch

Klawervlei
Tel: 021-865 2746
Email: terrainvest@bluewin.ch
URL: www.klawervlei.com
By appointment only
Situated in Stellenbosch

Klein Constantia
Tel: 021-794 5188
Email: info@kleinconstantia.com
URL: www.kleinconstantia.com
Opening time: 09h00 Monday to Saturday
Closing time: 17h00 Monday to Friday;
  13h00 Saturdays
Situated in Cape Town

Kleine Zalze
Tel: 021-880 0717
Email: quality@kleinezalze.co.za
URL: www.kleinezalze.com
Opening time: 09h00 Monday to Sunday
Closing time: 17h00 Monday to Saturday;
  14h00 Sundays
Situated in Stellenbosch

Kleinfontein
Tel: 021-864 1202
Email: kleinfon@iafrica.com
URL: www.kleinfontein.com
By appointment only
Situated in Wellington

KWV Wine Emporium
Tel: 021-807 3007
Email: the_wine_emporium@kwv.co.za
URL: www.kwv.co.za
Opening times: 09h00 Monday to Saturday;
  11h00 Sunday
Closing times: 16h00
Situated in Paarl

WESTERN CAPE

WINE WINE WINE WINE WINE WINE WINE

La Bourogne
Tel: 021-876 3245
URL: www.labourogne.co.za
By appointment only
Situated in Franschhoek

La Bri Vineyards
Tel: 021-876 2593
Email: info@labri.co.za
URL: www.labri.co.za
Opening time: 10h00 Monday to Friday
between October and April
Closing time: 12h30
Situated in Franschhoek

La Couronne Wine Estate
Tel: 021-876 3939
Email: info@lacouronne.co.za
URL: www.lacouronne.co.za
Opening time: 09h00 Monday to Saturday;
10h00 Sunday and public holidays
Closing time: 16h00 Monday to Saturdays
15h30 Sunday and public holidays
Situated in Franschhoek

La Motte Wine Estate
Tel: 021-876 3119
URL: www.la-motte.com
Opening time: 09h00 Monday to Friday;
10h00 Saturdays
Closing time: 16h30 Monday to Friday;
15h00 Saturdays
Situated in Franschhoek

Laborie Wine Estate
Tel: 021-807 3390
Email: pienaaf@kwv.co.za
URL: www.laborie.co.za
Opening time: 09h00 Monday to Saturday;
11h00 Sundays; Closed on Sundays from
May to September
Closing time: 17h00 Monday to Saturday;
15h00 Sundays
Situated in Paarl

Landskroon
Tel: 021-863 1039
Email: madelief@landskroonwines.com
URL: www.landskroonwines.com
Opening time: 08h30 Monday to Friday;
09h00 Saturdays
Closing time: 17h00 Monday to Friday;
13h00 Saturdays
Situated in Paarl

L'Avenir Vineyards
Tel: 021-889 5001
Email: info@lavenir.co.za
Opening time: 10h00 Monday to Saturday
Closing time: 17h00 Monday to Friday;
16h00 Saturdays
Situated in Stellenbosch

Lanzerac Winery
Tel: 021-847 2200
Email: ednac@lourensford.co.za
URL: www.lanzeracwines.co.za
Opening time: 11h00 Monday to Friday
Closing time: 15h00
Situated in Stellenbosch

Lievland Wine Eastate
Tel: 021-875 5226
Email: info@lievland.com
URL: www.lievland.co.za
Opening time: 09h00 Monday to Friday;
10h00 Saturdays and Sundays
Closing time: 17h00 Monday to Friday; 16h00
Saturdays and Sundays
Situated in Stellenbosch

Linton Park Wines
Tel: 021-873 1625
Email: info@lintonparkwines.co.za
URL: www.lintonparkwines.co.za
By appointment only
Situated in Wellington

L'Ormarins
Tel: 021-874 9000
URL: www.southernwines.com
Opening time: 09h00 Monday to Friday;
10h00 Saturdays
Closing time: 16h30 Monday to Friday;
14h30 Saturdays
Situated in Franschhoek

Louisvale
Tel: 021-865 2422
Email: winery@louisvale.com
URL: www.louisvale.com
By appointment only
Situated in Stellenbosch

Malan de Versailles
Tel: 021-873 1766
URL: www.wellington.co.za
By appointment only
Situated in Wellington

Middlevlei Wine Estate
Tel: 021-883 2565
Email: info@middelvlei.co.za
URL: www.middelvlei.co.za
Opening time: 10h00 Monday to Saturday
Closing time: 16h30
Situated in Stellenbosch

Mont du Toit
Tel: 021-873 7745
Email: kelder@montdutoit.co.za
URL: www.montdutoitwines.co.za
Opening time: 08h30 Monday to Friday
Closing time: 16h30
Situated in Wellington

Mont Rochelle Mountain Vineyards
Tel: 021-876 2770
Email: info@montrochelle.co.za
URL: www.montrochelle.co.za
Opening time: 10h00 Monday to Friday
Closing time: 18h00
Situated in Franschhoek

Moreson
Tel: 021-876 3055
URL: www.moreson.co.za
Opening time: 11h00 Monday to Sunday
Closing time: 17h00
Situated in Franschhoek

Morgenhof Estate
Tel: 021-889 5510
Email: info@morgenhof.com
URL: www.morgenhof.com
Opening time: 09h00 Monday to Friday;
    10h00 Saturdays and Sundays
Closing time: 17h00
Situated in Stellenbosch

Muratie Wine Estate
Tel: 021-865 2330/6
Email: info@muratie.co.za
URL: www.muratie.co.za
Opening time: 10h00 Monday to Sunday
Closing time: 17h00
Situated in Stellenbosch

Nabygelegen
Tel: 021-873 7534
Email: avalonwines@icon.co.za
URL: www.nabygelegen.co.za
Opening time: 08h30 Monday to Friday;
    09h00 Saturdays
Closing time: 17h00 Monday to Friday;
    13h00 Saturdays
Situated in Wellington

Napier Winery
Tel: 021-873 7829
Email: sales@napierwinery.co.za
URL: www.napierwinery.co.za
Opening time: 08h30 Monday to Friday
Closing time: 17h00
Situated in Wellington

Neethlingshof
Tel: 021-883 8988
Email: info@neethlingshof.co.za
URL: www.neethlingshof.co.za
Opening time: 09h00 Monday to Friday;
    10h00 Saturdays and Sundays
Closing time: 17h00 Monday to Friday;
    16h00 Saturdays and Sundays
Situated in Stellenbosch

Nelson's Creek Wine Estate
Tel: 021-869 8453
Email: info@nelsonscreek.co.za
URL: www.nelsonscreek.co.za
Opening time: 09h00 Monday to Saturday
Closing time: 17h00 Monday to Friday;
    14h00 Saturdays
Situated in Paarl

Overgaauw Estate
Tel: 021-881 3815
Email: info@overgaauw.co.za
URL: www.overgaauw.co.za
Opening time: 09h00 and 14h00 Monday to Friday; 10h00 Saturdays
Closing time: 12h30 and 17h00 Monday to Friday; 12h30 Saturdays
Situated in Stellenbosch

Paarl Rock Brandy Cellars
Tel: 021-807 3390
Opening time: 08h00 Monday to Friday
Closing time: 17h00
Situated in Paarl

Perdeberg Winery
Tel: 021-869 8244
URL: www.perdeberg.co.za
Opening time: 08h00 Monday to Friday; 09h00 Saturdays
Closing time: 17h00 Monday to Friday; 13h00 Saturdays
Situated in Paarl

Plasir de Merle
Tel: 021-874 1071
Email: plasirdemerle@capelegends.co.za
URL: www.plasirdemerle.co.za
Opening time: 08h30 Monday to Friday; 10h00 Saturdays (November to March)
Closing time: 17h00 Monday to Friday; 16h00 Saturdays (November to March)
Situated in Franschhoek

Rhebokskloof
Tel: 021-869 8386
Email: info@rhebokskloof.co.za
URL: www.rhebokskloof.co.za
Opening time: 09h00 Monday to Sunday
Closing time: 17h00
Situated in Paarl

Rickety Bridge Winery
Tel: 021-876 2129/3669
Email: sales@ricketybridge.com
URL: www.ricketybridgewinery.com
Opening time: 08h00 Monday to Friday; 09h00 Saturdays and public holidays
Closing time: 17h00
Situated in Franschhoek

Robertson's Wine Valley
Tel: 023-626 3167
Email: manager@robertsonwinevalley.com
URL: www.robertsonwinevalley.com
Situated on Route 62

Ruitersvlei Wines
Tel: 021-863 1517
Email: wines@ruitersvlei.co.za
URL: www.ruitersvlei.co.za
Opening time: 10h00 Monday to Friday
Closing time: 16h00
Situated in Paarl

Rupert & Rothschild Vignerons
Tel: 021-874 1648
Email: info@rupert-rothschildvignerons.com
URL: www.rupert-rothschildvignerons.com
By appointment only
Situated in Franschhoek

Rust en Vrede
Tel: 021-881 3881
Email: info@rustenvrede.com
URL: www.rustenvrede.com
Opening time: 09h00 Monday to Saturday
Closing time: 17h00 Monday to Friday; 16h00 Saturdays
Situated in Stellenbosch

Saxenburg Wines
Tel: 021-903 6113
Email: info@saxenburg.com
URL: www.saxenburg.com
Opening time: 09h00 Monday to Saturday; 10h00 Sundays
Closing time: 17h00 Monday to Friday; 16h00 Saturdays and Sundays
Situated in Stellenbosch

Seidelberg Wine Estate
Tel: 021-863 5200
Email: info@seidelberg.co.za
URL: www.seidelberg.co.za
Opening time: 09h00 Monday to Friday; 10h00 Saturdays and Sundays
Closing time: 18h00
Situated in Paarl

Simonsig Estate
Tel: 021-888 4900
Email: wine@simonsig.co.za
URL: www.simonsig.co.za
Opening time: 08h30 Monday to Saturday
and public holidays
Closing time: 17h00 Monday to Friday; 16h00
Saturdays and public holidays
Situated in Stellenbosch

Simonsvlei
Tel: 021-863 3040
URL: www.simonsvlei.com
Opening time: 08h00 Monday to Friday;
08h30 Saturdays; 11h00 Sundays
Closing time: 17h00 Monday to Friday; 16h30
Saturdays; 15h00 Sundays
Situated in Paarl

Spier Cellars
Tel: 021-809 1100
Email: info@spier.co.za
URL: www.spier.co.za
Opening time: 09h00 Monday to Sunday
Closing time: 17h00
Situated in Stellenbosch

Stony Brooke Vineyards
Tel: 021-876 2182
Email: info@stonybrook.co.za
URL: www.stonybrook.co.za
By appointment only
Situated in Franschhoek

The Company of Wine People
Tel: 021-881 3870
Email: info@thecompanyofwinepeople.co.za
URL: www.thecompanyofwinepeople.com
Situated in Stellenbosch

Uiterwyk Wine Estate
Tel: 021-881 3711
Email: mawine@absamail.co.za
URL: www.uiterwyk.co.za
Opening time: 10h00 Monday to Saturday
Closing time: 16h30
Situated in Stellenbosch

Villiera
Tel: 021-865 2002/3
Email: wine@villiera.com
URL: www.villiera.co.za
Opening time: 08h30 Monday to Saturday
Closing time: 17h00 Monday to Friday;
13h00 Saturdays
Situated in Paarl

Vredenheim Estate
Tel: 021-881 3878
Email: wine@vredenheim.co.za
URL: www.vredenheim.co.za
Opening time: 08h30 Monday to Friday;
09h00 Saturdays
Closing time: 17h00 Monday to Friday;
14h00 Saturdays
Situated in Stellenbosch

Wamakersvallei
Tel: 021-873 1582
Email: sales@wamakers.co.za
URL: www.wellington.co.za
Opening time: 08h00 Monday to Friday;
08h30 Saturdays
Closing time: 17h00 Monday to Friday;
12h30 Saturdays
Situated in Wellington

Waterford
Tel: 021-880 0496
Email: info@waterfordestate.co.za
URL: www.waterfordestate.co.za
Opening time: 09h00 Monday to Friday;
10h00 Saturdays
Closing time: 17h00 Monday to Friday;
15h00 Saturdays
Situated in Stellenbosch

Welbedacht
Tel: 021-873 1877
Email: wine@welbedacht.co.za
URL: www.welbedacht.co.za
Opening time: 09h00 Monday to Friday;
10h00 Saturdays
Closing time 17h00 Monday to Friday;
13h00 Saturdays
Situated in Wellington

Wellington Cellar
Tel: 021-873 1163
Email: wellingtoncellar@iafrica.com
URL: www.wellington.co.za
Opening time: 08h00 Monday to Friday
Closing time: 17h00
Situated in Wellington

Windmeul Cellar
Tel: 021-869 8043
Email: windmeul@iafrica.com
URL: www.mindmeulwinery.co.za
Opening time: 08h00 Monday to Friday;
09h00 Saturdays
Closing time: 17h00 Monday to Friday;
15h00 Saturdays
Situated in Paarl

Wine Concepts
Tel: 021-426 4401
Email: kloofst@wineconcepts.co.za
URL: www.wineconcepts.co.za
Situated in Stellenbosch, Newlands &
Cape Town

Zanddrif Vineyards
Tel: 021-863 2076
Opening time: 09h00 Monday to Friday
Closing time: 17h00
Situated in Paarl

Zandwijk
Tel: 021-863 2368
Opening time: 08h30 and 13h30 Monday
to Friday
Closing time: 12h30 and 17h00
Situated in Paarl

Zevenwacht
Tel: 021-903 5123
Email: info@zevenwacht.co.za
URL: www.zevenwacht.co.za
Opening time: 08h00 Monday to Friday;
09h30 Saturdays and Sundays
Closing time: 17h00
Situated in Stellenbosch

Wine Routes

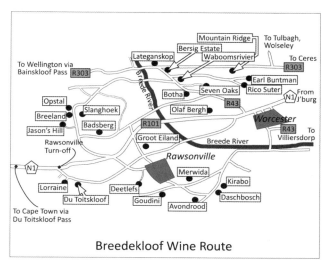

Breedekloof Wine Route

Breedekloof Wine Route
Just 90km from Cape Town, this wine route stretches west-east from Gouda to
Montagu and north-south from Tankwa Karoo National Park to McGregor.

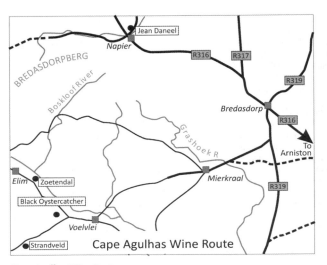

Cape Agulhas Wine Route

Most of the farms can be found in the village of Elim which lies on the peninsula of this, the southernmost tip of Africa.

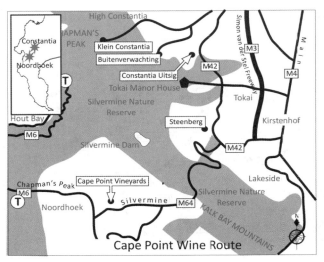

Cape Point Wine Route

This relatively new route covers 30 hectares and includes the vineyards of Noordhoek, Scarborough and Red Hill.

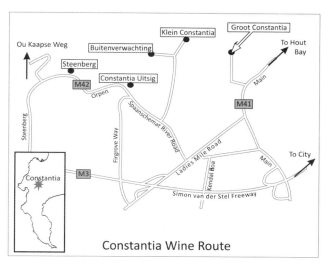

Constantia Wine Route

Constantia Wine Route

Minutes from the city centre this route reaches up the eastern slopes of the Constantiaberg Mountains. The Constantia Valley is made up of three famous estates: Buitenverwachting, Groot Constantia and Klein Constantia.

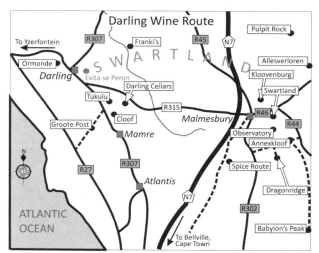

Darling Wine Route

The town of Darling is a leisurely hour's drive north of Cape Town, southeast of the West Coast National Park, and is home to five wine cellars.

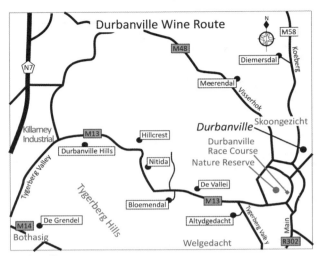

Durbanville Wine Route
20km northeast of Cape Town this wine route is often overlooked yet nine
estates lie on the rolling Tygerberg hills.

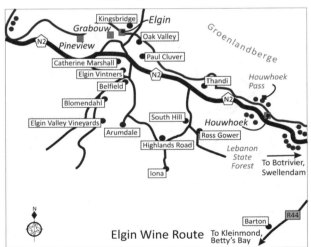

Elgin Wine Route
The town of Elgin lies to the south of the Hottentots Holland Nature Reserve
and the Elgin Valley, crowded with fruit orchards and vineyards which
produce predominantly fruity wines. This valley in the Cape Overberg is
only a 45-minute drive from Cape Town.

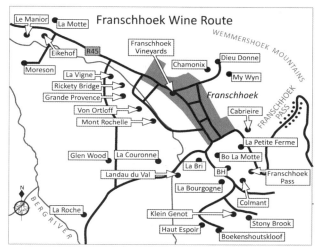

Franschhoek Wine Route

300 years after the French Huguenots settled in this valley it is now home to over 30 wine cellars. Franschhoek is a beautiful, historic town and is a 50-minute drive from Cape Town. A Cap Classique route has now been launched in the valley too—4km of sparkling wine heaven.

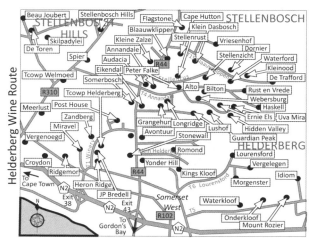

Helderberg Wine Route

Near the town of Somerset West and 15 minutes from Cape Town International Airport, this route is nestled in the Helderberg Mountains and has both a mountainous and maritime climate.

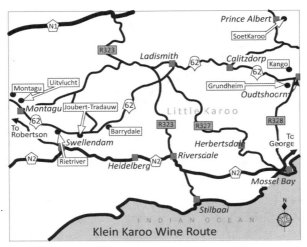

Klein Karoo Wine Route

Klein Karoo Wine Route

In this semi-arid area vines grow in the ravines, kloofs and valleys of the rugged mountains that form its landscape. The Klein Karro is bordered in the west by Montagu and Uniondale in the east. The Langeberg Mountains form its southern perimeter with the Garden Route and the Swartberg to the north. Route 62 runs through the Little Karoo and accommodates 16 cellars.

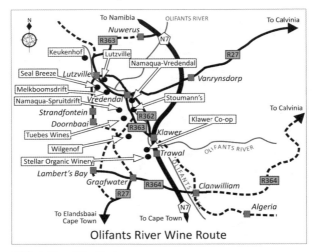

Olifants River Wine Route

Olifants River Wine Route

Citrusdal, situated 180km north of Cape Town, is the start of this route and thus necessitates a longer trip than most of the other routes. Meandering along the Olifants River for 120km this is one of the country's most beautiful regions and wine tasting should definitely be combined with taking in the breathtaking scenery of the Cederberg.

Paarl Vintners Wine Route

Nelson's Creek · Oude Denneboom · Anthony Smook · Perderberg · Domaine Brahms · Windmeul · Ridgeback · Rhebokskloof · Landskroon · Seidelberg · Fairview · Zandwijk · Glen Carlou · Baksberg · Juno · Pontac Manor · Paarl · Nwanedi · Boland · Nederberg · Vendome · The Mason's · Laborie · Simonsvlei · Val de Vie · Freedom Hill · Klein Parys

To Malmesbury · To Tulbagh · To Ceres · Wellington · Du Toitskloof Pass · Huguenot Toll Tunnel · To Worcester, Beaufort West, Johannesburg · To Durbanville · To Cape Town · To Stellenbosch · To Franschhoek

R45 · R303 · R301 · R44 · R312 · R101 · R310 · N1

Paarl Vintners Wine Route

50km northeast of Cape Town the town of Paarl is home to many of the country's foremost wine producers and is the world's first 'red' route.

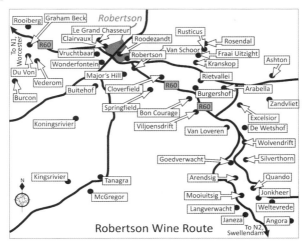

Robertson Wine Route

In the heart of Route 63 this is the country's longest wine route, starting an hour and a half's drive from the Mother City, including the towns of Ashton, Bonnievale, McGregor and Robertson.

287

Stellenbosch Wine Route
Just 45 minutes from Cape Town, Stellenbosch represents over 300 wineries. Although the area is relatively small, the number of wineries has necessitated a number of sub-routes, namely: Bottelary Hills, Devon Valley Vintners, Helderberg and Simonsberg-Stellenbosch. Bottelary Hills produces excellent red wines. Devon Valley Vintners lie to the west of Stellenbosch and focuses on red wines although they have also produced some enviable premium white and sparkling wines. Simonsberg-Stellenbosch is known as 'Cabernet country'.

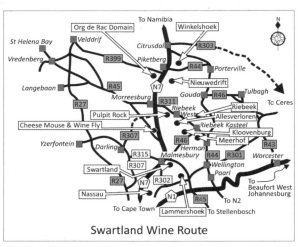

Swartland Wine Route

Swartland Wine Route
This route starts in Darling and extends 65km as the crow flies in a northeasterly direction to Porterville, through the Swartland, named for the renosterbos that typifies the landscape. The vineyards hug the Berg River and mountain valleys. The region is known for its full-bodied reds and fortified wines.

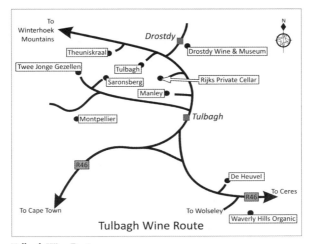

Tulbagh Wine Route

Tulbagh Wine Route

50km north of Wellington and 80km from Cape Town, Tulbagh is surrounded on three sides by mountains. Picturesque and quaint, this area has placed itself prominently on the map by the string of international awards its wines have recently won.

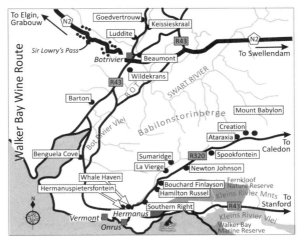

Walker Bay Wine Route

As the crow flies, the southern point of Walker Bay, Gans Bay, is 80km from Cape Point but only a 45-minute drive from Cape Town. The route boasts over a dozen wineries in and around the whale-watching town of Hermanus.

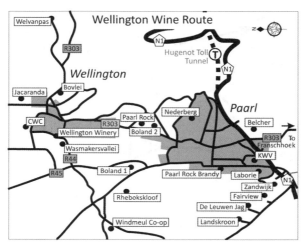

Wellington Wine Route

Ideally situated, at a leisurely two hours' northeast of Cape Town,
Wellington is a much-celebrated wine region. The town lies at the foot
of Groenberg Mountain and the region is the 'birth place' of 90 percent
of the country's vines with much of the landscape taken up by nurseries.
Connoisseurs can enjoy a a 3-day hike through vineyards, orchards and
indigenous fynbos, which includes wine tasting and samplings of cheeses
and olives, with stayovers at one of the four farms.

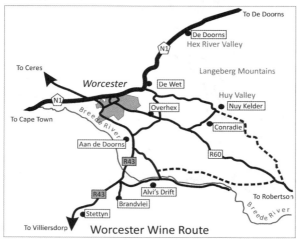

Worcester Wine Route

The town lies in the Breede River Valley and is only an hour's drive from
Cape Town. The district is the largest in terms of wine-growing area and
volume, producing almost 30 percent of the country's wines and spirits.

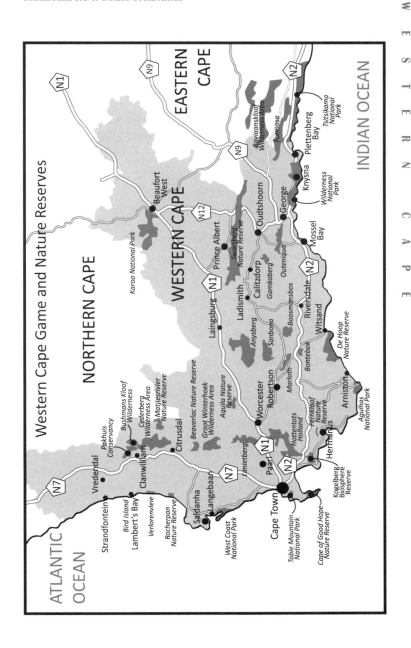

Game and Nature Reserves (including National Parks)

CapeNature
Tel: 021-659 3400 (head office)
Tourism reservations and bookings:
National callers: 0861-CAPENATURE (227 362 8873)
International callers: 0027-861-227 362 8873 / 0027-21-659 3500
URL: www.capenature.org.za

CapeNature Reserves

West Coast:
  Cederberg Wilderness Area
  Bird Island Nature Reserve
  Rocherpan Nature Reserve
  Groot Winterhoek Wilderness Area

Winelands:
  Limietberg Nature Reserve
  Jonkershoek Nature Reserve
  Assegaaibosch Nature Reserve
  Hottentots Holland Nature Reserve
  Vrolijkheid Nature Reserve

Overberg:
  Marloth Nature Reserve
  Kogelberg Nature Reserve
  Walker Bay Nature Reserve
  Salmonsdam Nature Reserve
  De Mond Nature Reserve
  De Hoop Nature Reserve
  Grootvadersbosch Nature Reserve
  Boosmansbos Wilderness Area

Cape Karoo:
  Anysberg Nature Reserve
  Swartberg Nature Reserve
  Gamkaberg Nature Reserve

Garden Route and Little Karoo:
  Outeniqua Nature Reserve
  Goukamma Nature Reserve
  Keurbooms River Nature Reserve
  Robberg Nature Reserve

South African National Parks
Tel: 012-426 5000
Email: reservations@sanparks.org
URL: www.sanparks.org

SANParks Reserves
Agulhas National Park
Bontebok National Park
Karoo National Park
Table Mountain National Park
West Coast National Park
Wilderness National Park

Other Parks

Aquila Nature Reserve
Tel: 021-431 8400
Email: res@aquilasafari.com
URL: www.aquilasafari.com

Beaverlac Nature Reserve
Tel: 022-931 2945
URL: www.beaverlac.co.za

Bushmanskloof Wilderness
Tel: 021-481 1860
Email: info@bushmanskloof.co.za
URL: www.bushmanskloof.co.za

Fernkloof Nature Reserve
Tel: 028-313 8100
URL: www.fernkloof.com

Inverdoorn Game Reserve
Tel: 021-434 4639
E-mal: info@inverdoorn.co.za
URL: www.inverdoorn.co.za

Kagga Kamma Private Game Reserve
Tel: 021-872 4343
Email: info@kaggakaam.co.za
URL: www.kaggakamma.co.za

Ko-Ka Tsara Game Reserve
Tel: 023-415 2753 / 416 1666
Email: info@kokatsara.co.za
URL: www.kokatsara.co.za

Matjiesrivier Nature Reserve
Tel: 022-931 2088
Email: cederberg@cnc.org.za
URL: www.cederberg.co.za

Sanbona Wildlife Reserve
Tel: 041-407 1000
Email: reservations@mantiscollection.com
URL: www.sanbona.com

Waenhuiskrans Nature Reserve
Tel: 028-425 5020
Email: bredasdorp@capenature.co.za

Entertainment

AfroBeat Drumming
drumming circles and performances
Tel: 084-566 0531
Email: info@afrobeatdrumming.co.za
URL: www.afrobeatdrumming.co.za

Asoka Son of Dharma
bars and lounges
Tel: 021-422 0909
URL: www.asokasonofdharma.com
Address: 68 Kloof Street, Cape Town

Baraza
cocktail bar
Tel: 021-438 1758
URL: www.baraza.co.za
Address: The Promenade, Victoria Road,
    Camps Bay, Cape Town

Barmooda
bars and lounges
Tel: 021-447 6752
URL: www.barmooda.co.za
Address: cnr Lower Main &
    Station Road, Observatory, Cape Town

Blues Bar
cocktail bar
Tel: 021-426 5042
Address: 108 Kloof Street, Cape Town

Bossa Nova
nightclub
Tel: 021-425 0295
URL: www.bossanova.co.za
Address: 43 Somerset Road, Greenpoint,
    Cape Town

Buddhabar
bars and lounges
Tel: 021-434 4010
URL: www.buddhabar.co.za
Address: 39 Main Road, Greenpoint,
    Cape Town

Cubaña
bars and lounges
Tel: 021-683 4040
URL: www.cubana.co.za
Address: Aska House, Main Road, Claremont,
    Cape Town

Dizzy's
bars and lounges
Tel: 021-438 2686
URL: www.dizzys.co.za
Address: 39 & 41 The Drive, Camps Bay,
    Cape Town

Ferryman's Tavern
bars and Lounges
Tel: 021-419 7748
URL: www.waterfront.co.za
Address: cnr East Pier & Dock Roads,
    V&A Waterfront, Cape Town

Ignite
nightclub
Tel: 021-438 7717
Address: The Promenade, Victoria Road,
    Camps Bay, Cape Town

M-Bar & Lounge
bars and lounges
Tel: 021-424 7247
URL: www.metropolehotel.co.za
Address: 38 Long Street, Cape Town

Mink
cocktail bar
Tel: 021-422 3262
Address: 24 Shortmarket Street,
    Greenmarket Square, Cape Town

Oblivion
bars and lounges
Tel: 021-671 8522
URL: www.oblivion.co.za
Address: 22 Chichester Road, cnr 3rd N
    Chichester, Harfield Village, Cape Town

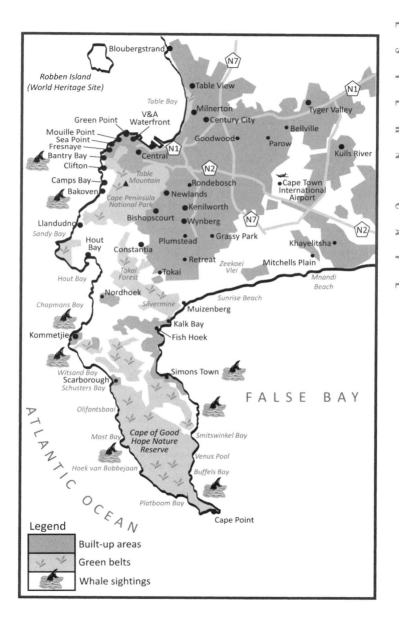

Obz Café
cocktail bar
Tel: 021-448 5555
URL: www.obzcafe.co.za
Address: 115 Lower Main Road,
    Observatory, Cape Town

Opium
nightclub
Tel: 021-425 4010
URL: www.opium.co.za
Address: 6 Dixon Street, De Waterkant,
    Cape Town

Planet Champagne Bar
bars and lounges
Tel: 021-483 1000
URL: www.mountnelson.co.za
Address: Mount Nelson Hotel,
    76 Orange Street, Gardens, Cape Town

Pulse
nightclub
Tel: 021-425 4010
URL: www.pulse.co.za
Address: 23 Somerset Road,
    Green Point, Cape Town

Rhodes House
nightclub
Tel: 021-424 8844
URL: www.rhodeshouse.com
Address: 60 Queen Victoria Street,
    Gardens, Cape Town

Springbok Pub
nightclub
Tel: 021-671 4251
Address: 1 Sport Pienaar Road, Newlands,
    Cape Town

Tin Roof
nightclub
Tel: 021-674 6888
Address: cnr Main & Stegmann Roads
    (opposite Steers), Claremont, Cape Town

Grand West Casino
gambling
Tel: 021-505 7777
URL: www.grandwest.co.za
Address: 1 Vanguard Drive, Goodwood,
    Cape Town

Annual events

Calitzdorp Port Festival
Tel: 044-213 3326
Email: boplaas@mweb.co.za
URL: www.sappa.co.za
Held every July

Cape Town International Jazz Festival
Tel: 021-422 5653
URL: www.capetownjazzfest.co.za
Held every March

Clan William Wild Flower Festival
Tel: 027-482 2024
Email: cederberg@lando.co.za
URL: www.clanwilliam.info
Held every August / September

Hermanus Whale Festival
Tel: 028-313 0928
Email: Email: info@knysna-info.co.za
URL: www.whalefestival.co.za
Held every September

Knysna Gastronomica
Tel: 044-302 5749
Email: gastronomica@theboatshed.co.za
URL: www.gastronomicakny.co.za
Held every September

Knysna Oyster Festival
Tel: 044-382 5510
Email: info@knysna-info.co.za
URL: www.oysterfestival.co.za
Held every July

Klein Karoo National Arts Festival
Tel: 044-203 8600
Email: info@kknk.co.za
URL: www.kknk.co.za
Held in Oudtshoorn every April

Lambert's Bay Crayfish Festival
Tel: 027-432 1000
Email: lambertsinfo@mweb.co.za
URL: www.kreeffeeslambertsbaai.co.za
Held every March

Madame Zingara's Christmas in July
URL: www.madamezingara.com
Held in Cape Town every July

Pink Loerie Mardi Gras
Email: info@pinkloerie.com
URL: www.pinkloerie.com
Held in Knysna every May

Prince Albert Agricultural Show
Tel: 023-5411 366
Email: princealberttourism@intekom.co.za
URL: www.patourism.co.za
Held every September

Prince Albert Town & Olive Festival
Tel: 023-5411 366
Email: princealberttourism@intekom.co.za
URL: www.patourism.co.za
Held every April / May

Riebeek Kasteel Olive Festival
Tel: 022-448 1368
URL: www.riebeekvalley.info
Held in the Riebeek Valley every May

Sedgefield Lakes Festival
Tel: 044-382 5510
Email: info@knysna-info.co.za
URL: www.visitknysna.co.za
Held every March

Spier Summer Festival
URL: www.spierarts.org.za
Held in Stellenbosch every
   December–March

Tulbagh Goes Dutch
Tel: 023-2301348
Email: tulbaghinfo@lando.co.za
URL: www.tulbaghtourism.org.za
Held every April

Wacky Wine Weekend
Tel: 023-626 3167
Email: manager@robertsonwinevalley.com
URL: www.wackywineweekend.com
Held in Robertson every June

Kids

Laser Quest
Tel: 021-683 7296
URL: www.tygerbergonline.com/laserquest
Situated in Tygerberg, Cape Town

Ratanga Junction
Tel: 0861-200 300
Email: info@ratanga.co.za
URL: www.ratanga.co.za
Situated in Century City, Cape Town

Tiny Tourists
Tel: 082-264 0553
Email: kath@tinytourists.com
URL: www.tinytourists.com

Shopping www.mallguide.co.za

Bayside Shopping Mall (Tableview)
Tel: 021-557 4350

Canal Walk (Century City)
Tel: 021-529 9600

Capegate (Brackenfell)
Tel: 021-981 2288

Cavendish Square (Claremont)
Tel: 021-657 5620

Constantia Village
Tel: 021-794 5065

Green Point Market
Tel: 021-914 7218

Green Market Square (Cape Town CBD)
Tel: 021-426-1052

Hout Bay Community Cultural Centre
Tel: 021-790 2273
Email: izikoll@gmail.co.za
URL: www.izikoll.co.za

Kirstenbosch Craft Market (Newlands)
Tel: 021-799 8800

N1 City Mall (Northern Suburbs)
Tel: 021-595 1170

The Pan African Market
Tel: 021-426 4478
Email: info@panafrican.co.za
URL: www.panafrican.co.za

Tulbagh Farmers Market
Tel: 023-230 1742
Email: thingsilove@global.co.za
URL: www.thingsilove.co.za

Tyger Valley Mall
Tel: 021-914 1822
URL: www.tygervalley.co.za

Willowbridge Lifestyle Centre (Tyger Valley)
Tel: 021-914 7218

Restaurants

Bloubergstrand
Café Blouberg
international cuisine
Tel: 021-554 4462
Address: 20 Stadler Road

Ons Huisie
international cuisine
Tel: 021-554 1553
Address: Stadler Road

On the Rocks
international cuisine
Tel: 021-554 1988
Address: 45 Stadler Road

Camps Bay
Azure Restaurant
international cuisine
Tel: 021-437 9029
Address: 12 Apostles Hotel & Spa,
    Victoria Road

Blues Restaurant
international cuisine
Tel: 021-438 2040
Address: The Promonade, Victoria Road

Bungalow
international cuisine
Tel: 021-438 0007
Address: Shop 2A, The Promenade,
    Victoria Road

Paranga
international cuisine
Tel: 021-438 0404
Address: Shop 1, The Promenade,
    Victoria Road

The Kove
international cuisine
Tel: 021-438 0004
Address: Shop 2B, The Promenade,
    Victoria Road

Tuscany Beach
international cuisine
Tel: 021-438 1213
Address: 41 Victoria Road

Canal Walk
Annapurna
Indian cuisine
Tel: 021-555 3595
Address: Shop 427, La Piazza

Braza
Portuguese cuisine
Tel: 021-555 0335
Address: Shop 425, La Piazza

Qing Sushi Bar
sushi
Tel: 021-555 1682
Address: Shop 96

Cape Town
Addis In Cape
Ethiopian cuisine
Tel: 021-424 5722
Address: 41 Church Street

Baran's Theatre Restaurant
Middle Eastern cuisine
Tel: 021-426 4466
Address: 36 Burg Street, cnr
    Shortmarket Street, Greenmarket Square

Biesmiellah
international cuisine
Tel: 021-423 0850
Address: Icon House Foreshore,
    Lower Loop Street

Bo-Kaap Kombuis
Cape Malay cuisine
Tel: 021-422 5446
Address: 7 August Street, Bo-Kaap

Bowl Restaurant
international cuisine
Tel: 021-469 1900
Address: 31 Adderley Street

Bukhara
Indian cuisine
Tel: 021-424 0000
Address: 33 Church Street

Catu
Irish bar
Tel: 021-424 7453
Address: 38 Hout Street

Da Capo Ristorante
Italian cuisine
Tel: 021-423 1234
Address: 52 Shortmarket Street

Five Flies
international cuisine
Tel: 021-424 4442
Address: 13-16 Keeroms Street

Gold Restaurant
African cuisine
Tel: 021-421 4653
Address: Gold of Africa Museum,
    96 Strand Street

Headquarters
steakhouse
Tel: 021-424 6373
Address: Heritage Square,
    100 Shortmarket Street

Kubo's
Japanese cuisine
Tel: 021-421 4360
Address: 48 Riebeek Street

Lapeng Restaurant & Bar
international cuisine
Tel: 021-425 5030
Address: 44 Strand Street

Maharajah
Indian cuisine
Tel: 021-424 6607
Address: 230 Long Street

Marimba
international cuisine
Tel: 021-418 3366
Address: cnr Coen Steytler &
   Heerengracht, Foreshore

Mesopotamia Kurdish Restaurant
Kurdish cuisine
Tel: 021-424 4664
Address: cnr Long & Church Streets

Nonna Lina Ristorante
Italian cuisine
Tel: 021-424 4966
Address: 64 Orange Street

Savoy Cabbage
international cuisine
Tel: 021-424 2626
Address: 101 Hout Street

Snoekies
South African seafood
Tel: 021-426 4000
Address: 31a Long Street

Synergy
cosmopolitan
Tel: 021-481 4000
Address: cnr Wale & Burg Streets

The Africa Café Restaurant
Tel: 021-422 0221
Address: 108 Shortmarket Street

The Gallery Café
international cuisine
Tel: 021-426 6119
Address: 172 Long Street, cnr Pepper Street

Thirty 7
international cuisine
Tel: 021-412 9999
Address: The Westin Grand Cape Town
   Arabella Quays, Lower Long Street

Tratoria Luigi
Italian cuisine
Tel: 021-790 1702
Address: Main Road

Westin Exclusive Club
international cuisine
Tel: 021-412 9999
Address: 19th Floor, The Westin Grand Cape
   Town Arabella Quays, 1 Lower Long Street

Century City
Taiwan City
Chinese cuisine
Tel: 021-555 3081
Address: Shop 421 Canal Walk

Claremont
Ashton's at Greenways
international cuisine
Tel: 021-761 1792
Address: 1-5 Torquay Avenue

Hong
Japanese cuisine
Tel: 021-683 6700
Address: Stadium on Main, Main Road

Perima's
international cuisine
Tel: 021-671 3205
Address: 5 Newmarket Place, cnr Lansdowne
   & Belvedere Roads

Clifton
La Med
international cuisine
Tel: 021-438 5600
Address: Glen Country Club, Victoria Road

Constantia
Buitenverwachting Restaurant
international cuisine
Tel: 021-794 3522
Address: Klein Constantia Rd

Catharina's Restaurant
contemporary
Tel: 021-713 2222
Address: 10802 Steenberg Hotel,
   Constantiavalley

Cape Malay Restaurant
South African cuisine
Tel: 021-794 2137 .
Address: The Cellars Hohenort Hotel,
  93 Brommersvlei Road

Tango's
steakhouse
Tel: 021-712 6631
Address: Cristy Centre, Kendal Road,
  Constantiaberg

The Greenhouse
contemporary
Tel: 021-794 2137
Address: The Cellars Hohenort Hotel,
  93 Brommersvlei Road

Durbanville
Bloemendal Restaurant
international cuisine
Tel: 021-975 7575
Address: M13 / Racecourse Road

Fish Hoek
Napoli Trattoria
Italian cuisine
Tel: 021-782 6992
Address: cnr Main & Station Roads

Gardens
Aubergine
cosmopolitan
Tel: 021-465 4909
Address: 39 Barnet Street

Café Paradiso
French cuisine
Tel: 021-423 8653
Address: 110 Kloof Street

Maria's Greek Restaurant
Mediterranean cuisine
Tel: 021-461 8887
Address: 31 Barnett Street,
  Dunkley Square

Oasis
breakfast and buffet
Tel: 021-483 1948
Address: 76 Orange Street

Sinn's Restaurant
international cuisine
Tel: 021-465 0967
Address: Wembley Square, McKenzie Drive

The Cape Colony
African and Asian cuisine
Tel: 021-483 1948
Address: 76 Orange Street

Vintage India
Indian cuisine
Tel: 021-462 5106
Address: Gardens Centre, cnr Mill &
  Buitenkant Streets

Zucca
Italian cuisine
Tel: 021-423 7331
Address: 84 Kloof Street

Green Point
1800° Grillroom
steakhouse
Tel: 021-430 0506
Address: Cape Royale, Main Road

Andiamo Deli
Mediterranean cuisine
Tel: 021-421 3687/8
Address: Cape Quarter, 72 Waterkant Street

Beluga
contemporary
Tel: 021-418 2948/9
Address: The Foundry, Prestwich Street

Benkei
Japanese cuisine
Tel: 021-439 4918
Address: Shop 3, Paramount Place,
  105 Main Road

Bouillabaisse
contemporary
Tel: 021-418 0440
Address: The Rockwell, Schiebe Street

Chef Ristorante
Italian cuisine
Tel: 021-419 6767
Address: 3 Rose Street

Crêpe Suzette
Parisian pancake parlour
Tel: 021-418 0443
Address: The Rockwell, De Waterkant,
  Schiebe Street

Fiesta
Mediterranean cuisine
Tel: 021-418 5121
Address: Shop A12, Cape Quarter,
  72 Waterkant Street

Pigalle Restaurant
Mediterranean cuisine
Tel: 021-421 4848
Address: 57 Somerset Road

Tank
Japanese & Mediterranean cuisine
Tel: 021-419 0007
Address: Cape Quarter, 72 Waterkant Street

Hout Bay
Chapmans Peak Hotel
Mediterranean cuisine
Tel: 021-790 1036
Address: Chapmans Peak Drive

Mariners Wharf
seafood
Tel: 021-790 1100
Address: Hout Bay Harbour

Moullie Point
Pepénero
Italian cuisine
Tel: 021-439 9027
Address: No 1 Two Oceans Beach,
  18 Bay Road

Wafu
Asian cuisine
Tel: 021-433 2377 / 434 5134
Address: 2nd floor, cnr Beach Road &
  Surrey Place

Wakame
Asian cuisine
Tel: 021-433 2377 / 434 5134
Address: 1st floor, cnr Beach Road &
  Surrey Place

Mowbray
Curry Quest
Indian cuisine
Tel: 021-686 3175
Address: 89 Durban Road, Little Mowbray

Muizenberg
Fogeys Railway House Restaurant
international cuisine
Tel: 021-788 3252
Address: Station Building, 177 Main Road

Newlands
Barristers
grill & Mediterranean cuisine
Tel: 021-671 7907
Address: Cardiff Castle, cnr Kildare Road &
  Main Street

The Silver Tree Restaurant
international cuisine
Tel: 021-762 9585
Address: Kirstenbosch Botanical Gardens

The Square
international cuisine
Tel: 021-6574545
Address: Vineyard Hotel & Spa.
  Colinton Road

Observatory
Diva Caffe Ristorante
Italian cuisine
Tel: 021-448 0282
Address: 88 Lower Main Road

Pancho's
Mexican cuisine
Tel: 021-447 4853
Address: 127 Lower Main Road

The River Club
Mediterranean cuisine
Tel: 021-448 6117
Address: Liesbeek Parkway

Rondebosch

Star Dust
Mediterranean cuisine
Tel: 021-686 6280
Address: 165 Main Road

Sea Point

3 Thirteen
international cuisine
Tel: 021-430 7777
Address: 313 Beach Road

Fujiyama
Japanese cuisine
Tel: 021-434 6885
Address: The Courtyard, 100 Main Road

Harvey's
international cuisine
Tel: 021-434 2351
Address: 221 Beach Road

Rive Gauche
French cuisine
Tel: 021-430 1200
Address: 20 London Road

Saul's
steakhouse
Tel: 082 449 3025
Address: 118 Main Road

Tarkaris
Indian cuisine
Tel: 021-434 4266
Address: 1st Floor Tarkaris Centre,
    305 Main Road

Simon's Town

Bon appétit
Tel: 021-786 2412
Address: 90 St. George's Street

Seaforth Restaurant
Tel: 021-786 4810
Address: Seaforth Beach, Seaforth Road

Strand

Surfside
international cuisine
Tel: 021-853 2748
Address: Strand Pavilion, Beach Road

V&A Waterfront

221 Waterfront
international cuisine
Tel: 021-418 363
Address: Shop 221 Upper Level,
    Victoria Wharf

Balduccis
Italian cuisine
Tel: 021-421 6002/3
Address: Shop 6162, Lower Level,
    Victoria Wharf

Balthazar Restaurant
steakhouse
Tel: 021-421 3753
Address: Shop 153, Lower level,
    Victoria Basin

City Grill
steakhouse
Tel: 021-421 9821
Address: Shop 155, Victoria Wharf

Dodge City
70s diner-style
Tel: 021-555 3462
Address: 130A Lower Level, Victoria Wharf

Emily's
international cuisine
Tel: 021-421 1133
Address: Suite 202, The Clock Tower

Jewel of India
Indian cuisine
Tel: 021-419 8397
Address: 6264 Victoria Wharf

Maze
South African cuisine
Tel: 021-431 5222
Address: Dock Road

Meloncino
Mediterranean cuisine
Tel: 021-419 5558
Address: Shop 259, Upper Level

Nobu
Asian cuisine
Tel: 021-431 5111
Address: Dock Road

Panama Jacks on Quay 500
international cuisine
Tel: 021-447 3992
Address: Quay 500, Cape Town Harbour

Paulaner Bräuhaus
German cuisine
Tel: 021-418 9999
Address: Shop 18 / 19, Clock Tower Precinct

Quarterdeck
South African cuisine
Tel: 021-418 3281
Address: Portswood Road

Quay Four
international cuisine
Tel: 021-419 2008
Address: Quay Four

Sevruga
contemporary
Tel: 021-421 5134
Address: Shop 4, Quay 5

Shoreline Café
contemporary
Tel: 021-418 8645/6
Address: Dock Road

Signal
contemporary
Tel: 021-041 7080
Address: West Quay

The Greek Fisherman
seafood
Tel: 021-481 5411
Address: Shop 157, Victoria Wharf
Shopping Centre

Woodstock
Chandani
Indian cuisine
Tel: 021-447 7887
Address: 85 Roodebloem Avenue

Chains and Franchises

Bihari
Tel: 021-702 2975

Cape Town Fish Market
Tel: 021-555 1950

Cattle Baron Steak Ranches
Tel: 021-948 5260

Col'cacchio Pizzeria
Tel: 021-551 1658

Cubana
Tel: 021-421 1109

Jimmy's Killer Prawns
Tel: 021-552 5000

John Dory's Fish & Grill restaurant
Tel: 021-552 6443

Ocean Basket
Tel: 021-555 2331

Primi Piazza
Tel: 021-552 0055

Accommodation

www.tourismcapetown.co.za
www.westerncapeaccommodation.co.za
www.sa-venues.com
www.wheretostay.co.za
www.safarinow.com
www.cape-accommodation.co.za
www.capestay.co.za
www.allcapeaccommodation.com
www.westerncape.com
www.south-african-hotels.com
www.westerncapehotelandspa.co.za
www.cape.hotelguide.co.za
westerncape.lodgesafaris.com
www.sleeping-out.co.za
westerncape.guesthouses.co.za

Cape Town
Hotels

Cape Town Lodge Hotel
Tel: 021-422 0030
Email: internet@capetownlodge.co.za
URL: www.capetownlodge.co.za

Fountains Hotel
Tel: 021-443 1100
Email: reserve@fountainshotel.co.za
URL: www.fountainshotel.co.za

Lagoon Beach Hotel
Tel: 021-528 2000
Email: reservations@lagoonbeachhotel.co.za
URL: www.lagoonbeachhotel.co.za

The Devon Valley Hotel
Tel: 021-865 2021
Email: info@devonvalleyhotel.com
URL: www.devonvalleyhotel.com

B&Bs, Guest Houses & Self-catering

Bonani B&B
Tel: 021-531 8352
Email: mandisa@bonanibandb.co.za

Cape Vue Guesthouse
Tel: 021-876 2524
Email: cvguesthouse@mweb.co.za
URL: www.cvguesthouse.com

Mountview Spa & Guest House
Tel: 021-434 3335
Email: info@mountviewspa.co.za
URL: www.mountviewspa.co.za

The Highstead Manor
Tel: 021-439 6040
Email: highstead@isales.co.za
URL: www.thehighsteadmanor.co.za

Verona Lodge Guest House
Tel: 021-434 9477
Email: info@veronalodge.co.za
URL: www.veronalodge.co.za

Villa Sunar
Tel: 021-551 7390
Email: info@villasunar.co.za
URL: www.villasunar.co.za
Situated in Cape Town

Other
Hotels

Garden Route Casino Hotel & Spa
Tel: 044-693 2800
Email: pinnaclbo@katleisure.co.za
URL: www.katleisure.co.za
Situated in Mossel Bay

NH Plettenberg Bay
Tel: 044-533 3572
URL: www.nh-hotels.co.za
Situated in Plettenberg Bay

Protea Hotel
Tel:0861-119 000
Email: reservations@proteahotels.com
URL: www.proteahotels.com

Spier Hotel
Tel: 021-809 1100
Email: info@spier.co.za
URL: www.spier.co.za
Situated in Stellenbosch

The Graywood Hotel
Tel: 044-382 5850
Email : reservations@graywood.co.za
URL: www. graywood.co.za
Situated in Knysna

The Misty Collection
Tel: 028-313 8460
Email: misty@hermanusmistybeach.co.za
URL: www.hermanusmistybeach.co.za
Situated in Hermanus

Windsor Hotel
Tel: 028-312 3727
Email: info@windsor-hotel.com
URL: www.windsor-hotel.com
Situated in Hermanus

Lodges

Crayfish Lodge
Tel: 028-384 1898
Email: info@crayfishlodge.com
URL: www.crayfishlodge.com
Situated in Hermanus

Garden Route Game Lodge
Tel: 028-735 1200
Email: reservations@grgamelodge.co.za
URL: www.grgamelodge.co.za
Situated in Albertinia

Ilita Lodge
Tel: 044-620 4143
Email: info@ilitalodge.co.za
URL: www.ilitalodge.co.za
Situated in the Great Brak River

Stanley Island
Tel: 083-276 6929
Email: info@stanleyisland.com
URL: www.stanleyisland.com

Treehouse Forest Lodge
Tel: 044-532 7703
Email: treehouse@tiscali.co.za
URL: www.treehouselodge.co.za

B&Bs, Guest Houses & Self-catering

3 Colours Blue
Tel: 044-690 3981
Email: 3coloursblue@absamail.co.za
URL: www.3coloursblue.co.za
Situated in Mossel Bay

326 @ Pringle
Tel: 028-273 8050
Email: gladys5@btopenworld.com
URL: www.326pringle.com
Situated in Pringle Bay

African Oceans
Tel: 044-695 1864
Email: info@africanoceans.co.za
URL: www.africanoceans.co.za
Situated in Mossel Bay

Agapé Stone Cottage
Tel: 028-435 7292
Email: agapecottage@mweb.co.za
Situated in Hermanus

Baleana Bay
Tel: 028-384 2190
Email: res@baleanabay.co.za
URL: www.baleanabay.co.za
Situated in Hermanus

Bridgewater
Tel: 044-382 1418
Email: bridge@mweb.co.za
URL: www.bridge-water.co.za
Situated in Knysna

B @ Home
Tel: 044-690 5385
Email: info@b-at-home.co.za
URL: www.b-at-home.co.za
Situated in Mossel Bay

Babette's
Tel: 028-514 2406
Email: brigidm@telkomsa.net
URL: www.atbabette.com
Situated in Swellendam

Bartholomeus Klip Farmhouse
Tel: 022-448 1829
Email: bartholomeus@icon.co.za
URL: www.bartholomeusklip.com
Situated in Hermanus

Cape Agulhas
Tel: 028-435 7975
Email: agulhasguest@telkomsa.net
Situated in Cape Agulhas

Dolphin B&B
Tel: 022-742 1944
Email: info@dolphinza.com
URL: www.dolphinza.com
Situated in Brittania Bay

Excelsior Manor Guesthouse
Tel: 023-615 2050
Email: guesthouse@excelsior.co.za
URL: www.excelsior.co.za
Situated in the Breede River Valley

Hermanus Esplanade
Tel: 028-312 3610
Email: info@hermanus.co.za
URL: www.hermanusesplanade.co.za
Situated in Hermanus

Klippe Rivier
Tel: 028-514 3341
Email: info@klipperivier.com
URL: www.klipperivier.com
Situated in Swellendam

La Fontaine
Tel: 028-312 4595
Email: lafont@itec.co.za
URL: www.lafontaine.co.za
Situated in Hermanus

Mermaid Guesthouse
Tel: 028-435 7767
Email: mermaid.sb@telkomsa.net
URL: www.webtown.co.za
Situated in Hermanus

Milkwood Lodge Guesthouse
Tel: 028-314 1736
Email: milkwbb@hermanus.co.za
URL: www.hermanusbedandbreakfast.com
Situated in Hermanus

Moolmanshof B&B
Tel: 028-514 3258
Email: info@annascollection.com
URL: www.annascollection.com\
Situated in Hermanus

Nautilus Cottage
Tel: 028-312 4955
Situated in Hermanus

Pelagus House
Tel: 028-312 4955
Email: pelagus@hermanus.co.za
URL: www.pelagus.co.za
Situated in Hermanus

Puza Moya
Tel: 022-772 1114
Email: info@capesport.co.za
URL: www.capesport.co.za
Situated in Langebaan

Sandals Beach Villa
Tel: 028-314 1116
Email: sandals@getaway-gateway.co.za
URL: sandals.getaway-gateway.co.za
Situated in Hermanus

The Alexander
Tel: 044-384 1111
Email: info@alexanderhouse.co.za
URL: www.alexanderhouse.co.za
Situated in Knysna

Villa Blu
Tel: 028-314 1056
Email: info@villablu.co.za
URL: www.villablu.co.za
Situated in Hermanus

Villa Mulligan
Tel: 044-382 0414
Email: markus@villa-mulligan.com
URL: www.villa-mulligan.com
Situated in Knysna

Warners Guest House
Tel: 044-382 9964
Email: gasthof@global.co.za
URL: www.warners.co.za
Situated in Knysna

Whale Waters Guest Lodge
Tel: 028-384 0550
Email: info@whalewaters.co.za
URL: www.whalewaters.co.za
Situated in Hermanus

Camping

Chapman's Peak Caravan Park
Tel: 021-783 1634
Situated in Cape Town

Driehoek Camping
Tel: 027-482 2828

Nuwerus Rest Camp
Tel: 027-482 2831
Email: info@cederbergexperience.co.za
URL: www.cederbergexperience.co.za

Starling Backpackers
Tel: 044-533 9108
Email: info@starlingbackpackers.co.za
URL: www.starlingbackpackers.co.za

Tsitsikama Backpackers
Tel: 042-281 1868
Email: stay@tsitsikammabackpackers.co.za
URL: www.tsitsikammabackpackers.co.za
Situated in Tsitsikama

Wolfkop Nature Reserve
Tel: 083-775 0144
URL: www.wolfkopnaturereserve.co.za

Tours

100 X 100 Africa
Tel: 073-217 0109
Email: leigh@100x100africa.com
URL: www.100x100africa.com

A2B Tours
Tel: 083-258 4769
Email: info@a2btours.co.za
URL: www.a2btours.co.za

African Eagle Day Tours
Tel: 021-464 4266
Email: daytours@aecpt.co.za
URL: www.daytours.co.za

Andulela Tours
Tel: 021-790 2592
URL: www.andulela.com

Atlantic Shuttle & Tours
Tel: 021-705 1074
Email: atlanticshuttles@vodamail.co.za
URL: www.atlantictours.co.za

Abang Africa Travel
Tel: 021-426 1330
Email: info@abangafrica.com
URL: www.abangafrica.com

Babi's Tours & Transfers
Tel: 021-361 2202
Email: phaks@babistours.co.za
URL: www.babistours.co.za

Back Road Safaris
Tel: 044-690 8150
Email: info@backroadsafaris.co.za
URL: www.backroadsafaris.co.za

Baz Bus
Tel: 021-439 2323
Email: info@bazbus.com
URL: www.bazbus.com

Bok Bus
Tel: 082-320 1979
URL: www.bokbus.com

Bonani Tours
Tel: 021-531 4291
Email: ourpride@mweb.co.za
URL: www.bonanitours.co.za

Brian's Birding
Tel: 021-919 2192
Email: info@brians-birding.co.za
URL: www.brians-birding.co.za

Camissa
Tel: 021-162 6199
Email: ops@gocamissa.co.za
URL: www.gocamissa.co.za

Cape Big 5 Safaris
Tel: 0861-244 348
Email: info@greenmarketsquare.net
URL: www.capebig5safaris.com

Cape Capers
Tel: 021-448 3117
Email: tourcape@mweb.co.za
URL: www.tourcapers.co.za

Cape Convoy
Tel: 021-531 1298
Email: info@capecovoy.com
URL: www.capeconvoy.com

Cape Eco-tours
Tel: 021-919 2282
Email: info@cape-ecotours.co.za
URL: www.cape-ecotours.co.za

Cape Escape and Explore
Tel: 021-885 2394
Email: info@capeescapeexplore.co.za
URL: www.capeescapeexplore.co.za

Cape Escape Tours
Tel: 021-447 9240
Email: cescape@mweb.co.za
URL: www.cape-escape-tours.co.za

Cape Friendly Tours
Tel: 021-694 0115
Email: cape@capefriendlytours.co.za
URL: www.capefriendlytours.co.za

Cape of Good Hope Tours
Tel: 021-686 3117
Email: daysout@iafrica.com
URL: www.capeofgoodhopetour.co.za

Cape Rainbow Tours
Tel: 021-551 5465
Email: info@caperainbow.com
URL: www.caperainbow.co.za

Cape Sightseeing Tours
Tel: 021-433 0091
Email: wjacobs@foxtransport.co.za

Cape Tours with Mac
Tel: 082-259 9950
Email: Mackenzie@thewildcoast.co.za
URL: www.capewithmac.com

Cathy's Tours
Tel: 021-393 4896
Email: cathystours@absamail.co.za
URL: www.personalcapetowntours.com

Cape Town Carriage Company
Tel: 082-575 5669
Email: info@ctcco.co.za
URL: www.ctcco.co.za

Charlo's Tours
Tel: 021-715 6607
Email: cadams@xsinet.co.za
URL: www.charlostours.co.za

Chapman's Peak Drive
Tel: 021-790 0778
Email: info@chapmanspeakdrive.co.za
URL: www.chapmanspeakdrive.co.za

Chelsea Morning
Tel: 021-422 3108
Email: rschelsea@iburst.co.za
URL: www.chelseamorning.co.za

Coffee Beans Routes
Tel: 021-424 3572
Email: tours@coffeebeans.co.za
URL: www.coffeebeans.co.za

Destin Africa
Tel: 021-462 5844
URL: www.destinafrica.co.za

Discover Cape Town
Tel: 021-534 3705
Email: yasmin@discover-capetown.co.za
URL: www.discover-capetown.co.za

Drive Direct Tours
Tel: 021-535 4404
Email: colin@drivedirect.co.za
URL: www.drivedirect.co.za

Dune Tours & Adventures
Tel: 083-409 7055
Email: keith@dunetours.co.za
URL: www.dunetours.co.za

Elains Cape Eco Tours
Tel: 021-842 3715
URL: www.elainscapeecotours.com

Elle Tours
Tel: 072-707 1192
Email: info@elletours.com
URL: www.elletours.com

Endeavour Safaris
Tel: 021-556 6114
Email: sales@endeavour-safaris.com
URL: www.endeavour-safaris.com

Explore Paradise Tours
Tel: 021-424 8356
URL: www.paradiseeploreers.rezgo.com

Ezizwe Tours
Tel: 021-697 0068

Fairview Touring
Tel: 021-715 2855
Email: Fairview@iafrica.com
URL: www.fairviewtouring.com

Flint's Tours
Tel: 082-902 2935
Email: info@flintstours.co.za
URL: www.flintstours.co.za

Footsteps to Freedom
Tel: 083-452 1112
Email: info@footstepstofreedom.co.za
URL: www.footstepstofreeedom.co.za

Friends of Dorothy Tours
Tel: 021-465 1871
Email: info@friendsofdorothytours.co.za
URL: www.friendsofdorothytours.co.za

FS Tours
Tel: 082-569 8299
Email: nstevens@mtnloaded.co.za
URL: www.fstours.co.za

Garden Route Adrenaline Tour
Tel: 021-421 8987
Email: info@adrenalinetour.co.za
URL: www.adrenalinetour.co.za

Gourmet Wine Tours of South Africa
Tel: 021-705 4317
Email: sflesch@iafrica.com
URL: www.gourmetwinetours.co.za

Grape Escapes
Tel: 021-855 5726
Email: rosian@telkomsa.net

Grass Route Tours
Tel: 021-464 4269
Email: grassroute@iafrica.com
URL: www.grassroutetours.co.za

Happy Holiday Tours
Tel: 021-855 2108
Email: Gudrun@happyholidays.co.za
URL: www.happyholiday.co.za

Hennie's Wine Adventures
Tel: 021-556 8594
Email: info@henniesadventures.co.za
URL: www.henniesadventures.co.za

Hotspots 2 C
Tel: 079-983 0812
Email: info@hotspots2c.co.za
URL: www.hotspots2c.co.za

Hylton Ross Exclusive Touring
Tel: 021-511 1784
URL: www.hyltonross.com

idiscover Tours
Tel: 021-872 4728
Email: johan@idiscover.co.za
URL: www.idiscover.co.za

Ingulube Tours
Tel: 076-535 2978
Email: touringulube@yahoo.com
URL: www.ingulubetours.co.za

Inkululeku Tours
Tel: 082-555 3453
Email: info@inkululekutours.co.za
URL: www.inkululekutours.co.za

Inverdoorn Game Reserve Safaris
Tel: 021-464 4266
Email: daytours@aecpt.co.za

Isango Tours
Tel: 021-872 9578
Email: info@isangotours.co.za
URL: www.isangotours.co.za

Izotsha Tours
Tel: 021-553 3480
Email: bbest@new.co.za
URL: www.berribest.com

M & H Tours
Tel: 021-797 2992
Email: madniah@imaginet.co.za
URL: www.mhtours.co.za

Mike Bosch Tours
Tel: 021-434 1956
Email: info@mikeboschtours.co.za
URL: www.mikeboschtours.co.za

Nature Safaris
Tel: 021-975 7017
Email: caflodge@iafrica.com
URL: www.campsafrica.com

Navigators Four-wheel Drive Adventure
Tel: 021-689 1825
Email: info@navigators2wd.co.za
URL: www.navigators4wd.co.za

Oakes Travel & Tours
Tel: 021-794 4554
Email: nathan@oakestraveltours.co.za
URL: www.oakestraveltours.co.za

Ocean to Ocean Shuttle & Tours
Tel: 021-593 3397
Email: pand@telkomsa.net

Other Side of Cape Town Tours
Tel: 021-715 4740
Email: info@andytours.co.za
URL: www.andytours.co.za

Randy's Tours
Tel: 021-706 0166
URL: www.randystours.com

Roots Africa Tours
Tel: 021-987 8330
Email: rootsafrica@xsinet.co.za
URL: www.rootsafrica.co.za

WESTERN CAPE

San-Lee Tours
Tel: 021-705 9266
Email: san-lee@telkmosa.net

Silvermine River Wetlands Tour
Tel: 079-391 2105

Sizwe Nation Tours
Tel: 073-019 7473

Soul Touring
Tel: 021-551 0467
Email: info@soultouring.com
URL: www.soultouring.com

South Sun Tours
Tel: 082-775 1556
Email: suleiman@southsuntours.co.za
URL: www.southsuntours.co.za

Springbok Atlas
Tel: 021-460 4700
Email: tours@springbokatlas.com
URL: www.springbokatlas.com

Stadler Tours
Tel: 021-786 5975
Email: cilla2clive@telkomsa.net

Stigma Tours
Tel: 021-556 8727
Email: info@stigmatours.com
URL: www.stigmatours.com

Tana Baru Tours
Tel: 021-424 0719
Email: tanabarutours@webmail.co.za
URL: www.tanabarutours.co.za

The Wine Bus
Tel: 021-859 1989
Email: info@adventurewinetours.co.za
URL: www.adventurewinetours.co.za

Tour De Lux
Tel: 021-913 5301
Email: tourdelux@mweb.co.za
URL: www.tourdelux.com

Usiwa
Tel: 021-790 8549
Email: usiwa@mweb.co.za

Wanderlust
Tel: 021-462 4252
Email: info@wanderlust.co.za
URL: www.wanderlust.co.za

Western Discovery Tours
Tel: 022-931 3547
Email: info@westerndiscovery.co.za
URL: www.westerndiscovery.co.za

Wine & Whale Tours
Tel: 021-852 6545
Email: wineandwhales@telkomsa.net
URL: www.wineandwhales.co.za

Wine Desk
Tel: 021-405 4550
Email: waterfront@winedesk.co.za
URL: www.winedeskwaterfront.co.za

Wow Cape Town Tours
Tel: 021-697 0174
Email: rharper@polka.co.za
URL: www.wowcapetowntours.com

Xama Adventures
Tel: 021-685 735
Email: xama.sa@mweb.co.za
URL: www.xama.co.za

Your Tour
Tel: 021-551 1086
Email: post@yourtour.co.za
URL: www.yourtour.co.za

Zibonele Tours & Transfers
Tel: 021-511 4263
Email: info@ziboneletours.com
URL: www.ziboneletours.com

Out to Sea

Africa's Ocean Safaris
Tel: 044-533 4963
Email: info@oceansafaris.co.za
URL: www.oceansafaris.co.za

Barron Charters
Tel: 021-421 4471
Email: info@barroncharters.com
URL: www.barroncharters.com

Big Game Fishing Safaris
Tel: 021-674 2203
Email: skipper@gamefish.co.za

Classic Cape Charters
Tel: 021-418 0782
URL: www.capecharters.co.za

Circe Launches
Tel: 021-790 1040
Email: info@circelaunches.co.za
URL: www.circelaunches.co.za

Cruise IQ
Tel: 021-421 5565
Email: info@cruiseiq.co.za
URL: www.cruiseiq.co.za

Drumbeat Charters
Tel: 021-791 4441
Email: drumbeatcharters@intekom.co.za
URL: www.drumbeatcharters.co.za

Hermanus Whale Cruises
Tel: 028-313 2722
Email: hermanuswhales@lantic.net
URL: www.hermanus-whale-cruises.co.za

Hooked on Africa Fishing Charters
Tel: 021-790 5332
URL: www.hookedonafrica.co.za

Nauticat Charters
Tel: 021-790 7278
Email: nauticat@mweb.co.za
URL: www.nauticatcharters.co.za

Strandloper Safaris
Tel: 021-650 4520
Email: info@strandlopersafaris.co.za
URL: www.strandlopersafaris.co.za

Tigger 2
Tel: 021-790 5256
Email: tigger@netactive.co.za
URL: www.tigger2.co.za

Waterfront Boat Company
Tel: 021-418 5806
Email: info@waterfrontboats.co.za
URL: www.waterfrontboats.co.za

White Shark Projects
Tel: 021-405 4537
Email: info@whitesharkprojects.co.za
URL: www.whitesharkprojects.co.za

WESTERN CAPE

Car & Bike Rentals

Active Car Rental
Tel: 021-557 3551
Email: info@activecarrental.co.za
URL: www.activecarrental.co.za

Adelphi Rent a Car
Tel: 021-439 6144
Email: adelphi@intekom.co.za
URL: www.adelphi.co.za

Avis
Tel: 0861-021 111
URL:www.avis.co.za

Base 4 Helicopters
Tel: 021-934 4405
Email: info@base4.co.za
URL: www.base4.co.za

Budget
Tel: 0861-016 622
URL: www.budget.co.za

Cape Bike Rentals
Tel: 072-250 1691
Email: www.capebikerentals.com
URL: www.capebikerentals.com

Car Hire WP
Tel: 021-797 0940
Email: info@carhire-wp.co.za
URL: www.carhire-wp.co.za

Click Car Hire
Tel: 021-551 9515
URL: www.sa-venues.com/explore/
  clickcarhire

Drive Direct
Tel: 021-535 4404
Email: colin@drivedirect.co.za
URL: www.drivedirect.co.za

Drive South Africa
Tel: 0860-000 060
URL: www.drivesouthafrica.co.za

Easy Wheels
Tel: 021-949 4499
Email: cars@fairestcapecarhire.co.za
URL: www.easywheels.co.za

Europcar
Tel: 0861-131 000
URL: www.europcar.co.za

First
Tel: 0861-011 323
URL: www.firstcarrental.co.za

Hertz
Tel: 0861-600 136
URL: www.hertz.co.za

Motor Classic
Tel: 021-461 7368
Email: info@motorclassic.co.za
URL: www.motorclassic.co.za

On The Move
Tel: 086-007 2765
Email: donne@rbsolutions.co.za
URL: www.rbsolutions.co.za

One Stop Car Hire
Tel: 021-903 0150
Email: 1stop@vodamail.co.za

Point 2 Point Shuttle Services
Tel: 021-951 4099
Email: info@p2pshuttle.co.za
URL: www.p2pshuttle.co.za

Rent A Harley Davidson
Tel: 021-853 6794
Email: courtenay@ironhorse.org.za
URL: www.ironhorse.org.za

Scenic Car Hire
Tel: 021-439 1698
Email: scenic@mweb.co.za
URL: www.sceniccarhire.com

Status Luxury
Tel: 021-510 0108
Email: info@statusluxuryvehicles.com
URL: www.statusluxuryvehicles.com

Vineyard Car Hire
Tel: 021-761 0671
Email: info@vineyardcarhire.co.za
URL: www.vineyardcarhire.co.za

Emergency Numbers

All Emergencies
107

Crime Stop
0800-11 12 13

Tourism Assistance SA Police
021-421 5115

Ambulance
10177 or 1022

Rescue Services – Sea
021-449 3500

Rescue Services – Aviation
021-937 1116

Mountain Rescue Service
10177 or 1022